LINKS TO THE COURSES PLAYED

www.stromnessgc.co.uk

www.bathgate-golfclub.co.uk

www.anstruthergolf.co.uk

www.aberdourgolfclub.co.uk

www.northberwickgoldclub.com

www.shiskinegolf.com

www.standrews.org.uk

www.crailgolfingsociety.co.uk (for Balcomie)

www.gigha.org.uk

www.machrihanishgolfclub.btinternet.co.uk

www.glenbervie-golf-club.com

www.forresgolf.com

www.freenetpages.co.uk/hp/beauchiefgolf/

www.royaldornoch.com

www.moraygolf.com

www.crudenbaygolfclub.com

www.dollargolfclub.com

www.golfhouseclub.org (for Elie)

www.lundingolfclub.co.uk

www.tobermory.co.uk (for Iona)

See also:

www.spiritualgolf.com (for Fairway to Heaven)

Also by Andrew Greig

POETRY

Men on Ice

Surviving Passages

A Flame in Your Heart (with Kathleen Jamie)

The Order of the Day

Western Swing

Into You

This Life, This Life: New & Selected Poems 1970–2006

MOUNTAINEERING

Summit Fever

Kingdoms of Experience

NOVELS

Electric Brae

The Return of John MacNab

When They Lay Bare

That Summer

In Another Light

Preferred Lies

*A Journey into the Heart
of Scottish Golf*

ANDREW GREIG

Thomas Dunne Books
St. Martin's Press ⚏ New York

THOMAS DUNNE BOOKS.
An imprint of St. Martin's Press.

Quote from "Friends" by W. B. Yeats reprinted with permission from A. P. Watt Ltd on behalf of Michael B. Yeats.
Quote from *Sonnets to Orpheus* by Rainer Maria Rilke, translated by Don Paterson © Faber and Faber Ltd.
Poetry extracts from "The Hollow Men" by T. S. Eliot reproduced courtesy of Faber and Faber Ltd.
"A Long Shot" on p. 281 taken from *This Life, This Life: New & Selected Poems 1970–2006* by Andrew Greig (Bloodaxe Books, 2006).

www.stmartins.com

Library of Congress Cataloging-in-Publication Data

Greig, Andrew.
    Preferred lies : a journey into the heart of Scottish golf / Andrew Greig.—1st U.S. ed.
        p. cm.
    ISBN-13: 978-0-312-37299-6
    ISBN-10: 0-312-37299-X
    1. Golf—Scotland. 2. Greig, Andrew. 3. Brain—Wounds and injuries—Patients—Scotland. I. Title.

GV984.G74 2007
796.35209411—dc22

                                                            2007035936

First published in Great Britain by Weidenfeld & Nicolson,
an imprint of The Orion Publishing Group Ltd

First U.S. Edition: December 2007

10 9 8 7 6 5 4 3 2 1

This one is for Lesley

Acknowledgements
and Thanks

This book could not exist without the people I met, talked and played golf with. In particular I want to thank: Trevor Dunk and Mark Trippett (Beauchief); Duncan Robertson (North Ronaldsay); Alastair McLeish (Bathgate); Liz Duff (Aberdour); Patrick Rayner and David Huish (North Berwick); Fiona Brown ('I have to stay rotund for the hugs I get!') and Colin Bannatyne (Shiskine); Rhona Grant, Hamish Todd, 'Plumber' Brown and John Bannatyne (Gigha); David and Sandy (Glenbervie); Mike and Jenny Gilderdale (Elie); Don Paterson (Princes Street Gardens); Vin Harris and David Hares (Machrihanish etc.); Graeme Lennie (Balcomie); Sandy Aird (Forres); Joan Shafer and John Talbott (Dornoch etc.). Also the special people who shared their lives and golf with me at 'Fairway to Heaven': Paul, Tim, Maria, Nick, Tony, Bruce, Blair, Cynthia, Gisela, Fritz, Torsten, Rainer; Guenter Schnorr (Dollar).

Also a warm, admiring *Fore!* to the humane and liberating golf writings of Michael Murphy, Fred Shoemaker, Michael Konik and Bob Rotella, as they play down the fairway ahead.

Contents

You must begin again   1

1 ST 'Laird' (North Ronaldsay)   5
The cronies play Billowness   15

2 ND 'Travesty' (North Ronaldsay)   17
The missing links   25

3 RD 'Aliosaurus' (Bathgate)   27
Playing Anstruther through the night   38

4 TH 'Duff' (Aberdour)   41
On giving up golf   52

5 TH 'The Shining' (North Berwick)   56
Bringing it all back home   65

6 TH 'Jewel' (Shiskine)   69
A ghost hole, and other ploys   84

7 TH 'Initiation' (St Andrews Old Course)   88
On golf, sex, and the joy of timing   99

8 TH 'Good Isle' (Gigha)   102
Golf heaven, no caddy-carts admitted   116

9 TH 'Brothers' (Glenbervie)   120
A 6 iron to the green   132

10TH 'Gilders' (Elie) 135
A round with Rilke 157

11TH 'Colum Cille' (Iona) 163
Interlude: on Friendship Bridge 173

12TH 'The Shot' (Lundin Links) 178
Why golf is unnecessary 184

13TH 'Shades' (Stromness) 187
The budgie who golfed 193

14TH 'Big Easy' (Forres) 196
A British-sized ball 209

15TH 'Equanimity' (Old Moray) 212
And your bird can swing 219

16TH 'Extraction' (Cruden Bay, Nairn) 222
Off a tight lie 235

17TH 'The Zard' (Royal Dornoch, Forres) 239
End of the fairway 253

18TH 'Return' (Dollar) 256
Endgame 274

So great a sweetness flows
I shake from head to foot

W. B. Yeats

Nothing on Earth can enlarge the sweet spot –
but we can enlarge the area of forgiveness

Mark Trippett, pro at Beauchief, Sheffield

You must begin again

So the day came when I climbed into the loft and came down
with a former life. The cobwebs clinging to the bag came away
with a stiff brush; the grooves in the club faces were filled with
fragments of long-gone days from *before*. At the sink, I gave them
a quick scrub, but the soil and grass were impacted solid.

Some time back I had passed on my climbing gear to my eldest
stepson Joe, a passionate climber, much better than I'd ever been.
With Mal Duff dead on Everest, I wasn't going on big mountains
again. I'd nearly given Joe the golf clubs too, but not quite.
Instead they'd been lugged about on all my moves, last to be
loaded, first to be shoved away in a corner. It was a wonder I
could still lay my hands on them.

I slung the bag over my shoulder and stepped out into the
bright Orkney morning, thinking the wonder was I could lay my
hands on anything.

Six months earlier, the walk from my house to the Ness had been
a challenge. Though my memory and concentration had
improved since I'd finally left hospital, I was still a hollow man,
gutted and enfeebled. In the city: too much stimulation, more
input than I could handle. Back in Orkney there were fewer
things, and bigger: sky, sea, the hills of Hoy across the water.
How I needed those simplicities.

Day after day while convalescing I took the walk along the

narrow street that runs through our town of Stromness, twisting slightly as it follows the shoreline's contours, then opening out as the houses stop. I loved the next stretch, walking above the unbreakable water, smelling salt and seaweed, watching the light bend over Scapa Flow.

Then the road dips down to shore level, past the old boatyard and finally on to the Point of Ness.

On my early outings, I had to rest there. Not-dying takes it out of you in many ways. After a while my eyes would turn from the sea to the golf course laid out above the Sound of Hoy. I took to leaning over the wall, watching golfers tackle the 16th hole. My shoulders began to turn involuntarily as they drove off; my hands twitched as I watched the approach shots into that complex green. I analysed the swings as they drove off next to me on the 17th. I could see why this one hooked, and that one topped; felt satisfaction at the good player's timing, that precise *keesh!* as the ball flew . . .

One afternoon I was leaning over the dyke. The mower was out on the hill and the smell of cut grass travelled downwind, and mingled with the sweet rot of seaweed. I watched a foursome playing and thought: *My God, surely I can do better than that.*

So that morning came when I went into the loft, then carried my bag of clubs over my shoulder to the Stromness course, just as I had done as a lad in Anstruther some forty years earlier, and it may have been the bright warm April morning, or the rattle of the clubs behind my back, but I felt hopeful, full of curiosity, excited for the first time in a long time.

I admit my heart was beating fast as I pushed open the little brown gate and stepped onto the course.

We've seen it in films: the gunfighter, the priest, the ice climber, returning to their old accomplishment. It begins with the equipment, strange yet so natural in the hands again: holster, chalice, crampons. From a broken zip pouch I take out a couple of balls – a bit scuffed, but good enough. A few golf tees. Then the flattened, wizened blue golf glove. My father's voice in my inner ear: *It helps remind you the game's played wi' the left hand.*

The glove is cold, worn and slightly musty, but still fits. Standing at the 1st tee, I look around. Apart from two children on the swings and the distant tractor-mower, there's no one about. Good, because this could go horribly wrong.

I choose to play safe and take out the 4 iron. Hands fall into place on the rubber grip. I take a few cautious swings. I could think about pivot, shoulder, weight transference, hip turn, wrist release, but my body seems to know fine what to do.

Quick check to see no one's looking, then I do some yoga stretches. When I watch my youngest stepson Leo, I see he moves in a subtly different way from me. He bounds, flops, lounges, jumps up, all quite fearless and unmeditated. Injury never crosses his body's mind.

I tee up the ball, wonder if that's too low and I might miss altogether, so tee up higher. A couple of faster practice swings. This feels good, the whole kinetic sensation of it. I'm not telling my body to do all these complex things. I just think: *Go*, and it does what comes naturally. Like the first times Lesley and I made love, cautious and gentle, after I came out of hospital.

The gunfighter moves into the street; the priest approaches the altar; the climber clips in — as I step up to the ball, everything becomes very clear. The scuffed dew on the fairway says I'm not the first person out today. Sun warm on my neck as I bend over the ball. Terns peeping by the Ness, gulls tilting over the hill, bairns calling on the swings. I'm alive, surrounded by golf course, sea, life. I'm living in *after*.

I swing. Arm socket and neck jerk as the club head meets little resistance. I look up to see the ball rising near-vertically, veer right, land over the wall in someone's garden.

What a very silly game.

I'm shaking my head, part mortified, part amused, as I tee up another ball — a bit lower this time. Should have trusted myself more.

OK – no laughter at the back. There is no one at the back. This is just a silly, fun thing I'm trying out because I'm still on the planet and need to recover more than my physical health.

This time the ball flies up that brae like a slingshot, straight and true. I lift my bag and walk up the fairway with golden warmth coursing from my wrists to my heart. The course is alive, I'm alive, I have just hit a proper golf shot, and the first lark of the year is singing way high up.

I think on my dad, last seen seventeen years after his death, when he came to me while I lay in a coma in Hallamshire Hospital Intensive Care. It had been good to see him. He had told me to picture walking up the first fairway at Anstruther, and that helped me hang on.

I look round the glittering course. *Dad, I wish you were here to enjoy this.*

Then I stop mid-stride because I swear to Golf I hear his voice, his real live voice, throaty and amused. *But I am.*

When a man's deid, he's deid, my father would say. I tend to agree with him. Yet all I have ever written starts from voices within, and they are true in their way. As I hit then followed the flight of that little dimpled planet, and set off after it in some kind of erratic, jubilant pursuit, I sensed I was on the track of something, though I had no idea it would take so long to get there.

It wasn't so much that I took up golf again; truth is, it took me up.

It takes me up still.

'Laird'

(NORTH RONALDSAY)

North Ronaldsay: outermost of the Orkney Islands off the north coast of Scotland. Approx. 3 miles by 1 mile. Pop. c.62, plus 3,500 rare-breed North Ronaldsay sheep. Also numberless birds and seals. The island is surrounded by the longest drystone wall in the world, to keep the seaweed-eating sheep on the beach.
*Trees – few, none taller than 15 feet. Hedges – none. Buildings over one storey – 3. 1 **golf course, privately owned, open to all.***

As I walk across the island from the house of the Old Laird, the wind bears a dog's bark from the other coast, the faint groan of a digger up by the lighthouse a couple of miles off, and the high, thin mewing of innumerable seabirds.

The birds, the surrounding sea, the wind over grass – they are ever-present as one's heartbeat and breath, so constant they are not so much sounds as conditions of existence. When they stop, you're probably dead or have left North Ronaldsay.

The grey sky had rolled back like an eyelid while we were inside listening to Mr Robertson talk about his course, and I'm now walking with a handful of golf clubs under a vast blue stare. There is no cover on this little island. From here it's possible to look back towards the Bird Observatory at one end, see a volunteer bend over a bird-ringing trap, then look north and watch the post van stop by the lighthouse at the other end.

At any moment of the day any inhabitant would have a pretty good idea where all other inhabitants or visitors were, and what they'd be up to. If you want to locate one person on North Ronaldsay, just ask any other. Remote islands are the very last places a recluse should seek.

To my wife Lesley, though she thrives on many aspects of our Orkney life, this absence of privacy is horrifying. To me, it's good to be constantly in a social network, knowing others and being known. I admit this sits rather oddly with my preference for solitary golf – true golf, as I think of it. Les has gone to explore the other side of the island, and I am here to discover this course alone, and that's just fine with both of us.

A rust bucket with four wheels attached comes up behind. I step off the road as it trundles by. The driver lifts a hand in greeting, I return the salute. Why does he greet me? He doesn't know me. He greets me because I am here and he is here, and we are on the same island.

As the car dwindles and I climb over the gate through the dyke, I think maybe it's because of this little bundle of golf clubs I'm carrying in my hand. Maybe he greets me as one golfer does another, fellow members of the same singular, suffering, exultant fraternity.

I jump down from the gate onto short-cropped springy turf, then I'm standing on one of the world's oddest and most remote golf courses, surrounded by 360 degrees of uninterrupted horizon under a vast blue sky. It's late July, the day is warm for the North Isles, the sun is full on my face, and I'm outrageously and unreservedly happy.

The 'clubhouse' is a battered shed perched on breeze blocks. It is slightly skewed, and faded and tattered as everything is here by wind, salt and light. There is no starter, no tee-off booking, no queue at the first tee. In fact, there is no identifiable tee.

There are also no golfers, and no greenkeepers other than the three hundred-odd North Ronaldsay sheep cropping the fairway. A number of poles, black and white and canted at strange angles, some bearing faded tatters of material that might once have been flags, are planted in the midst of turf. According to the sketch-map on the back of the scorecard, the nearest one marks the 9th green.

Scanning the course against the needle-bright light, I begin to understand there are no 'greens' as such, no 'fairway', no 'rough'. It's all an undifferentiated One, like the original world, the world before language. There is only undulating links turf, bounded by the ocean on one side and a great stone dyke on the other. It makes the simple Stromness course seem like Augusta.

Is this really a golf course at all? I climb three concrete steps, pull sharply on the old wooden door. After brief resistance, it gives, and I step into the empty hut that just yesterday was the nerve-centre of the world-unknown North Ronaldsay Open Championship.

A strew of assorted golf clubs, propped on the table or splayed on the floor, some bent, all seaweed-dark with rust. Three very tired golf bags. A box of old balls. A bundle of pale-blue score cards: *North Ronaldsay Golf Links: Rules and Scoring Card*.

I pour coffee from my flask, look out the window at the sheep and the sea, then pick up a card to read the Local Rules:

The seashore is not a bunker.
A ball may be lifted free and dropped not nearer the hole
when lying on kelp ware, in beach marks, or in wheel tracks.

PLEASE KEEP ALL GATES AND THE
DOOR OF THE GOLF HOUSE CLOSED

Pinned up on a wall is a yellowed list of the charges for playing this unique course:

Residents £5 per calendar year.
Non-residents £3 per day, including scorecard.
£10 per week, including 7 scorecards.
Clubs plus bag £1 per day.
Hon. Sec. Peter Donnelly, Sanger.

I put aside for the time being the question of where I might leave my fee, peel away the tape I'd used to bind my few clubs together for the fifteen-minute plane flight from Kirkwall. I've brought 5, 7 and 9 irons, putter. The irons are my own, cavity-backed, graphite-shafted. They look conspicuous in these surroundings. The putter is my father's, a hickory-shafted Ben Sayers blade, heavy and ribbed along the sole. Folding my fingers round its rectangular black grip, worn smooth with use, I feel again his huge hands wrapped over mine as he teaches me the overlapping grip.

I select one of the wooden clubs lying on the floor of the hut, a 3 wood or 'spoon', as I still think of it. My dad gave clubs their old names, their proper names, the ones he'd grown up with around the Great War. The 2 wood was a 'brassie', the 3 wood a 'spoon'. The irons I've brought today he might loosely cry a 'mashie', 'mashie-niblick', 'niblick'.

Standing in this little hut, the names seem right. Just glancing out the window at the sheep scurrying over the 9th 'green', it's clear this doesn't call for precision golf. It calls for a long iron to mash the ball with, a general-purpose club and a pitching club, as well as a wooden-shafted putter, and a lot of instinct, improvisation and hoping to luck.

I pick up the clubs in one hand, stuff a scorecard into my pocket, and step from the hut onto the links.

I feel dreamy yet unusually awake and alert. It's a state that descends on me on golf courses, part of what has brought me back to the game after thirty years. A sense of the past, my own and golf's, trails thin and high above me along with the few scattered clouds.

I consult the sketch on the back of the scorecard to ascertain roughly where the first tee might be, then decide which leaning pin out there most likely marks the 1st green.

A few stretches and swishes, then settle over the ball. Unless I top this horribly, I'll clear the nearest group of sheep that unconcernedly graze the first hole. The more distant ones will have to take their chances as the ball comes down. These sheep have survived unchanged from late Neolithic, so they can take a few golf balls raining from the sky. This is mad. Is this golf at all?

But the pin is there, 182 yards away, and I'm here. The day is so bright, the wind is warm; along the length of Linklet Bay, the turquoise water is mind-alteringly clear.

I focus on the ball, the smudge of earth on the back of it. Arctic terns dive overhead as the breeze pats my face. My father's voice: *Keep your head still, lad. Dinna press.* The first two Commandments of Golf, eternally true, always being broken.

Here we go –

Something happens, that's all that can be said of it. The body winds up, releases, wrists kick, arms follow through – and inside and out something has happened. I look up, find the ball high, near-invisible in the white light. Caught in the breeze, it drifts further out right, falls among a scatter of sheep.

I pick up my little handful of clubs and set off.

This 1st hole is called 'Khylas' – must be the same Mount Kylash I remember in Tibet from our Everest Unclimbed Ridge expedition in 1985. The Old Laird told us his grandfather, who effectively owned the whole island, had created the course in the 1880s after serving as an engineer with the army in India. As we shook hands on parting, Duncan Robertson added, 'It's the name of a sacred mountain in the Himalayas that my grandfather once visited. Which may seem rather odd because the hole is completely flat. I think he meant that for him that hole was Heaven. Do enjoy yourself.'

As I find my ball, flick away the nearest dry sheep turds and a bit of rabbit skeleton, I think the laird's grandfather wasn't far wrong. There's no mountain, sacred or otherwise, in sight, but there is a white-sand beach a mile long on my right where seals have lain up, a mild breeze that comes clean all the way from Newfoundland, warm sun, mottled turf the colours of faded camouflage trousers. Above all there is space, a vast dazzling openness redolent with sea and grass and sheep, and I've a cleek in my right hand, a ball at my feet and a canted pin up ahead. It is indeed heavenly.

The shot goes roughly as intended, but my ball drops short of the pin, kicks right and stops abruptly. I've just learned two things: the ground though very dry is quite spongy. Probably to do with the sheep. The links of my childhood would be like concrete in this weather. Secondly, the air is so clear it falsifies judgement of distance. That lighthouse looks just a couple of big tee shots away, though it has to be nearly two miles.

The ball's now some 20 yards from the pin. Am I on the green or not? There is no green, just a stout metal pole keeled over towards the horizon. Do I putt this, pitch it up, or run it in?

I opt for the orthodox shot, flip the ball up with the 9 iron. Ball lands, jumps sideways. Right. No more high pitches.

I stoop down, clear a path to the hole through the light dry sheep droppings, the odd pebble and bone. God knows how they played the Open yesterday in this. Already the winning score of 39 over the nine holes, by a nephew in 'the laird's party', seems a decent achievement. Must wash my hands afterwards. On a normal golf course you do that because of the various chemicals sprayed; here it's because of the rabbits and sheep.

My first putt scutters along, bounces right then left, ends up a couple of feet from the hole. Which looks a bit bigger than standard. Which given the state of this non-green green, all lumpy, sheep-trodden, unrolled and uncut, is probably necessary.

To my surprise the next putt goes in the hole. I pick it out. A 5 at a 182-yard hole, normally a par 3, though my card gives it as a par 4. I can see I'm going to have to adjust my notions of what's possible here.

It's absurd but even here, alone and unobserved, I really want to do well. That second shot, the misjudged pitch, irritated me. Already I am erecting targets, expectations, aspirations. Though this is just an exploratory round on a sort of golf course, and no one's watching, I've already invested in outcomes. And that, sure as golf is golf, will bring frustration and disappointment.

Call it human nature. Call it the karmic wheel, the hoop of fire, attachment, the source of all suffering. Or just call it Golf.

As I biff my way up the long 3rd hole ('Long Hole', par 5), I'm thinking of my father's Anstruther golfing pals when he'd retired there. Mr Duncan and Jimmy Gilmour. In their seventies and never very good golfers in their youth (judging by their curt, prodding swings), these taciturn, canny men had played the course for decades. They knew every wrinkle, every hazard, and how to adjust their abilities to it.

On a short course like Anstruther, full of little quirks, ambushes and oddities, such men should not be taken on lightly as they poke and prod their way around in two hours twenty minutes. On the few occasions when as a teenager I played with them, though I was always driving past them off the tee and my swing was far more rhythmic and free than theirs, at the end of the round we had scored much the same.

They were of a different age, those men. They're long gone, skeletal in the ground or scattered as ashes.

As I putt out the 3rd 'green', I look down at my hands. Dad taught me this grip. He taught me many things, most of them through golf. How to win, how to lose. How to behave towards the people you play with. The importance of knowing one's game and limitations, the necessity of self-control. *You're no' here to chatter, you're here to play golf.*

I shake my head to clear it of these ghosts, then cajole the ball into the hole with his putter.

Alternating between bafflement and incredulity, frustration and pleasure, I leisurely explored the North Ronaldsay links. 'Long Hole' seemed very long into the firm breeze. 'Burn Hole' had a faint watery depression running across it. 'Short Hole' was indeed short at 99 yards (a pleasurable short iron drifting downwind like a dandelion seed, felt and looked lovely but went way past the pin – I over-adjusted for the clarity of the air).

Some of the tees were marked by half-buried little concrete markers, others I couldn't find at all. The course was apparently not at its best. When the laird's grandfather founded the course for himself and his visitors, before coming up for the summer he'd pay a crofter to clear the fairways and roll the greens. And there were additional holes, now lost, played over the great sheep dyke.

Mr Robertson had blamed the deterioration on 'the socialist government who gave the tenants all these rights in the 1880s'. I drank his tea and said nothing. It didn't seem the time to opine that the Crofters Act of 1883 was a fine, long-overdue piece of legislation that finally gave crofters some security in their lives.

From one point of view Duncan Robertson is a largely absentee feudal laird who deep down regards the island as his family's personal kingdom. He could be regarded as an exemplar of everything that's retrograde in landownership in Scotland, especially the Highlands and Islands.

Then again he was humorous, courteous, hospitable. And though he doesn't play golf himself, the course remains open to all. He seemed a kindly and decent man, which for me weighs more than political views. In the days when I climbed hard and had to entrust another person with my life, I learned that opinions are froth. Only how we behave has weight. *Will this person leave me on the mountain?* What we say afterwards in tents and bars may be entertaining but largely foam from the mouth.

At the 7th, playing directly towards the sea, my ball ended up within the ribcage of a rabbit skeleton. I decided to prefer (improve) the lie of my ball without penalty, so lifted and dropped it a foot away. No getting away from mortality, even here. Maybe especially here.

This was 'Carlos' Hole'. I wondered who Carlos was; it seemed an oddly exotic name for the far north. I imagined a homesick Spaniard, descendant of some shipwrecked sailor from the Armada. (The following day Peter Donnelly laughed and told me Carlos was a well-loved dog, buried on the course under a marker of his own.)

At the long 8th, 'Linklet Hole', I tried the wooden club I'd borrowed from the 'clubhouse', and heaved one ball onto the beach, the next into the sea. I let the sea have my second ball as a form of local taxation, but found the other in a pool near where the seals had indignantly retreated, leaving low shining hollows as they dragged themselves to the water. I could have done with the bizarre club the laird had shown me: a very old wooden-shafted club with a rusted head that had a circular hole in the middle of its face. I'd looked at it, mystified. The hole was slightly smaller than a golf ball. It looked like some ancient agricultural implement from some long-lost art.

'A water iron,' Duncan Robertson had said. 'I think my grandfather had it made for playing off the beach.'

Then I was at the 9th. Found the tee, decided on the mashie-niblick. Scaffed the tee shot horribly, worst shot of the round. But my second was sweet, restoring my mood, ended up some 20 feet from the pin. I cleared away various pebbles, a bone or two, wool and sheep and rabbit droppings, looked at the putt. I wanted this par, the second one of the round. Even alone and playing each shot just for the interest and pleasure of it, still these little goals, hopes and anxieties. The turf was lumpy as usual, the ball could go anywhere.

I remembered a technique developed on our scarred putting green in Anstruther: hitting the ball on the up to deliberately impart top-spin. That might help hold it on the line. I steadied over my dad's putter, remembering him. The ball ran smartly with little diversion, finished a foot away, a tap-in for par.

I looked around, but there no witnesses apart from a few sheep.

Still, it's what you do when no one's looking that counts. I took my packed lunch from the hut and sat down in the sun and wind, feeling as wide open as the world around me.

The cronies play Billowness

On a brisk April morning, they are playing the short 2nd on Anstruther, by Billowness where the green sits below the squat War Memorial. My dad in his tweed jacket and plus-fours, pipe clenched between his teeth, looks increasingly like the great Harry Vardon as he waits his turn to play. Jimmy Gilmour and Mr Duncan wear gardening trousers and old windcheaters. All three have flat bunnets, pulled down firmly against the stiff breeze.

Jimmy Gilmour's prodded tee shot has just kicked off the rim of the bunker and finished near the pin. He smiles, shakes his head: undeserved.

Below his stubby white moustache, Mr Duncan says something as he steps in turn onto the tee; they all chuckle quietly. Mr Duncan stabs with his wood, the ball wobbles low then trundles onto the edge of the green. He brushes his moustache, looks satisfied. It'll do.

My father tees up his ball, a Dunlop 65 he found in the rough a month back. He looks up, then down, waggles the club once. The others stand still and silent, as they should. Dad is wearing heavy green woollen stockings and his old brown golf shoes. In his bag beside the tee is the putter I'm using today.

He swings, pulls his shot a bit, always a problem for him. His ball runs past the left-hand bunker, leaving a simple approach to the pin. He may get down in two from there.

He nods philosophically, shoulders his bag, and the three elderly men set off steadily towards the green, Jimmy Gilmour limping with his gammy leg from the Great War.

Unhurried, absorbed yet not that bothered – there's no money on these games, they just notice who has won – they'll get round Anstruther with a minimum of fuss. There will be the pleasure of a good shot, disappointment at a poor one, quiet laughter and head-shaking at a piece of luck, maybe the pleasure of finding a good ball in the rough.

As always, they play briskly, with few words and some brief chuckles. No hanging about, just walk up to the ball, hit it and walk on. They don't use scorecards but keep the score in their heads. Each expects to get through a month using one ball, and will be quietly satisfied to get through a round with the same golf tee.

If there's time, there'll be a quick pint at the Craw's Nest afterwards, where the best score will pay. They share a very Scottish sense that good fortune must come with a penalty, and a bad day is best cheered by a free drink. Then it'll be home for lunch, agreeing to play again in a couple of days.

If I say golf courses are haunted places, I mean it is we who are haunted. I can only watch, believing and not believing, as by the 2nd green above the Billowness, on a brisk bright grey morning in Eternity, my father glances at the hole once, then bends over his putter.

2ND

'Travesty'

(NORTH RONALDSAY)

I drink with one hand, run the other through salt-stiffened hair. My fingers linger a moment on the tube just under my scalp on the right side, then drift to find the two shallow depressions in my skull. It's a reminder, if I ever need one.

I've been writing about my brain injury indirectly, through fiction. But *In Another Light* is finished now and there's a gap left. Which gives me time to play a bit until I discover what comes next. Agent and editor would like to see another novel, but I'm tired of living in make-believe, and a bit resentful of all those days spent in the shed with a bright world untasted outside. I'd rather be out playing golf, or walking by the sea, or upstairs making love with my wife.

One thing this tube in my head tells me is I've only so many days. What do I want to do with them? It's a simple enough question.

I throw my sandwich crust to an enterprising sheep, reckoning it would enjoy a change from seaweed. I live much of my life in a daze, cut off from the present by the internal dialogue commenting, judging, remembering and anticipating. On a golf course I seem to abruptly *come to*, like with Lesley when our eyes meet across the breakfast table. Why is that? Can we make it happen more often?

17

Back to golf, though these inner conversations are very much part of the game. What have I learned from this preliminary reconnaissance round? The course, as always, is a given. It can't be adapted, I must adapt to it.

I need to alter my distance judgement to allow for the clarity of the air. And pitching the ball in high towards the pin doesn't work. So it's back to the low pitch-and-run shot of my childhood, the classic Scottish seaside links shot from an age before watered greens and the lofted wedge. After dozens of hours spent practising that shot with all the tunnel-vision fanaticism of a teenage boy, maybe some of that knowledge still resides in my wrists and arms.

Then the top-spun putt to help the ball hold its line – that will help.

The biggest adjustment is mental. I'll stop treating this as a travesty, a hopelessly run-down modern golf course, and play it as it is. That's the only way to deal with the sheep turds, the random bounces, ruts, pebbles, bits of bone, the lost tees, the missing pin. Think of par for each hole as at least one more shot than usual and try to make that. (After all, what we now call 'bogey', meaning one over par, used to actually *mean* par. It was par for the time.)

The alternative is frustration and constant irritation. *Play the course*, my father used to say. *Play it as it lies, not as how you want it to be*. How much of his life-guidance was couched in terms of golf.

These sheep now, they're adapted. Short-bodied, wiry creatures like little goats, their fleece in corkscrew twists like half-unravelled dreadlocks. They spend much of their time on the seashore at low tide, eating the soft bright-green seaweed. Their digestions are adapted to it, and it's believed they're unchanged from the Neolithic period.

They also happen to taste great. I'll be eating North Ron lamb tonight at the Bird Observatory, looking forward to it already.

I stand up, stretch away the stiffness that's setting in already. Think sheep. Think adaptation. Here goes.

This time I allow for the crosswind, and my tee shot at the 1st flies and bounces, finishing some 30 yards from the flag. On any normal course one would entertain ambitions to get down in two from here. On any normal course this would be given as a par 3. But here the R & A guidelines are firmly – and rightly – laid aside. Where a pitch may jump in any direction, and holing any putt longer than a couple of feet is uncertain, this really is a par 4. Bogey 4, right?

Fine. I reach back into my childhood memories, pitch-and-run the ball to within 15 feet. Again top-spin helps the first putt hold its line better. Tap in for a 4.

Yes, it feels like I'm playing golf. The word *travesty* is being carried away on the breeze in the direction of Norway. Adapt, accept. Play it as it lies.

The 2nd *is* a par 3, a mere 146 yards. I locate a likely teeing area. Demarcated tees didn't come into golf till the late nineteenth century; before then players hit off at one or two club lengths from the previous hole. This added to the scarring and unevenness around the greens, making reliable putting impossible.

I improvise the tee shot, gripping the mashie well down the shaft. Mishit the ball out to the right, a poor shot made worse by a bad bounce.

How quickly one's moods shift on a golf course, buoyancy followed by irritation at the shortcomings of course and self. As I walk after the ball, keeping my eye on where I think it ended up among the wool and gull feathers, I can watch my mind churning away.

In golf, with its many pauses, its often lengthy walks between one shot and the next, there's time to watch thoughts and emotions shift, merge and succeed each other with all the inevitability and impersonality of thin clouds across this bound-less sky. It's a meditation of sorts. Instead of watching my breath, *mindfulness of breathing*, this is *mindfulness of golfing*.

Figuring out what to do with this awareness – of how desire creates anxiety creates tension that leads to poor shot which makes for irritation, which is silly because it's only a golf ball for God's sake and the day is beautiful – well that's Scottish Presbyterian Buddhist stuff and it's going to take a lifetime to work it out.

My ball is sunk in a small eroded sandy hollow in the turf, probably made by sheltering sheep. The word *travesty* floats back a little way from Norway. No, no, it's only a bunker. A natural bunker like all the early ones were. The kind of natural feature from the founding links of Leith, Musselburgh and St Andrews, in imitation of which the rest of the world's bunkers are manufactured.

This course isn't a pain in the neck, it is an *ancestor*. I shuffle my walking shoes in the sand, get the feel of its weight and texture. The pin's some 40 yards off. Once again I revert to an improvised shot from my youth. Lay open the face of the 9 iron, hit it neither clean nor scoop totally underneath, hard down onto the back of the ball. Waggle once or twice, trying to remember how this goes. How often did I practise this into the falling dusk, how many years ago?

Steep arc. Don't stop on it. Go –

– Now that gave a real jolt of pleasure, direct and unarguable as my annoyance of a few minutes ago. Ball flies out true, runs as intended, finishes near enough. Two putts. A 4. One over par, but still the pleasure of making that one shot right.

I'm camping in the ruins of a once-fine golf game, so I must take pleasure from the shots that come out right. In my competitive Hot Boy Golfer days, I got so wound up that a round would be ruined by one missed putt or one poorly thought-out pitch, and I'd walk home fretting. Now I'm free to enjoy the good bits and let the bad go.

Still, a decent score would be nice . . .

Which starts to look more possible after the 'Long Hole'. According to the laird, this was once over 600 yards long before a great storm truncated it. Discarding the borrowed wood, I hit a 5 iron straight, a second 5 iron straight, then a 7 iron to 15 feet. My putt – clang! – hits pin and goes in.

A birdie. Blimey. Can't be many of them on this course. A rising warmth spreads through my system like whisky, a silent inner *Thank you!* rises to the great Whatever. Of course, this mood will pass like the others, but it's still good to be here to have it.

My hand goes of its own accord to the hard little bulge of the tube in my head. The colloid cyst that lodged itself where my brain fluid should drain is still in there. That blocked drain had built up the pressure in my head, leading to violent headaches then unconsciousness then a coma, trending towards death as my brain was compressed. After hours lying on a trolley while people wondered who I was and what to do with me, only a good guess by a consultant neurosurgeon saved my life. Mr Jellinek seemed very pleased when he told me about it later, the police escort as he dashed across Sheffield to operate – 'I'd always wanted to have one of those.' I was pretty pleased about it too.

Two days after he'd opened up my skull and installed an external drain – a plastic tube that dripped a clear yet slightly greasy fluid into a plastic bag that reminded me of the kind goldfish come in at the fair – my surgeon sat on the end of my bed to discuss what to do next. He could operate to remove the cyst but he couldn't guarantee not affecting my centres for memory and abstract reasoning – did I need them in my work? 'Now and then,' I croaked. So he decided to leave the cyst and install a bypass shunt to drain cerebral fluid into my abdomen, which seemed like a good idea to me. The shunt seems to have taken; it'll outlast me. It'll still be intact when my bones are powder. The knowledge isn't depressing so much as the context in which all my days are happening.

'Burn Hole', 'Short Hole', 'Gravity Hole' go by without trauma. I'm adapting to how to play this course. Just get the ball reasonably close, don't expect or try too much. Concentrate on each shot, then let the mind wander in between, uplifted by this vast green and blue openness, a hint of the curve of the Earth on that horizon . . .

Score 5, 4, 5. If only I'd got here a day earlier, I could near have won the Open yesterday. Because it really is open; all you have to do is turn up. Apparently one group of seven were volunteers from the Bird Observatory, most of whom had never played golf before. It took them five hours to get round the nine holes; admittedly that included a long break for alcoholic refreshments in the old car parked at the 4th. Then the ceilidh party afterwards, from which the island is still recovering. Wish I'd been there.

No, don't think like that. Just enjoy being here today, each shot, each challenge, then accept each outcome.

With this enlightened (if only momentarily) outlook, I steal another birdie at the par 4 7th, the one named after the much-loved Carlos: mashie iron downwind, then the niblick to 15 feet, palm away the sheep droppings, and the top-spun putt comes to rest against the pin. Move the pin gently, ball falls in.

At this point it comes to me: this course is not a travesty of golf but its more characterful and worldly ancestor. Like these scuttering wee sturdy sheep, it's much more tasty than the contemporary version.

Then the epiphany comes. Looking around for a likely site of the next tee, with the nearby shore resounding all the way up the island, the island itself resting in an improbably turquoise-to-indigo sea, I realise it's the manicured courses of much modern golf, landscaped and planted so beautifully with trees and ponds, with their colour-coded distance markers, their artificial bunkers shored and raked, their greens watered and rolled to eliminate every bit of moss or crab grass, aiming for the perfect course where there is no unevenness, no unexpected breaks, no pebbles, rabbit skeletons or sheep's droppings or distracting seagulls, indeed the complete banishment of all animal life – *they are the travesty.*

I try the borrowed 3 wood at the 8th, push it heavily out right, the result no fault but my own. (It's a Scottish game, for sure.) But redeemed by a soaring mashie iron, the first truly timed shot of the day, the kind that sings through wrist and arm as shoulders and hips rotate, the weight transfers into the impact, and the club gives and the ball flies like both are living things meeting and parting.

I find my ball some 12 feet from the hole. Crouch down to sweep the turf. For the first time, I inspect the putt from both sides of the hole. The greens here don't have much borrow as such, they're just lumpy. Hit it firm and hope.

Ball runs fast, hits back of cup, hops up, falls in. Another birdie, third of the round. I look around, dazed and incredulous. Of course no one's watching apart from a few indifferent sheep. Absolutely nothing's at stake here – I mean, it's not the North Ronaldsay Open, is it?

But still the day has become so bright.

The 9th is a straightforward hole, 164 yards, playing back towards the club hut and the dyke. With the wind shifting, it's a soft mid-iron. Another improvised shot, the kind all the early golfers would have known – club face slightly open, gripping down the shaft – floats and stotts into the general area of the canted flag. That's all I'm trying for, the general area. This isn't target golf. This is canny, philosophical, improvised. In the old days, players must have endlessly encountered good and bad luck, much more so than now. It must have been part of the mood, texture, the *taste* of the game, yet another reminder for the Presbyterian-at-leisure of the mysterious ways of the Almighty.

Dad's old putter, with its heavy, chunky head and wooden shaft, seems right for these conditions. Two putts it is.

Done.

Time to head back, find Lesley and my stepson Leo, who set out this morning down the other side of the island for the kind of long self-communing daunder a teenager needs to take. Golf isn't my life, they are.

I return the 3 wood to the hut, pull the door shut behind me, climb the gate across the great sheep-barring dyke then set off across the island for the Bird Observatory. I'm happy and empty in my head, tired in my feet, knees, ankles, back. Despite how much I get from golf now I've come back to it, I play only sporadically and am not properly fit for it. I still swing pretty much as I did at Leo's age, only I'm not fifteen any more.

Walking back across North Ronaldsay, quietly replaying the round and the notions and memories that came with it, I glimpse my next possible project. It may not be a good career move – I really should write another novel – but from the outset it's not a career but a life I've been after. If I ever doubt the wisdom of that, I finger one of these dents in my skull where the drill went in, and know that my life is too short and uncertain to waste on such trivialities as a career.

Golf isn't life. It's just a small, radiant corner of it, like a chip of mirror-glass, the kind where if you bring it close enough and examine carefully from a number of angles, you can see the whole of your eye, and a surprising amount of the world around you.

The missing links

On my desk today, next to my notebook, I have the scorecard from that second nine-hole round, sweat-smudged, grass-stained. Something smiled on me that day. In a wintry Sheffield shed, I feel the light, the air, the dry spongy turf, hear the sea breaking.

Behind the scorecard is a print of one of the earliest photographs of golf. It's 1858, a young man named Robert Chambers is putting to win an early version of the British Amateur Championship. A semicircle of some forty people in frock coats, flat bunnets and stovepipe hats crowd round him. His caddie is carrying what looks like five clubs slung in the crook of his arm, as I did that day on North Ronaldsay.

Look more closely. Though Chambers's stance is away from the ball and it looks as if he's about to play a full shot and the turf is coarse and uneven, he's clearly putting. Then, recognising the memorial on the low hill behind the crowd, I realise with a shock Chambers is on the 18th green at St Andrews Old Course. And this championship green is indistinguishable from the fairway, being tufted, unrolled and unwatered, and it looks remarkably like those in North Ronaldsay.

Eighteen fifty-eight was also the year Allan Robertson became the first man to break 80 at St Andrews. The condition of the non-greens – more than the wooden-shafted clubs and the 'guttie' ball used then, which could be surprisingly effective – explains why that took so long to happen.

I think now of the North Ronaldsay links not as a perversion, travesty or poor relation of golf, but as a unique survival of the game as it was in its first 400 years. The original links at Leith, Musselburgh, St Andrews, Aberdeen, Gullane, all the way along the East Coast of Scotland, were common land, open to use by all, including sheep, cows, rabbits. Those animals were the only greenkeepers, as they are in North Ronaldsay. And those democratic, non-exclusive origins flavour the practice and perception of the game in Scotland to this day.

Playing North Ronaldsay was like coming face to face with the missing link we'd believed extinct, or running into Robert Johnson playing the Blues at a crossroads in the Mississippi Delta – strangeness and bemusement tinged with recognition, giving way to delight at encountering the true source.

If you're minded to encounter the source and origin of golf, don't go to St Andrews, Carnoustie or farcically exclusive Muirfield, try to get on the ballot for a tee off place, pay £100 a round as well as a bundle for accommodation. Use the money to fly to Orkney then from Kirkwall to North Ronaldsay with four clubs, a putter and a few balls; stay at the Bird Observatory then play as many rounds as you feel like. Play for nothing at all but the playing of it and you'll be playing true golf, the original game, drinking from the clear source.

'Aliosaurus'

(BATHGATE)

'Al, I'd like to play golf with you at Bathgate.'

A pause, then Alastair's voice down the line, his Lowland Scots accent like steel wool scouring a rusty putter.

'Why me? Why Bathgate? I havenae played there in twenty year.'

'I'm thinking of writing an odd sort of golf book.'

Another silence. Al always tended to consider before he spoke; not many of us did in 1970. We did a lot of stoned blethering while he, our mature student pal, stood straight and clean-shaven, clutching a whisky tumbler before the coal-effect electric fire of his and Senga's council flat.

'It'll be an odd buke that wants me in it. Aye, sure.'

In his teens young Alastair McLeish was torn between notions of becoming a golf professional, or a revolutionary Marxist. Only in Scotland could such a career choice present itself.

He was born into the industrial working class of Bathgate, Central Scotland. His family had always been political. The heroes of his childhood, some of them relatives, had fought fascists in Spain or the police in the General Strike. Looking round his town, he felt life had to become better for the folk there, and that could only be done by ultimately resolving the class struggle.

Yet there were other local heroes, like the legendary Eric Brown, leading Scottish professional for many years, Ryder Cup captain. And young Bernard Gallacher hitting the headlines, winning tournaments and making good money. For along with the workingmen's clubs, the focus of Bathgate life was its golf course.

Assertively working class, surrounded by factories, the slag heap and coal bing, the rubbish dump, the quarry, this was another kind of Scottish golf course, where the game was cheap, hard fought, heavily wagered, well lubricated afterwards. For much of its hundred-year history, Bathgate has produced a stream of very tough, very fine golfers. The club has produced two Ryder Cup captains; nowhere else in the world can claim this.

I asked Alastair once why he thought this had happened. He paused, frowned, then the quick, rueful McLeish grin. 'I suppose we're awfy competitive buggers.'

When I want to counter the notion that golf is invariably elitist, the territory of the moneyed middle-classes, for posh folk and networking businessmen, I usually start with Bathgate and Al McLeish.

I woke in a B & B outside Linlithgow to a wet smirr of rain, drove to Bathgate through a chilly April dawn. *Dreich* is our word for it – our climate has made the word necessary, and its persistent, clinging gloom accounts for a lot of the Scottish mindset.

I was worrying about my mother. The other morning, before I'd left Anstruther, she had looked small and anxious in her nightdress in the hall, a husk of the enthusing, energetic woman I'd known all my life. 'I'm not feeling myself,' she kept repeating. An hour later, she abruptly reappeared, fully dressed, and briskly said she felt fine, there'd been nothing wrong with her. There are pluses to having a failing memory.

So I'd left, as she'd insisted, but I still felt wrong. A bad son. I owed her everything and I wasn't with her. I was driving in the wrong direction.

I reminded myself that playing golf throughout Scotland for a possible book would be an opportunity to see her more often. And to catch up on old friends. Recent events had made it clear we must take those opportunities to see the people that matter to us, while they're still there, while we're still here. But being away from Sheffield and Orkney meant more time away from Lesley, and life was too short for that too.

These games of golf were not going to be pure pinball.

But there was Al waiting on the corner, and a real pleasure to see him. We've been pals for over thirty years. As he gets in the car, a brief firm handshake – Bathgate men don't do hugging. He looked and sounded unchanged: still the short, crinkly hair, weathered face, quizzical expression. Same windcheater, straight trousers, lace-up shoes as he'd had in the 1970s when we first met.

Though only a few years older than the rest of us doing English and Philosophy, from his dress, his outlook, his manner, his situation, he might as well have been another generation. 'Uncle Al' was married, to the lovely, down-to-earth, sardonic Senga who could hold her own with him in the alcohol and opinion stakes. They had a tidy council place of their own rather than our squalid smelly rented flats. She had an office job! They ate proper meals of meat and two veg at regular times!

'So how's yer heid these days, Andrew?'

'Still there,' I replied, and managed to keep my hand from going to my temple. 'Some days I forget stuff, and I get confused more easily.'

He looked at me closely, then nodded. 'Na, we're jist getting older!' I laughed and turned off for the golf course.

We were booked on the 1st tee at 7.30. Al had insisted on this time to get an uncluttered round. It was cold, still not fully light, still drizzling. But Alastair seemed stunned at what he saw.

'Christ, it never used tae be like this!'

Young trees everywhere, shivering in the breeze. The fairway was lush but well cut; the tee itself was manicured, smart new tee box; pathways of artificial matting led off the tee; new clubhouse and pro shop; distance markers and irrigation outlets. The 18th green was large, looked firm, well kept. No sign from here of the factories, coal bings, rubbish tips I remembered from 1974 when we'd last played here together. It was what my father would have called *sprush*.

Alastair gazed upon it and shook his head, somewhere between wonder and regret.

'Blow me! You could almost call it beautiful.'

Even more bizarrely to me, already other golfers were appearing. Playing occasionally in Orkney this last while, I'd got used to the idea that during the week I could pretty much just walk along to the course on impulse and play any time. Here people were queuing up at 7.30 on a poor morning. It seemed golf had changed while I'd been away.

So we took a few hurried swings and prepared to set off. In the damp half-light, it was a world away from last summer in North Ronaldsay and the Stromness course. Down in Sheffield I'd recently joined the Beauchief (pronounced 'Beechief') club, a resolutely non-posh municipal parkland course, and had played a few times there in fine spring weather. It had been exhilarating, joining my first golf club since 1969 and discovering a new type of course. But English spring and Scottish spring are two different beasts, and now I was stiff and cold and anxious not to disgrace myself.

Al slightly mishit a safe, short drive. I sliced mine so badly it was nearly a shank, through the trees on the right into deep wet rough. I felt ridiculous, annoyed with myself, acutely disappointed – the usual. My second ball was well enough struck but ran into a bank of thick rough on the left of the fairway.

I lost both those balls, dropped another and hit it from the fairway, so that was an end to any legitimate scoring for the day. There'd been no discussion of handicaps, and whether we were playing against each other. We were just playing, that was understood. Anyway, as I realised after losing three balls in the first four holes, my game was falling asunder like a decrepit ship, taking my mood down with it.

'Aye, Scottish Protestants,' Al remarked after struggling himself in the opening holes. 'We're perfectly able to torture ourselves without any assistance.'

The game which had seemed so delightful, so easy, in North Ronaldsay and Stromness last summer, so enjoyable at Beauchief, had become difficult verging on impossible. I had a couple of pars at the 3rd and 4th, then something that might have been a 9. For the next hole, my scorecard simply has: ?

I was not happy. Tried to laugh it off, but I was not happy. The drizzle on my glasses warped my vision; I was cold and stiff, had no timing at all, felt out of touch, out of sympathy with the game. This golf book, if I ever wrote it, would be a farce. I should go back to making things up, I could invent a wonderful round of golf.

I focused on my friend. His swing had never been beautiful, but it was crisp, unadorned, straightforward as the man himself. He didn't feel he was in good touch, fretted over his driving and his putting, but he was scoring pretty steadily.

'What you playing off these days, Al?'

'Eight. I'd hoped it would be lower, after ma retirement, like.'

From where I stood, knee high in sodden grass, eight was pretty good for a man in his mid-fifties. But in golf as in life, Al always wants things to be better. Even as we played, he tried out a new putting grip, altered his length of backswing for short pitches, experimented with his stance on the tee.

A character note, in keeping with his political idealism. Because for all the collapse of the Soviet Union and the whole communist dream, in our supposedly post-political age Alastair

McLeish is still an unrepentant Marxist humanist. Whether it's a putting stroke or people's lives, things are rotten and surely should be, *can be*, better.

'I gave up golf several times in the last thirty years,' he remarked. 'It's only fairly recently I've come back tae it.'

'Too busy?' I asked sympathetically.

'I just found myself standing over a putt one day and I couldnae see the point in it.' He shook his head, then came the rueful grin. 'I suppose I mean I wasnae playing well.'

We began talking about the disappointments and frustrations of golf, the mystery of why it all goes horribly wrong. Al mentioned a friend whose handicap had gone from 5 to 22 in three years for no apparent reason *and he still hadn't given up.*

'I'd have packed it in.'

'I'd hae just shot masel.'

Discussing why we play well one day and are incompetent the next made my poor round so far seem less a cause of pain and more an interesting topic.

After all, I thought, this book can't be about me as a special golfer. No point kidding myself: I was once quite good and now I'm average. I won't be handing out handy golfing tips for lowering handicaps. I don't even have a handicap to lower. I have only delights and tribulations, encounters and experiences to relate, not solutions.

Right there on Bathgate golf course, as the rain became diluted by diffident sunlight, I realised my concern has always been with how things are, not how things should be.

The 8th at Bathgate is one of a number of demanding, satisfying par 3s on the course. Just 131 yards, teeing off inside a stand of trees, playing towards a narrow green flanked by bunkers, backed by more trees. I dried my glasses, looked at it.

I'd like to hit a good shot here; the hole deserves it.

The round's not so far gone that it can't be rescued and renewed. I've got to believe that. I do believe that.

My 8 iron is my first real golf shot of the day, finishing 20 feet from the pin. Even I couldn't three putt from there.

Both feeling more cheerful with the sun now drying us and the course, at the next hole we each had another regulation par. Still, Al suggests I try changing my putting stroke because I'd been struggling earlier. As I stare at him in disbelief, I realise another difference between us.

While he constantly tries to find a new solution, when I'm struggling I try to put things right by *returning* to what worked before. I want to recover a lost rightness. My character note, I suppose.

Our mood is lifting with the sky. At the tree-lined 10th (it seems they've planted 10,000 trees since we last played here, as well as removing the bings, heaps, quarries and dead factories) a decent 3 wood is followed by an 8 iron to 2 feet. First birdie of the day.

'You're playin some good golf, Andy.'

Though he's always been a better player than me, I want his respect.

He has mine. These last thirty years have been a struggle for him. In his teens he realised he wasn't going to reach Bernard Gallacher's standard, so turning professional was off the agenda. And he never did become a university lecturer in political philosophy – staff numbers at the universities went into rapid reverse just at the time we graduated. Instead he taught media studies ('maistly to a bunch of bored laddies who didnae want to be there but had to be for their module – I slipped in a wee bit Marxist propaganda when no one was looking') at Robert Gordon Technical College (now rebranded as a university) in Aberdeen.

Factories closed, the unions disintegrated. The Soviet Union collapsed, the Berlin Wall came down. Al had long spoken out against the perversion of Communism the Soviet Union had become, but still it was painful to see the noble dream go out with a whimper. Only his and Senga's son Malcolm, born after many years together, was a consolation of those years.

At Robert Gordon he'd always been in opposition. A shop steward, he fought several bruising campaigns against unjust dismissals, slashed resources and general administrative stupidity. Some he won, some he lost. It certainly stopped him ever getting promoted. He finally took early retirement and now does some caddying for interest and cash, plays regular golf medals at his fine course Murcar, reads a lot. He tells me that in the last six months he's read sixty novels.

'What kind?'

'Austrian novels.'

'There are sixty Austrian novels?'

'Oh aye. They're quite serious, like.'

Still thinking about Al and the life-disappointments he's had to endure, I make a horrible mess of the 11th. Heave my drive some 40 yards. Shaken and embarrassed, I top my next shot way over the green into the undergrowth.

This is a terrible place.

All the way round, Al has exclaimed over the changes since he was last here. The greens are much bigger – and faster, cut shorter with the new mowers. There are matted trolley tracks everywhere. Sprinkler heads dotted around fairways and greens. Whole stands of trees, new leaves sparking with water in the sunlight. Little coloured posts which he says are distance markers. Rakes in every bunker. When I top a shot into the burn, there's the long-handled scoop to get the ball out. Really, the course is quite transformed. It was always a decent one; now it's a different sort of decent one. It's happening all over the country; golf is changing.

He liked Bathgate when it was an unambiguously urban industrial course for an unambiguously industrial proletariat. Though the greens are amazing, this new smartness makes him uneasy. Has the membership changed, or just its expectations?

The majority of Bathgate folk, he admits, are significantly better off than thirty years ago – but at what cost?

By now the day is fine, almost warm. The timing finally comes back and I hit a series of good 3-wood drives that bring some more pars. At the 505-yard-long 15th, I actually hit three consecutive good shots, something rare since my teens. Another par.

At the 16th I chance the driver. The ball sings down the middle of the fairway. 'Hey, no bad, Andy!' Which is high praise among Scots. It matters to me that Al sees I can actually play golf, if only in flashes. The couple of times we went round together here while at university, it was much the same. By that time I scarcely played and was reliant on muscle memory that once in a while came right. There were so many interesting things to do other than play golf, and I tried lots of them.

But now I could be being paid – well, paying myself – to play! I picture Dad's face at this new development; he'd have been right amused. I wonder what he'd say about Mum. Am I doing right by her? Are my brothers and sister? She keeps losing things. Her short-term memory is a riddle things fall through. The other day she assured me potatoes take only a couple of minutes to boil. Does it just suit me to go along with her insistence she wants to live on her own, in her own house, or is that her right?

Even in the special protected space that is a golf course, life has a way of finding you.

Still, a good drive is there to be played. I look at the ball, let each dimple come into focus. Let the grass, the green ahead and the sun drying my shirt displace the rest for a while. So lucky to be here at all, remember that. We're all in temporary accommodation here – my dad, mum, myself, Al, Lesley.

So be it. My 9 iron clicks, that sweet give in the hands as the ball rises and drops on the green. Then a long holed putt: another birdie. What a great course.

How much a round is flavoured by its ending, like music by its final chords. On the last hole, finally a drive that everything got right behind: weight, legs, shoulder, arms, wrists. No effort at all and my old ball flies a good 260 yards on that slow fairway. Then a high straight wedge to 12 feet.

I'd like to say I holed it, but I have to say things as they are, not as they should be.

'I really enjoyed that,' Al says as we shake hands. 'I make it we both came back in 38 – no so bad for a couple of old-timers early in the season.'

Outside the clubhouse, Al goes over to an elderly short man, touches his shoulder.

'Davy . . .'

Man looks at Al, stares. Then: 'Jesus Christ, what the fuck?! Ali!' Shakes his hand warmly. Again, inside the clubhouse in the spacious bar, a tubby bald man jumps up. 'Al! What the fuck! Whaur ye been aa these years?'

'Aberdeen,' Al says simply.

'Whit the fuck for?'

'God knows.'

As they catch up, I reflect the membership possibly hasn't changed that much. Bathgate is still no one's idea of an exclusive country club.

Driving back to my mother's next morning with the aching head and slightly poisoned feeling that follows an evening with the McLeishes, I'm thinking still about Alastair's approach to golf and politics.

He dreams, as most golfers and nowadays few citizens do, of improvement. He imagines things really can be better. This has yielded him a lifetime of striving and disappointment, with little victories in between. The world has changed and he has refused to adapt. A friend nicknames him 'Aliosaurus'.

'It's rather noble,' I'd suggested last night.

'He's just stubborn,' Senga snorted. 'Ali cannae change. He

doesn't like new foods, or to try new activities, or see films he knows he doesn't like, even though he hasnae seen them.'

She looked at him and shook her head, amused, despairing, affectionate. They've been married for ever; I heard this same complaint thirty years ago.

Al frowned into his whisky, sorting out his retort. He looked like a man quizzed by the world on a daily basis, and each day he gives back what he knows is the right answer, and each time the world refuses it.

He can see the painful joke of his position. He knows 'the working class' doesn't really exist here any more, that most people would rather consume than have justice, equality, even freedom. But he knows this is wrong, just as he knew my putting stroke was wrong and had to correct it (thus ruining my putting for the rest of the season till a Tibetan Buddhist undertaker made good the damage – but that's for later).

But what stays with me still, as I drive back to my mother who at eighty-four cannot hope for improvement, is Alastair's response to Senga's chiding. He looked up from his glass, baffled, sincere.

'I have to believe we can improve. That things can become better for people, that we're no helpless victims of history. And that one day I'll break par on Murcar.'

I drive on to Anstruther, wondering how short my mum's short-term memory will be today, if I should stay longer and more often, dreading the day she won't be there. I can't disagree with Al or his sincerity. It's just that up ahead wait things no politics, medical science or good round of golf can solve: human love and loss.

Blow me, you could almost call it beautiful.

Playing Anstruther
through the night

I opened my eyes to see blue eyes looking down at me. The dead
who had kept me company had gone.

'You're in a hospital,' she said slowly. 'You've been very ill.
You're all right now.'

She looked worried. I wasn't worried, I had come back to the
world with no baggage whatsoever, not even my name. But I had
hers.

'Lesley,' I said.

She nodded. I felt pleased.

'Back.'

'Yes. You're in Intensive Care.'

'Oh, good.'

When they'd contacted her in Guildford, they had warned that
I mightn't be alive when she got back to Sheffield. That journey
took six hours, with delays, missed connections. I can scarcely
imagine what that was like. Meanwhile I was out of it, drifting in
some kind of ante-chamber that I thought of as *blue shadowlands*.
It's worth recording that though it was often unpleasant, the
unspoken immanence of death wasn't terrifying.

It helped that my father came and talked about playing golf on
Anstruther, then Mal Duff, reminding me of setting out on a
bright, hard morning in Glencoe, then Anthea Joseph, who
drank gin, laughed and told her outrageous stories about Bob,

Paul, Jimi, Van Morrison, Fairport. In different ways, they had helped me hang on. It didn't strike me as odd they were all dead.

When Lesley finally got to the hospital, they told her I was still alive after the operation to relieve the pressure on my brain that was killing me. She was warned I might have significant brain damage. She wondered what she would do if I had – we had only been together for a year, no promises had been made. In those days it was still 'see how it goes'.

So there was a lot riding on my being able to look at her and croak 'Lesley'.

In Intensive Care and for the weeks afterwards in the neurological ward, the days weren't so bad. Long periods of boredom, with her visits the highlights, and friends come to say they were pleased I wasn't dead. I agreed, but couldn't tell them the other aspect of surviving: that nothing felt the same.

But nights were long, with panic circling nearby in the semi-dark lit by the nurses' night station. Pain in abdomen and my temple, fear of death or permanent brain damage, the prospect of being for ever lost to oneself and not knowing it, groping in some dull confused fog. Maybe my lover and friends were humouring me, privately mourning the damage. Maybe I had changed. How could I know? Would the shunt take this time, or would Mr Jellinek have to operate yet again, and this time remove the colloid cyst that was blocking my brain-drain? He'd warned me there'd be a risk of damaging my centres for reasoning and memory . . .

When the night fears prowled, I would hold them at bay by playing round Anstruther's modest 9-hole seaside course. Though my memory of recent things was hopeless, I found I could visualise each hole methodically, and feel again the worn club grips, smell cut grass, damp canvas bag, sunshine and rain. I'm fifteen. My parents are still alive, I have never been in love, I have never seriously lost. It's all in front of me. Achievement nil, aspiration infinite.

I'd play each hole in turn, visualising it minutely: the great slopes of the 1st and 7th; the abandoned coastguard station above our broken tidal swimming pool; the 5th a striking short hole, offering a choice between steep clinging gorse banks on the right, and straight ahead slopes and ridges all running the ball down towards the rocks and sea – bonnie enough but it's not a fair hole because there is no real golfing solution to the terrain, just trusting to luck or fate. Then again, some problems have no proper solution. Sometimes you have to hit and see, then take it from there.

Friends left me soothing music; a chaplain offered the comforts of religion; a little radio brought the World Service, with reports from far places and repeats from childhood. But through those long ward nights on the edge of panic, when I could no longer hold Lesley's face in my mind's eye, it was to picturing Anstruther golf course that I turned.

We all have a ground, a place that secures and defines us. I had not known that a little golf course would be mine.

After playing with Al McLeish at Bathgate, I finally went back to play Anstruther for real. I'd made the tea for Mum; we discussed John Keats's letters to Fanny Brawne ('We all felt she wasn't good enough for him'); I tried to keep my voice natural as I told her yet again where I'd just come from. Then I nipped off to the course.

The evening was full of shifting greys, and what we call 'fresh'. I stood on the 1st tee for the first time in many years, club in hand and no one in sight. The fairway swelled in a hill that had seemed so huge and distant when I was thirteen. This was what my father had offered me in *blue shadowlands*: the option of standing here again.

I teed up a ball, took a couple of brisk practice swings – then stopped with the driver helpless in my hand as I wept like a child.

Once that was done, I took a deep breath and drove off into the promised land.

4TH

'Duff'

(ABERDOUR)

What's changed? I wonder while I drive to meet Liz Duff at the Aberdour golf course, scene of her husband Malcolm's apoplectic encounters with those demons of golf that are in their own way as unforgiving as the demons of ice and snow. In my mid-thirties, curiosity, adventure and certain other things impelled me to put my neck on the block with Mal through Scottish winters and Himalayan summers. Now I'm happy to spend a day sweating up hills the unthreatening way, or find my challenges on a golf course.

Maybe it's maturity. Or perhaps I've just got older. Still, as Noël Coward remarked, getting older is frightful but consider the alternative.

This is going to be emotional for both Liz and me. Though it's seven years since Mal died in his tent on Everest with a book across his chest, this will be the first time since then that Liz and I have played golf together. He'll not get older, and we have. Yet there'll be much laughter today, there always is when memories and stories about Mal come up, and the extent of our laughter marks the depth of our loss.

Call it a memorial round to one of golf's great foozlers. A man baffled, disgusted, fascinated to find that his will-power, huge capacity for concentration, self-belief, physical and mental strength – that all these could not prevail over a little white stationary ball.

I get to Aberdour early. The day is breezy and warm, and there's plenty time to loosen up, try the practice putting green, hit some shots into the netting. I'm slightly raised, excited, almost nervous, but though this place is full of memories of Mal and the way things were back then, I don't feel the clutch and sink of loss.

Maybe it's because the present morning is so full. The first tee is perched high on the crown of the course, looking out over the glittering Firth of Forth, at the little islands and skerries, the gulls birling and the seals flopped on rocks. On the far side of the firth are the Bass Rock, Edinburgh, the Pentland Hills, North Berwick where I'll be playing next. Small sailing boats with bright sails tack improbably against the breeze.

The course itself is a strong, fresh green. Despite being near the sea, Aberdour is more a parkland than a links course. It's full of trees, big towering hardwood trees and lots of recently planted saplings. And it's sprusher and smarter than I'd remembered, from the tee boxes to the distance markers, the matting laid down for the trolleys to the irrigation covers. It seems to be happening everywhere. People pay more for golf now, expect better conditions and take longer about it.

'Hiya, Andy!'

And here comes Liz, beaming, looking tall and slim in white golfing slacks and a bluebell shirt. We hug then look at each other. Don't know what she sees but I'm looking at my old friend.

'So how's the brain these days?' she asks.

I'd seen the MRI scan slides. Amazing how much the grey matter can be compressed without quite killing, and mostly come back to shape. There are consequences, of course, only some of them physical.

'Unless my friends are being very kind, I'm almost back to normal.'

'That bad, eh?' she says, and hugs me again.

When Liz tees up on the first, laughs and says, 'Here goes nothing, Andy!' and our round begins, I think of course she's right. Mal is gone, and we're bound the same way. Here indeed goes nothing. Yet she's right to laugh. Today's course lies ahead of us.

The round opens with a short, spectacular descent to a bunker-surrounded green with two eroded rock stacks like horns behind, the Firth of Forth dark blue between them. I think Liz would like it recorded that she won the first two holes with a 3 at each of them ('Aye, and then the trouble started!').

As we approach the 1st green, Liz laughs and points at the seawall. 'Mal hated losing balls!' she says. 'Even during competitions he'd jump over there to look for his. And if he didn't find it, he'd come back later.'

My own game stutters from the start, from the opening 8 iron pushed right into a bunker to a series of 3 putts that make me wonder what's the point in trying to hit good shots when I just waste them on the greens. I abruptly lose confidence in my judgement of distance, how hard I want to hit the ball – once that's gone it's hard to recover. On the 4th, I manage to leave my first putt short, batter the next way past, then miss the return.

Four putts from 20 feet. Painful. I feel depression and sulk coming on, then dislike myself for it. The day begins to lose its shine.

Given that he was my teacher, mentor, and vastly my better first at climbing and then at trout fishing, I have to admit to being pleased I was effortlessly Mal's superior at golf on the few occasions we played. My drives would soar past his, my putter didn't stutter in those days. Bunkers were not for me an invitation to dig to Australia.

It wasn't that I was that good after fifteen years away from golf, more that at times he could be so bad. The harder he tried, the worse he got. He'd have a few good shots, even a few good holes, before disaster struck with a wildly shanked iron, or a muffed dribble into the bunker (he was as fatally drawn to bunkers). I saw the veins in his neck standing out, sensed the volcanic outburst he was struggling to suppress.

He couldn't believe it. He just couldn't believe it. All that strength, concentration, will-power – and still that ball trickled yet again back down into the sand. Mal was a great believer in self-control and course etiquette, which just made it worse (and more entertaining) when the explosion came.

At first he asked for a stroke every second hole. Then a stroke a hole. Then we agreed to stop in any way playing against each other.

I felt it brought a balance to our relationship. Struggling now round Aberdour with Liz, I see his face that time at Glenbervie when my explosion shot out of a deep bunker and flopped beside the hole in a shower of sand. I treasure that look yet. My closest male friend on the planet, the one who'd kept an eye out for me and brought me safely through many days in Scottish winter hills and two Himalayan expeditions to date, was seriously impressed.

'How d'you do that, youth?'

'Practice,' I replied. 'Lot of practice a long time ago. If you didn't keep dragging me off on your mad expeditions, I'd do it more often.'

'Ah yes,' he said. 'There's something I've been meaning to talk to you about . . .'

That was the day he outlined his proposal to climb Lhotse Shar with Sandy Allan. I'd come along, see Upper Nepal, guide a few paying members along, then climb and load-carry as high as sensible on the mountain, say 23,000 feet.

'Nothing to it, old chap. You'll enjoy Nepal after Baltistan and Tibet.'

'You told me that one person out of ten dies on every Himalayan expedition. This would be my third. That doesn't sound good odds.'

'But you'll be with me!'

'That's what I'm worried about.'

I lined up my drive, squinting into the shimmer down the long 9th. It seemed to go on for ever, as I'd once assumed I would.

'There might be another book in it,' he suggested.

I can't remember what happened to my drive after that magnificently timed piece of gamesmanship. I do know we went to Lhotse Shar, and that the walk in through Upper Nepal and the early stages of the climb were as life-enhancing and joyous as he'd suggested. And I know Mal got lucky when a sérac collapse round 7000 metres only fractured his skull, and that Sandy did well to get him off the big slopes alive. I know I've never written about it and it was my last big trip.

But I can't remember where my drive went, or his, or any other shots from that round on that sweltering afternoon at Glenbervie. I only remember the light, the deep-green trees and the bright-green greens, the heat and joy and ease of it, to be playing on my earliest golf course with my great pal as he outlined our next ploy.

It may have been that memory, or his amused presence somewhere in the air shimmering over the turf as Aberdour baked, but I began to play some golf. Some sweet straight tee shots cracked off the club face. Then a birdie 2 at the 12th, where a 6 iron soared just right, the ball finished a couple of yards from the pin. Took my time, looked at it from three angles, holed it.

I watched Liz swing. Now in her mid-fifties, she looked fit and well, still quick to laugh and make fun of herself, of us, of the world. But definitely a little more sobered and subdued than she used to be. Her swing had changed too. Liz used to play hockey and it showed in the way she played golf – a wide-legged, swift hard swipe, the club scarcely rising above shoulder level. Now her swing was long and slow, deliberate and unforced, letting the club do the work.

Her drive – at the 14th, I think, a green and pleasant tree-lined easy par 4 – clicked off sweetly. A flush of pleasure in her face as she held the follow-through position.

'Nice one, Liz!'

She laughed as she put her club away and we set off. 'See that bunker on the right? Malcolm said if I could drive past that, he'd buy me a trolley.'

'And?'

'Look at my trolley!'

So his name came up as we went round, in recollections, anecdotes, occasions we'd shared from riotous Hogmanays in Glencoe to a birthday celebration at Everest base camp. Talking about him brought laughter, nods and smiles. For a moment I involuntarily glimpsed his face in the blue sky, hair and beard tousled, looking down on us, that glint in his eye that signalled another daft ploy in the making.

But he's gone, of course. He's with us only in our stories and memories and laughter – which means he's with us quite a lot. I've known few people recollected as often as Mal Duff, and nearly always with laughter. When he and Liz were in full flight at a session in the Clachaig Inn, each competing and correcting the other's story, they were a hilarious double act.

We don't laugh as much or as loud as that now. (We don't drink as much either.) At the top of the course Liz stopped and looked round: deep green trees behind us, the course spread out down to the sparkling Forth where the breeze had failed and the little boats sat motionless.

'It's so beautiful here when the weather's like this,' Liz said. 'Sometimes when I've been a bit low I've come out here, and I look around. And something happens, then I feel better, even if my golf is rubbish.'

It's the understated *a bit low* that made me want to hug her. There'd been a string of family tragedies in Liz's life, long before Mal's death. Her resilience and lack of self-pity have always astounded me, yet there are times when the bounce goes.

We go back twenty years, we have a history. We have shared

innumerable nights in climbers' pubs, in freezing vans and sweltering airports. We have shared in ploys and plans that changed my life. We have done routes together in Glencoe, on Ben Nevis, the Lakes. We spent a night together in a very small snowhole with our friend Terry Dailey on the North-East Ridge of Everest at 21,000 feet. I have stood up to make my farewells to Mal in the church at Culross, unsure if I could speak at all until she caught my eye and gave a tiny nod.

So though we don't see each other that often, the connection is there, solid as a 10-millimetre rope running between climbing partners.

'I keep hearing Mal telling me to believe in myself,' Liz says as we near the end of the round. 'The trouble is, there's some things at work I know I'm no good at, and others I've just learned to bluff.'

She slices her drive into the rough on the right, sighs with disappointment. I don't insult her by saying 'hard luck'. Instead I nod in silent sympathy. My drive cracks into a tree, bounces out onto the fairway.

'Nicely judged, Andy,' Liz says drily.

I learned this much from my climbing days: mountains are not impressed by PR, spin, reputation or self-belief. They don't buy it. They don't buy into anything, so for once in your life, you're not selling.

Presidents, film stars, captains of industry get the truth from a golf course as much as plumbers and fishermen. They might as well be stripped naked. I like to think that's why they play – for that reality check in the midst of the unreality of yes-men, gofers, spin-doctors and publicity people.

Dissemble as much as you want afterwards (and on medal nights the clubhouse bar is knee-deep in horse manure), but at the time golf enforces honesty. There's no real prospect of blaming one's opponent. It's not even the course's fault. Though every golfer knows the sense of injustice at this pin placing, the wind direction or that lightning-fast green, nevertheless that is the course, there to be played. One might as well be indignant about the condition of the ice on the Ben, or be irritated by the height of Annapurna.

In a winter white-out on Ben Nevis, or looking at an avalanche-prone slope on the North-East Ridge of Everest, an overdose of self-confidence can kill you. Then again, without faith in our abilities, none of us would ever go very far, or get very high, or complete a book. The belief we can do this thing is one way of legitimately preferring our lie. It improves, without guaranteeing, our chances of a good result.

The difference is that the wrong call when climbing can be fatal, whereas in golf it means watching your ball plop into the water hazard.

When climbing, there's little time to reflect. The thinking goes on in the walk-in and the walk-out, digesting what has gone down as you head homewards. But in golf it's like there are two parallel games going on: part of me is absorbed in playing each shot, each hole at Aberdour, while somewhere else I'm processing things about the mountains' honesty, golf's honesty, mortality's honesty.

That's not playing golf, yet it's part of the experience. It would have to go in the book. I'm still not at all sure whether this book is a joke, a holiday, or the real thing I must do next. It's as if the book and I are on our third date and quite soon there's going to have to be a decision one way or another.

I come out of my dwam to Liz admitting she finds she gets more easily stressed and anxious as she gets older – work stuff, having to cold-call people, even making a meal for friends, or facing a putt in a golf medal.

'I just tighten up. *Here.*' She places her hand flat on her diaphragm. 'I don't want to, but I do. Do you find that?'

'All the time,' I say. 'Especially with short putts. But I've always thought of you as so confident and capable.'

She laughs ruefully. 'Glad it seems that way. Will you give me this putt?'

I glance at her ball, the hole. Maybe two and a half feet, with a little left-to-right borrow. I can see why she doesn't want to take it. Maybe we do get more anxious, less innocently sure of our abilities. Maybe we stop believing the world is on our side. Maybe we discover positive thinking doesn't stop bad things happening.

'It's given,' I say, tapping it away. 'There's no way you'd miss that.'

Consider the etiquette involved in playing partners giving each other putts. It's a mutual agreement to let each other off the hook. A bond, a co-conspiracy, a relaxation of standards. It also helps speed up the game.

Sometimes it's agreed overtly. Other times there's an unspoken trade-off, an exchange of favours: I'll give you yours if you give me mine.

I've noticed I give myself fewer short putts playing alone than I'll happily accept from someone I'm playing with. Playing alone I hole out nearly everything, but playing with pick-up partners on Beauchief in Sheffield, or with Liz, I'll happily take away my ball if they invite me to.

Al McLeish wouldn't give or take any remotely missable putts. That would be too lax by his standards, too soft for his strict conscience. At the other extreme I've played with people (who must remain unnamed) who pick up or offer putts of over three feet, at which point it gets silly.

Liz and I aren't here to give each other stress, so we're fairly generous. But still we know that for the game – for life – to have any value, there have to be challenges, uncertainties and the possibility of failure. Twenty years ago she left an utterly safe and predictable marriage to a financial consultant ('the kind of person who when we got back from one year's holiday would start planning the next') for a broke, climbing-obsessed, unpredictable, emotional, spontaneous, inspired dreamer of no fixed income or abode – that is, Malcolm. And never regretted it.

So she knows as well as I do what we can and cannot grant

ourselves. There's a moment at the last hole, 187 yards, par 3. Slight following breeze. I guess a 5 iron, murmur my current mantra *soft, straight,* and put it on the green, level with the pin but some 30 feet to the left. I've been three-putting all day. I really want to get down in two from here and finish with my fifth par for the round.

My approach putt runs past the hole. Maybe three feet. Liz has already secured her 4. We both look down at my ball. There's a slight pause.

'I think you ought to hole that, Andy,' Liz says. 'Just to round off the day.'

'If I miss it, it'll ruin my day,' I say, only half-joking. But I know she's right. If I pick up my ball, there'll be a niggling not-right, not-complete feeling. I'll have let myself off too easily.

Then again, miss this – there's a slope, and I've been putting poorly all day – and the whole day will sour. There's not a golfer alive, no matter how enlightened or light-hearted, who doesn't know the feeling that happiness rests on this outcome.

So I look at the putt. From one side, then the other. Might as well do this properly. Don't rush it, pretending I don't care, that it's so easy it's just a formality so if I miss it I can pretend it was just a tap-in. I've seen it so often, the ways we kid ourselves.

I do care. If I miss this I'll be pissed off. I care about lots of things, some of them in the past and unalterable. A few in the future. And right now there's this.

A slight left-to-right borrow. Aim for the edge of the cup. Hit it firm enough but not too firm.

Ball runs, curves in with that sweet gurgle. Yes. *Thank you.*

We shake hands, as is the custom at the end of a round. Then we hug, which isn't.

I make mountains out of molehills? I do. A drama out of a short putt? Yup. I've been in big mountains, bloody big life-threatening, life-altering mountains, and I know the difference between them and molehills. And still I like to engage closely with small things, and so let them be big.

What's gained by refusing to care much, be anxious, look closely into the world, yourself, life? What do you get by not reflecting or getting too interested, upset or excited, keeping it all in proportion?

What you get is a life spent among molehills.

You get losses too. Pains and sorrows that range from outrage at that green where I took four putts, to a husband and life-enhancing friend dying in a tent years before his time.

At Liz's that night, well fed and heavily watered with wine, I glance at one of a number of pictures of Mal on the bookshelf. It's taken in a bazaar, looks like Kathmandu, on one of his many expeditions. How much living he packed into those years! He's grinning at the camera, so present and engaged. I'm struck how young he looks. Alive, he was always more grizzled and weathered than me, but now we are leaving him behind. The age-gap between us grows like that between the man gone overboard and the ship sailing on.

'Goodnight, matey,' I murmur and totter off to bed. I dream of small sailing boats with bright sails off Aberdour, tacking resolutely up the Forth against the tide and breeze.

On giving up golf

I never took up golf.

It was just always there. Putters and golf balls lay round the house, so we children played with them. My father took a hacksaw and shortened the hickory shaft of an old niblick, wrapped the handle in tape and handed it to my brother David. When I was about seven, the niblick came down to me. Dad corrected my grip, and for the swing I watched David. As for David's swing: like Van Morrison's 'Astral Weeks', there is no accounting for it.

Chip shots on the back green grew to whacks across the river. Then I was deposited with some old clubs and balls on Glenbervie's practice hole, and told not to make a nuisance of myself while Dad and David played. After my grandfather died, David got his clubs and I got David's, in an old canvas 'pencil' bag. Then my first complete rounds at Dollar (I might play there again, maybe lay some painful ghosts) where the course became my refuge and escape.

You might as well ask when I took up using language.

When I play with people who have taken up golf as adults, I'm impressed and bemused. Learning to play golf is like learning Finnish – very odd, very difficult, unnatural to anyone but Finns. A golf swing isn't natural. The ball's not moving and nor are you, that's the sod of it. It's not a reflex game and there are no excuses. The humiliation is all your own.

I'm very thankful to have come from the one part of the world where playing golf is as natural as breathing, swearing, smoking, drinking, pessimism, eating fatty foods and dying early of heart disease: Scotland.

But I do remember giving it up – golf, I mean.

Back in Anstruther this morning at my mother's, I took the new dog – it's not going to work out, she's lovely but much too boisterous, keeps threatening to pull Mum over, running away; we're all worried about how to handle this – up past the old school. Looked in through the windows of the music room, where we held the folk club and performers sat, uncomfortably but ethnically, on straw bales, as tastes shifted from 'The Muckin of Geordie's Byre' to 'A Hard Rain's A-Gonna Fall'.

At fifteen I was still focused on golf and playing in tournaments. By sixteen, I'd begun playing guitar. Spare time that once was devoted to honing the chip shot went instead on acquiring finger-picking styles. Then rehearsing to get up on those straw bales and in a daze of adrenaline rush through 'Last Thing on my Mind' and 'It Ain't Me, Babe' (a sharp reprimand from the Folk Club president: 'That isn't a folk song. It's not even a protest song!')

For that matter, you could write your own songs. Everyone was at it. Donovan on *Ready, Steady, Go!* didn't look much older than me. Songs? Easy! Poems too, because I wasn't much of a singer.

Eight months is a long time at that age. By the autumn term in 1967, Henry Cotton, Walter Hagen and Arnold Palmer had been replaced as heroes by Bob Dylan, Ray Davies and Guillaume Apollinaire. I hadn't gone off golf, just run out of time for it. When I had played, my game was slipping and there wasn't time to put it right, with a new term of folk clubs coming up.

Standing looking in the window of that empty room with the dog whining impatiently, I could see into the corridor where Pete Smith, maths teacher and golf fanatic, once stopped me and asked when I'd be putting my name up for the Fife Boys team. Having won the school competition, the Anstruther Boys, the

Elie Boys and the Balcomie Gay trophy (oh innocent days!), there was no doubt what the next step would be.

And with my head full of lyrics, rehearsals and a new way of playing G7, I hesitated. Yes, I wanted to stay good at golf. I wanted to play for Fife. But . . . He insisted, the deadline was coming up – hadn't I seen the notice?

I managed to look at him, just, as I muttered, 'I won't be going in for it, Mr Smith,' then hurried off down the corridor.

The pup dog tugs, and we head on back to Mum's. While wondering how to put it to her that she really isn't capable of looking after this dog, I'm seeing still the expression on Pete Smith's face when I told him I wasn't going up for the Fife Boys. Disappointment, yes. He was disappointed in me. More than that: incomprehension.

But for me, hurrying to my typing lesson where I would painstakingly type out my latest Norman MacCaig and Mallarmé imitations, there was only faint guilt and regret. What I mostly felt was liberation.

I never played competitive golf again.

Golf wasn't really abandoned, it just drifted away. I still played once in a while, when the weather was a certain way and the impulse took me. Gradually golf tailed off to the occasional game, and then none. My clubs gathered cobwebs in their mildewed bag in the cupboard under the stairs.

Youth is pretty ruthless in pursuing its interests. The other week, Leo sold his PlayStation video games platform. These games had been the consuming interest of his life for as long as I'd known him.

'I haven't gone off it,' he said. 'It's just there's so many other things, with the youth theatre, and my band – well, three bands now – and my AS exams, and now I'm writing plays.'

I nodded, remembering.

'I thought: maybe I've sold out. I'm no longer a *player*. And then I thought: no, I'm just having a fit of integrity! I'm selling up because there's things I want to do more.'

I wish I'd had the wit and self-knowledge to have said that to Pete Smith when I turned away from golf that afternoon in the school corridor: '*Don't worry, Mr Smith, I'm just having a fit of integrity.*'

'The Shining'

(NORTH BERWICK)

Patrick Rayner always put me in mind of George Martin, the recording producer whom the Beatles nicknamed 'the Spitfire pilot'. His clean aquiline chiselled features, the floppy swish of fair hair, his upright boyish keenness, come from a different age.

I took to Patrick (as the Beatles enjoyed and respected George Martin) from the moment we met some twenty years back – as it happens, sitting at the controls of a sound studio. He's a radio drama producer for BBC Scotland. Later we worked together on a radio play I'd adapted about a Battle of Britain summer romance – love and death and the moment intensely lived, my usual themes.

Like myself, Patrick retained a boy's enthusiasm for fighter pilots. He sat at that mixing desk like it was his cockpit, coaxing performances, questioning, enthusing, pushing back the flop of hair that fell forward every time he leaned over the desk. We'd become friends, the kind who enjoy each other a lot, but remain too busy with their own lives to meet more than once in a while.

I was through at BBC Glasgow, doing promotional work for *In Another Light,* when he hailed me. I mentioned what I was contemplating writing next, and he lit up like Leo when he sees an opportunity for a day off school. Apparently he too played golf 'sporadically but keenly' when work and family allowed. He was a member at North Berwick; would I like to come and play as his guest?

I nearly said, 'Tally-ho, Patrick!'

It's a cool, windy and grey morning as Patrick and I leave his home in Portobello, on Edinburgh's shoreline. He's elated to be taking a day off mid-week. It feels like we're skiving school. Driving east along the coast road, he mentions that in his spare time he makes furniture, mostly from wood liberated from skips, using his father's old tools.

'It's sustained physical work, demanding close attention,' he says. 'Somehow that makes it a complete break from my usual life.'

'Like playing golf,' I suggest. 'Quite different from emptying your mind by taking a walk.'

Patrick nods vigorously. 'Instead you're filling your mind with something else.'

'Not so much displaced anxiety as displacing anxiety!'

We consider this as we drive past Musselburgh, probably the oldest playing golf course in Scotland and therefore in the world, still publicly owned. The first recorded women's tournament was played here in 1811, between local fishwives. Somewhat earlier, in 1567, Mary Queen of Scots played a round before surrendering to the Confederate Lords, which must have interfered with her short game. Or maybe it would have helped. Sometimes it does, having something else on your mind.

Thinking of this, I add, 'And sometimes playing golf is both concentrating and completely empty-headed.'

'Yes!' he thumps the wheel. 'And that's when you're really playing well!'

It had been like that at Beauchief the last time I'd been out. I'd met up with a strongly built Japanese lad, a former student in Sheffield. We talked a bit between shots, mostly got on with it, and for much of the round I felt both focused and empty, applied yet effort-free. This may or may not be Zen; all I know is it felt good and I played well. When it's like that it reminds me of good love-making or good climbing – your being is in your whole body, not just your head.

'You want to know the secret of golf?' Patrick says as we enter the seaside town of North Berwick. 'The true secret of golf is one day you play really well and the next day you play really crap – and you don't know why!'

The clubhouse at North Berwick is just right – formal and traditional but not stuffy. It's one of the major early Scottish links courses; people have been playing here for several hundred years. The dining room is panelled with old wooden lockers from the late nineteenth century. It remains an Open qualifying course, and the Scottish Boys has often been played here.

The locker-room smell is a heady blend of musty grass, damp leather shoes, old wood, spiced with notes of sweat and deodorant. Like me, Patrick plays golf in old trousers, shirt, weekend sweater – 'gardening clothes', he quips. His golf bag is slim, light, uncluttered, dates from his teens. He'll be carrying it, which I admire but don't emulate, being thirled – attached – to my trolley, which saves my back and feet a lot of stress.

His RAF father phoned him up at boarding school over thirty years ago: 'I've seen a set of clubs at Lillywhite's Sale for £35 – shall I buy them? You pay half?' I check them out: steel shafts, small heads, thin sharp blades. They're like the ones I played with as a lad, and now look frighteningly hard and unforgiving. He has a proper wooden 3 wood, and a metal driver his brother gave him after the head finally broke from his original persimmon driver.

Not even a golf glove. He likes the game simple and stripped down to its essentials, as it was when he started playing as a lad in the sixties, slipping onto the course through the gap in the fence with a few clubs and a couple of balls.

The starter's hut marries tradition with modernity – our 10.30 booking is checked off on computer. The course is fairly full but not crowded; just one couple wait to play off ahead of us.

I loosen up with the bends and stretches that have become essential, then stand on the 1st tee and shiver slightly in the brisk easterly off the sea. It looks great though – the undulating links stretch ahead of us; the Firth of Forth is grey-blue, a choppy sea, small boats with bright sails tacking. Volcanic basalt outcrops litter the channel: the Isle of May and the Bass Rock. Lots of little islands just offshore – Patrick points out Fidra, said to be the model of Stevenson's Treasure Island. The rounded red volcanic dome of North Berwick Law looms up behind us, topped by the whale's jawbone arch.

As we wait for our tee-off, the haze clears and the sun comes out, cautiously, provisionally, as befits a Scottish sun. It lights up the red sand of East Lothian, hits on the grey-white shavings off the wind-whipped metallic waves. Smell of the sea, seaweed, warming turf, rises into my face; the sound of the sea will be with us all day.

Oh yes.

The course layout is classic Scottish: eight holes out, a hole across, then nine holes back. Not so much a round as a flattened loop laid along that narrow strip of naturally short sandy turf between arable land and the sea that we call *links*. This is the low, bumpy, narrow cradle of golf.

Beach and the sea are on our right. I see dog-walkers and children playing, remember walking there with a girl on a shimmering, dazed afternoon . . .

I switch back to Patrick recommending a mid-iron off the tee, then a second shot up onto the rugged Port Garry outcrop that juts over the sea, where the first green lies hidden. Looks interesting. It's a wonderful moment: about to start on an unknown course, with no idea what's out there.

I watch his easy practice swing, the naturalness of stance and grip. He says he's played only twice this year, is horribly rusty, but there's years of muscle-memory there. He played plenty as a boy, confesses he went to St Andrews University largely because for £4 a year he could play on any of the four courses, which of course he did. A lot. (Brother David did the same; sometimes wish I had.) These days his handicap is 12, which is roughly what I'd guess mine to be if I had one.

He tees up. His stance is upright, narrow, relaxed. Reminds me a bit of brother David as he pauses, then hits the ball away nicely – rhythmic, without forcing, almost languid, elegant. His hair is made to be swept back in the wind: the Spitfire pilot.

Sweet relief when my shot ends up near his. The few living spectators and centuries of shades of earlier golfers nod judiciously. We have not come to desecrate these links; we are not wearing shorts or anything tartan, or using buggies, mobile phones or calculators. We're not great but we're not bad. Above all, we're here to quietly but whole-heartedly *participate*.

As we walk down the fairway, I suggest, 'We'll not play against each other, just play the course.' He agrees, and we stick to that. Throughout the round we'll observe 'the honour' – the person who had least strokes at the previous hole tees off first on the next – so we must be vaguely aware of who has done better.

I'm marking my scorecard to help me remember the round if it comes to writing it up later. I write so that I may pay more attention to the world. When I'm writing, the world, whether imagined, recalled or right in front of me, becomes sharper, brighter, focused and frankly more interesting.

This is what has brought me here, brought me back to golf – not healthful exercise or making business contacts, competing or sharing a laugh or lowering my non-existent handicap, but the world becoming close-up and personal again.

And talking of close, my ball for this second shot is on the tightest lie I've ever seen. Here the ball doesn't sit up nicely on stiff blades of grass. Instead there's a thin skim of yellowish turf over hard sand. The ball might as well be on a billiard table.

I'm faced with an interesting blind shot – and there's a lot of them on these undulating fairways, where over centuries turf has claimed the sand dunes left by a retreating sea, all hollows, mounds and gullies – over and across the promontory. Intimidated by that tight lie, I hit my 9 iron thin. After struggling up the rough brae, I find the ball in a dip over the green.

Automatically, I take out the 9 iron again.

'You'll not stop it on the green with that,' Patrick warns. 'This is pitch-and-run territory.'

Pitch-and-run: that takes me back. Back to adolescence, playing on the Elie links. No wedges then, no possibility of the high approach stopping dead on a lush watered green. In summer, approach shots had to land well short of the green then run in with the contours. That was the skill and feel of the game – reading the run of the fairway, finding the best way in, gripping an iron well down the shaft; the shot the old codgers of my youth were so exasperatingly good at.

So I do just that: use a 6 iron and run the ball up the bank. It kicks more than I'd expected, ends up some 10 feet from the pin. I tap the putt gently, it runs three feet past. Bloody hell, these greens are like a bowling alley, so hard and fast they might as well be lined in wood.

But this is a quality course and the gently tapped return putt holds its line and drops in.

'It's been a windy, dry month,' Patrick explains. 'This is quick for the time of year.'

On the 2nd fairway, off another frighteningly bare lie, my divot explodes in a puff of dust as I pull the shot into a bunker. Though it's only May, the fairway is pale, gleaming under the thin East Coast light. Distance is hard to gauge; the sharp breeze raising hairs along my forearms has cleared away the haze and the whole course is shining, almost hallucinatory as it humps and wrinkles into the distance along the bay.

It's a challenge, the right sort of challenge. This is what golf comes from, and in its core remains.

The modern sand wedge makes bunker shots straightforward. I get my feet well anchored, select the spot behind the ball: steep arc, hit smoothly through under the ball, which drops gently on the green amid its sand-shower, but runs on well past the hole.

OK, we're going to have to get used to this.

Patrick is playing steadily. Nice upright swing, he tends to push the ball a bit right. He's exhilarated, eyes shining, shirt-sleeves rolled up now: he looks forty-five going on fifteen.

Watching how he approaches each hole, I start to get the idea. We must negotiate with this course. No question of *shooting* a score; this isn't target golf. And the fairways and approaches are so undulating it seems that only on the tees do we play off a level stance. The greens are huge, warped, fast and true.

We have to play *with* this course, let its contours work for us, as golfers here have for hundreds of years in this brisk air, working their way with wooden clubs and feathery or gutta-percha balls, round, up, down, over the eroded dunes and outcrops.

I feel their presence, and kinship with them. Though recent developments in clubs and balls have changed the game vastly, this terrain still insists it will not be dominated. This still feels like Golf; here it is possible to still feel in touch with the game of Tom Morris, Braid and Donald Ross, Vardon and Jones.

A 6 iron at the 3rd lands well short of the green, runs with the slopes, finishing 20 feet from the hole. I'm beginning to get it.

The monstrous 50-foot putt at the 4th runs true, up the slope, down and across, curves back again as hoped, stops within a foot of the hole. We're dead chuffed to half the hole in 3.

'Proper golf,' Patrick comments. That's all we ask, to once in a while play proper golf.

With the fairways running so fast, there's no need to try for distance off the tee; it's just granted. So we use our 3 woods a lot and let the run do the rest. It's that kind of course; it responds to being thought out and treated with respect. Under these conditions, with the breeze behind, the 450-yard par 4s become a comfortable drive and 6 iron.

Feeling increasingly at home, I have a run of four pars and a birdie in six holes.

And still the course can jump up and bite you. More accurately, I bite myself. Confronted by an abyss between me and the green, I'm psyched out. Hands tighten, my swing lacks conviction, my head comes up, ball dribbles into the abyss. (Liz said it succinctly the other day at Aberdour: 'My anxiety that something may go wrong makes it go wrong. I know that – so why can't I stop it?') Centuries of golfers nod their heads sympathetically: *Aye, laddie, maun keep yer heid down.*

Things fall apart somewhat in the second nine. Maybe I'm tiring, slackening concentration. Or maybe the opposite, trying too hard, glimpsing the possibility of *a good score*. Fatal, of course. Nothing takes you out of the zone faster. I make a mess of a fascinating hole where a stone dyke runs at an oblique angle hard by the green, and though I'd like to have played it better, the problem the hole poses is so intriguing I'm not that distressed.

Patrick, on the other hand, gets steadily better. He strikes the ball cleaner, his drives lengthen, struck with more confidence. For today at least, he's consistent; unlike me, he gets round with no lost or out-of-bounds balls. He'd still be a very decent player if he could play more (at his best he played off 5 and it shows) but there are many other things in life besides golf. He loves his work and his family; a fortunate man who knows it.

'You know when you're a teenager,' he suggests after hitting a particularly sweet approach shot, 'and you play *a real golf shot*, you feel much older, connected to an adult world?' I nod, remembering playing with my father. 'Then in your fifties you hit a sweet one that turns out right, and you feel like a teenager again.'

Exhilarated by the ever-improving weather, the noble course itself, our mid-week escape from the world of work, the sea switching in an instant from gunmetal to indigo to the precise shade of my beloved's eyes, we have entered a better place. An innocence we'd once known, then mislaid along the way, is being restored to us.

There's another distraction in the incoming holes that head back along the shore. Among the shades of golfers past there is a girl in a white cotton dress, where we'd once walked in a hormonal dream by this golf course, exultant, tormented, not in our right minds. And many years after that, same beach by same seaside town, walking with Lesley, as hungry but more true as we sought somewhere to lie down and find each other.

Haunted places, golf courses. So many ghosts, so many human events. As the sun becomes fierce and high, and everything shimmers and warps, the course seems to rise upward and float free. If there are indeed places on Earth where another realm is near at hand, North Berwick links is one of them.

I pull myself together just as Patrick's golf gets a bit wayward, and finish with a couple of par holes. Big straight last drive, decent blind pitch up the big slope onto another wide true green. Though my ball is 25 feet from the hole and the green is warped in the links manner, I'm feeling at home here now, and don't even contemplate three-putting as I run my putt to a foot of the hole, tap in.

It's the taste of the last sip that we're left with, and the day is sweet in my mouth as we shake hands on the last green.

'Golf as it should be played,' Patrick comments. 'Terrific day, Mr Greig.'

'Top-hole, Mr Rayner.'

All the way on the drive home into the lowering sun, we're still flying.

Bringing it all
back home

I brought along my father's hickory-shafted putter that day, because the stamp on the blade was *Ben Sayers*, and I'd a notion Sayers had connections with North Berwick. In the pro shop David Huish, a very respected senior Scottish professional, turned it over in his big hands.

'It's a Benny.' He pointed at the little bird stamped alongside the name. 'A wren,' he said. 'All the Sayers putters had that.'

He carefully inspected the club as though it was an archaeological curiosity, which in a way it was. Ran his fingers along the serrated base. 'Interesting. The idea of this is to let the blade pass more easily over the grass – greens weren't cut as short in those days.'

He checked the leather grip, the airholes punched in it, the odd square shaft.

'Definitely early 1950s.' That figured. In 1947 my father returned to Scotland, to Bannockburn, began a family and started playing golf again. He probably bought this putter, along with a set of steel-shafted irons at John Panton's shop at Glenbervie. His old hickories came down to us.

So the putter is almost exactly my age. And I'm now the age my father was when I was born. He died four weeks before I went on my first Himalayan trip, and for the following years I was so busy and fully stretched that I really didn't think on him much.

There are reasons why he's so on my mind now. I'm holding one of them. And before that, the time he came to help me in *blue shadowlands* though he was dead.

David Huish was absorbed now, pointing out details I'd never noticed, like a near-invisible rivet securing the head to the shaft. When he started as an assistant pro in 1957, he had to learn to make, finish and repair clubs. It was part of the job, an extensive apprenticeship in centuries-old skills.

I said I remembered my father having little lead weights inserted into the head of his driver and brassie. Huish nodded, there was a lot of that. Golfers were always having their clubs adapted – new grips, new weighting, repairs and alterations. Nowadays you buy a new set.

He took us round the back, into a little locked workshop, long disused. He showed us the heavy pad for smoothing and flattening the leather grips. And hanging here, dim with dust and cobwebs, were implements he'd once handled every day, the punches, sanders, planes, drills, templates, vices.

With my dad's putter, he showed how he'd learned to shape a hickory shaft. 'See how it gets slimmer here? And becomes round? That took hours with the plane.' Then sanding to the right shape and thickness, the correct balance of strength and whip. That was a matter of fine judgement. Each club was a one-off; there was an art to matching a set.

'See the dark streaks in the wood here?' I'd always assumed it was just dirt in the grain, but no. The shaft was oiled, then dipped in pitch, then heated over a candle flame to make it sink in, then sanded off again – all to protect the wooden shaft from damp and rot.

Standing in that abandoned workshop, listening to David Huish, I sensed the passing of a skill, a knowledge, a laborious craft. He described the job of a modern club professional as being part instructor and part salesman of equipment he can never keep up with; whole new ranges of retail possibilities, clothes, gizmos, gadgets, stroke-savers, souvenirs, books, videos, as well as the actual hardware, the bewildering array of new clubs, the individual trophy drivers at several hundred pounds each – all in the spacious, well-lit saleroom of the modern pro shop. I smiled, remembering John Panton's little unheated hut at Glenbervie which sold scorecards, a few sets of clubs, balls and tees, and maybe some golf gloves.

Nice stuff, no doubt, and seductive. Hope springs eternal in the golfer. My father had lead weights inserted; I fingered a hollow-headed driver that will virtually hit the ball for me. Or these balls that will fly so far, so straight, almost self-guided smart missiles. Or this speciality wedge. And this Rescue club – who among us does not need rescuing? But the craftsman, the artisan who actually made, altered and maintained clubs as well as instructing on their use – he has gone.

Steel shafts took over from hickory so quickly in the years before the Second World War for good reasons. They were standardised, much quicker to make, reliable, cheaper, less subject to torque, hit the ball better. Bobby Jones won the Grand Slam in 1930 with a hickory set, and that was about the end of them. For some years after, some manufacturers painted the steel shafts brown, so they looked reassuringly like hickory. I still have an old brown-shafted driver in the loft.

Back in the shop, David Huish glanced at me then handed back my father's putter. 'You know, in the fifties, this was the Sayers factory and workshop. This club was almost certainly made *right here in this room.*'

The putter seemed to vibrate in my hand. I'd inadvertently brought it home.

'Do you use it at all?' he asked.

'Sometimes early in the season,' I replied, 'on an inland course. It's too heavy for faster greens.'

He agreed, pointing out what I'd been gradually becoming aware of, that these days irrigation and equipment means greens can be cut much shorter, rolled harder, so balls run faster and more true. For the money a round costs now, people expect the greens to be perfect. Which has left my father's putter redundant, a curiosity, a museum piece.

Except of course on North Ronaldsay, and the island courses I'm setting off to explore next. As we drove home, Patrick and I reflected on a day on a special course, a true links course of great tradition without being up itself. North Berwick had all the modern improvements but it remains the real thing, definitely one for the book.

'So you reckon you can finish this book?' he asked. 'When did you decide?'

In David Huish's shop, the moment I found out I'd brought Dad's putter home, my fingers wrapped round the worn grip, staring at the subtle rivet that held it all together.

6TH

'Jewel'

(SHISKINE)

Island golf, like island whisky, has a special tang, a slow burn and a long peaty finish that lingers long after it has gone down.

It is late evening in late May on Arran, the southernmost island of the Hebrides. The air is soft as moss, sweetened with sea-pinks, cut grass and seaweed. The breeze drifts over my face and arms, raising forearm hairs that glow in the low red sun over Kintyre. As I take a few swings to shake out the stiffness from North Berwick, Fiona Brown the starter and self-styled 'heid bummer' of the course, locks up for the night. 'Enjoy yersel!' she calls, and is gone.

I am alone on the 1st tee at Shiskine, Arran, with an empty, unknown course ahead of me.

The first fairway, pale yellow after a dry Spring, runs hollowed and humped alongside the ocean on my left; the green is tucked somewhere over a grassy mound, hidden as greens are on seven out of this course's twelve holes. At North Berwick the little waves had broken briskly, in a businesslike East Coast manner; here they seem to collapse gently onto the sand, forget themselves before fanning out among the orange legs of wading birds.

I decide to stand a little closer to the ball, and swing more upright. It feels there's more power, standing close to the ball and swatting the club past my chin. And here I feel closer to everything, readiness gathering in my hands and the power all around me.

It may be the different air of the West, the blending of small waves and peeping sandpipers, the happy solitude of what lies ahead, but I am utterly seduced at this first date, and I haven't even started yet.

My country is so concentrated that one day I played golf on the East Coast at North Berwick, then the next traversed it to Glasgow, turned south down the West Coast to Largs, took the ferry to Arran's port of Brodick, arrived and it was still only mid-afternoon. Time to walk along the seafront in hot sun, hunger at the bare rock crests of Goat Fell rising north of the town. Mal and I once came here to help a film crew realise a poem for solo woman rock climber that I'd written. I still feel the tug, but I don't go there any more.

I took the road known as 'The String Road' over and across the island – a high road twisting and turning like a grey tarmac river as it tumbles down to the other coast – and discover that Blackwaterfoot consists of a small pier, the Kinloch Hotel, a scattering of houses. Time still to have a shower, an early meal, chat to the waiter, the bar manager, the receptionist – all of whom play on Shiskine. It seemed where some rural parishes have a pub and a community centre, Blackwaterfoot has its golf and tennis club.

The course had been recommended to me by a non-playing Frenchman in Paris a few weeks earlier. Alain Gnaedig – whose translations make my writing seem more elegant, intelligent and profound than I suspect it actually is – leaned across a café table and said, 'If you write your curious golf book, Andrew, I suggest you go to Blackwaterfoot in Arran. The course is called Shiskine. It has just twelve holes, but if you go I think you will find something very special.'

So small a country is mine that there was still time after eating to go along to the golf course in the quiet of the evening, just for a look. Time to meet Fiona Brown and be uplifted, entertained, informed. Most starters I've known are rather sour, dour or officious men who, rather like school janitors who feel the school would run much better without pupils, believe their job would be ideal if only there were no golfers.

Fiona is definitely not one of them. She's had this position for twenty-five years, had the good sense to give up golf after back problems; she clearly has a ball, encouraging, chiding, bantering as she takes the money, hands out scorecards and advice, sells drink and sweeties, calls the tee-offs out through the window. A funny, chatty powerhouse, for most people she sets the tone of the club, along with the club manager she introduced me to, Fiona Crawford.

It's unusual to arrive at a club that immediately feels so easy, inclusive and warm-hearted. It's unusual for a golf club to be fronted by two women. 'Do you think that makes a difference?' I asked.

Fiona Brown looked at me, grinned, made a sweeping gesture of her arm that took in the starter's hut and her shop, the course, bowling green, tennis courts, the tearooms where the dances are held. 'What do you think?'

She also has for years run a Children's Hour where for that period Monday-Friday through summer, only elevens and under can play while they learn not only the basics of the game but also the rules and etiquette, the ethos of golf. Once they feel ready to have a handicap, they are welcome to do so and join the adult world. This seemed a healthy way to go about things.

As was Fiona's next suggestion: 'Look, it's such a bonnie evening and I'm closin' up soon – if you've got your clubs, why not just gang oot and have a wee whiz round on us? There'll be no one ahead or behind you, so it'll only tak you a couple of oors.'

And so it was that as the sun grew huge and red over the Kintyre peninsula, I hit a leisurely opening 3 wood down the undulating fairway and set off into a glowing jewel.

*

Ever since I didn't die on a trolley in the Hallamshire Hospital in Sheffield, and a surgeon made an inspired guess, drilled into my head to let the pressure out and my squashed brain began to re-expand, my memory isn't so good.

'Like a sieve' is apt – most of the events, faces and details of the day just run through it. What catches and sticks is ordinary, and precious. Glimpses of the day – two squirrels pursuing each other round a tree in a glimmering grey double helix, Leo flipping his trilby up along his arm onto his head and flashing a grin before setting off to school, the bone-white new moon in a blue-black permanent sky when I lock up the shed – they remain, glittering flakes in the bottom of the sieve.

Songs and their words, those I can remember without effort. Even the ones I don't like stick. Poems, likewise. And there are some holes on some golf courses that I can still walk myself through any time. A strikingly high proportion of those holes are on Shiskine.

Each hole on a golf course has a name as well as a number, but usually it doesn't register much. Even regular players often won't know the hole by its name, only its number. Of all the courses I played that year, only a handful of names have stuck, like 'Kylas' in North Ronaldsay, 'Crown' at Nairn, 'Foxy' on Royal Dornoch.

Most golf courses, however fine, have some fairly anonymous holes that resemble each other. There is no such hole on Shiskine. Here every name stayed with me from the outset, except perhaps the last, 'Kilmory', which I've just had to look up. A number is not adequate to holes of such character; only the name yields it up. Each is a one-off, like the course itself.

On the opening 'Road Hole', I found my ball in a hollow well down the fairway, climbed the grassy mound to spot the green with lots of spiny grass and a track behind it. I guessed at an 8 iron, hit it sweetly into the sea-silence of that place, found my ball in a dip over the green. Chipped back, two putts, struck by the quality of the green. This was no rustic North Ronaldsay.

I looked around, still feeling odd to be alone in this other-wordly place. I took out my notebook to record the hole, then changed my mind. At Bathgate and then North Berwick I'd begun to notice taking notes detracted not just from concentration on playing golf but also from actually *being there*. However useful it might be later, breaking off to jot things down took me away from where I actually was. And right now, here was the only place and time I wanted to be. I had no doubt I'd remember every shot of it, the surroundings, the soft incandescence blooming in the western sky, the curlew's long *pirl pirl* as it flew into the sun.

(Now, nine months later, writing this in Stromness, glancing out the window as a swirl of hail blows down gunmetal-grey Scapa Flow, I don't even have to close my eyes to be there again.)

So I put that notebook away and walked on to 'Twa Burns'. It was another blind hole; I checked the 'Course Descriptor' Fiona had handed me. The course was dotted by an eccentric mix of white tyres, posts, poles, bells and signalling devices to accommodate the invisible greens. It required an act of faith to hit some of those shots and *believe*.

I hit a bonnie drive over the first burn, up onto a big green wave with a bunker. I climbed the crest and looked down into a valley where a second burn ran in front of a big, sloping green. Humming high in my head, I hit my second shot, crossed the burn to find the ball again well past. Chipped back poorly. My long putt ran so true and smooth I didn't object to the hidden slope that took it right. Relief when the next putt held its line and dropped. Truly, the greens were a revelation, my idea of perfect for golf – fast and firm enough, yet not bone hard and lightning fast like North Berwick; intriguing, undulating yet true.

'Crow's Nest': everyone who's been to Shiskine remembers this hole, and I'm not surprised. I hit my tee shot blind, on trust, up a wild crag of rock, gorse, long coarse grass. I dragged my trolley up, found a hidden green on a little shelf, nestled under the cliff of Drumadoon. It's like trying to hit and stop a ball on the small roof garden of a three-storey house: tricky. I was still happily shaking my head as I took another bogey, wondering what this course would reveal next.

It offered up 'The Shelf'.

I'd never seen such a big drop to a hole. From the tee it fell vertiginously towards the sea, rocks and beach on the right. It's a shot any golfer really wants to make, the green way below yet so close I could almost throw my ball onto it. I pushed my soft 8 iron right, pitched and took three putts on the slowest green on the course.

And still came away smiling. The fact that I never played well on Shiskine and still love it beyond nearly all other courses is a testimony to how special it is.

'The Point' reminded me of Anstruther, teeing off near the sea, beach on my right all the way, fairway sloping down towards it. I made the mistake of looking at my card here instead of trusting my eyes; misread the distance, hit a good 3 wood that soared happily way past. At 212 yards, 'The Point' is an awkward, lovely, sea-bound hole, very links. It looks pretty and harmless – but isn't.

Most courses have a 'signature hole', the one that encapsulates and defines it. Nearly every hole on Shiskine is a signature hole. But 'Shore Hole' is one of Shiskine's signature signature holes, a really superb links number. The drive is parallel to the beach, long grass cresting the dunes, and the wooden out-of-bounds fence calling *This way!* Very inhospitable ground to the left. In a cross-wind, this would be a very difficult shot. But on that evening's warm breeze – a breeze.

Another punchy 3 wood – standing closer to the ball was really working. Once again, I'd discovered the secret of golf. (They drive clever rats into psychotic confusion that way. Next time out, the cheese is moved, and has to be discovered all over again somewhere else. We're not rats and this is self-inflicted. What's weird is we *enjoy* it. Scottish, you see.)

I followed that happy drive and found an unprepared-for big gully, like the gulf between two huge waves, yawning between my next blind shot and the two-tier green. It looked natural, complex, a real golf challenge. Out on the sand, terns scuttered upright like self-important waiters as I hit a pitching wedge onto the upper level, two putts. Dead chuffed to make my first par of that enchanted evening here. (Each time after that, rubbish. But rubbish on a gem doesn't stick.)

Even my mum, if she played golf, would remember 'The Himalayas'. It's all hill and no fairway. I looked at my Course Descriptor, read the name and thought, 'You're not kidding.'

In a sense, every shot on a new course is played blind. So I shrugged, took a 6 iron and whacked the ball over what had once been a 100-foot-high dune but is now thick with grass and gorse. I came round the side of it to see the green in a bowl with gorse and another burn beyond it. No sign of my ball – must have gone way over.

As I poked about in the rough, I thought every day is played blind, into the unknown. All we can do is choose our shot, then hit and hope. It's a bit scary, but keeps us alive. I never saw that ball again.

Though there was no one ahead or behind me, I used the weird lever-and-pulley system for signalling I'd left the green. What's that word, I wondered, for something made to measure, a one-off? *Bespoke.* This is a bespoke golf course.

After the enjoyable companionships of my last outings, it was good to be alone again, all quiet, dreamy, intense. I moved on through what my father called a *dwam*, a lucid dream, as I uncovered one hole after another, playing through an engorged sunset, which was followed by a conflagration in yellow, gold, saffron, scarlet, flamingo.

Looking at the drive ahead on 'Hades', I understood the relish in that name. The tee shot had to carry a forget-about-that-ball-pal gorse-filled chasm. Not difficult, but distracting. I hit my first poorish 3 wood (apparently mislaid the secret of golf again) into the bunker on the right. Got well set in there, noticing how the light was starting to go, and the birds' chirruping turning sleepy.

Felt very happy as I carved that ball out to 15 feet. Felt even happier as my putt ran absolutely clean and true for my only birdie of that first round. This greenkeeper should be cherished and bought malt whisky on a regular basis.

A real golf course – and Shiskine is that, not a toy or a curiosity – needs a par 5 to give it some backbone and gravitas. It's what Anstruther and Stromness lack, much though I love them. 'Drumadoon' is to my mind the other signature signature hole: a really classy, complex, visually satisfying 477 yards, with the burn and another great dip and rise coming into play, then a long angled slope up to a canted green. Took the opportunity to hit a decent fairway wood, chipped and got my par. A puff of breath, a silent *Thanks!* Thanks for everything, for here, for this, for being here at all. And somewhere inside my battered brain, an easing.

'Paradise': well, yes. I stood on the 10th tee at the top of the course, with a 360-degree panorama across Arran, the Sound, the Kintyre peninsula where a threequarter moon had silently risen like a blood grapefruit. The breeze had dropped to a whisper; sea and birds were hushed in the gloaming, that luminous summer dusk of the North.

Deep in my dwam, I pulled that tee shot slightly into the bunker, flipped the ball out, two putts. When I'd picked my ball up, it was faintly damp with the first dew. I was humming a pentatonic song left uncompleted from my chronically romantic adolescence: *Mary MacDonald was the only lover / Of my childhood dreams. / She alone knows how to compose the rose / That flows through hills and streams . . .*

' "Paradise", 150 yds', the scorecard read. It seemed closer than that.

(In autumn my Buddhist undertaker friend Vin Harris would hit, into a full-gale cross headwind, one of the shots of my year – a 5 wood that started slightly left, stayed out there through the buffeting, drifted in slightly as it fell and dropped 20 feet from the pin. A great golf shot, exactly as he'd envisaged it. Treasure those courses that give you such opportunities.)

'The Hollows', I quickly learned, is a very tricky 196-yard par 3. Played blind yet again, over a hill, down into a horrendous gorse-nurturing hollow, then back up into the green nestling in a small hollow of long spiny grass. As I scuffed out a 5, I could see there were many ways of making a mess of this hole, and I'd only begun exploring them.

The last hole, 'Kilmory', I played more or less by moonlight. Found my tee shot on the green some 35 feet from the pin. Palm flat on the grass: dew-damp. Adjusted for that and gave the ball a little extra, watched it roll dimly to a couple of inches from the hole.

I holed out, looked round the half-dark moonlit course, blessed it silently and left.

In the steaming bath at the Kinloch Hotel, with a large Ardbeg malt, I lay murmuring the litany of names, seeing the course and the shots and the setting rise up again before my eyes. That last hole, 'Kilmory', was the only slightly banal one on the course (sorry, Fiona; sorry, Mr Bannatyne) but that par had been a sweet finish.

I let the Ardbeg trickle down into my memory, warmth on warmth. A long day, a long finish, with a valedictory sweetness at the end of the salt. Sod the Lake Isle of Innisfree and its nine bean-rows; give me Shiskine and its twelve holes in early summer gloaming.

Next morning I enjoyed a big, leisurely breakfast to a three-quarter gale and spasmodic horizontal rain. The night before, Fiona Brown had left a message to say she'd arranged for me to play next morning with Colin Bannatyne, at eighty-three the club's oldest regularly playing member. I could be confident an old fella wouldn't go out in this. Still I went to the course just to meet him.

He was waiting in the lee of the clubhouse. From the moment we shook hands, he reminded me of my father and his generation

– his casual golfing clothes, the old windcheater, the cloth bunnet, his high cheekbones, bushy eyebrows, the elongated nose and ears that come with many years on the planet. He spoke in a way that has largely died out with his generation – a slow, deliberate, soft but firmly accented Scots, choosing his words with care. And always courteous yet direct, straightforward yet wry.

Dignity, that was the word. Though now an old man at the end of his playing days, he had it. When exactly did our generation mislay dignity?

'Och, it's no too bad, Mr Greig,' he said straight off. 'You just have to keep the ba' doon.'

On the first tee he seemed unperturbed by the lateral rain and the cold. He just pulled his bunnet down a bit tighter as he courteously invited me to play first. Yellow clots of spume from the breakers were birling across the fairway. I hadn't tackled this kind of wind since my teens.

At the top of my swing I staggered slightly but managed to get the ball away straight, then watched it being carried off onto the 12th fairway. Interesting.

When Colin Bannatyne began to swing, I thought he was having a seizure, or was afflicted with Parkinson's. First his hands slowly moved back a foot or more, the clubhead stationary; then an abrupt twitch, then a jerk followed by a kind of loop and a twist; another twist, a twirl then a soft dive through the ball as though spearing a fish, finishing with hands low and clubhead pointing somewhere else entirely.

The ball went quietly, low and straight, some 170 yards down the fairway. Throughout our round, that extraordinary swing never changed. Nor, as a rule, did the result.

'So who taught you to play?' I asked casually as we set off.

'My brither.'

'And did he swing like that?'

'Oh aye, just the same.'

At first I watched with horrified fascination. Then I started to look away in case it was contagious. But the result was effective, attuned to the course, the conditions and his age. Low prodding and a simple short game were what was required.

'I suppose you'll know this course quite well?'

He looked at me, then out at the waves thundering in. Rain and spray glistened on his weathered cheekbones as he nodded.

'I've played this course for seventy years. But know it? I suppose I do, a bit.'

Was this a day to play golf? Maybe not, but I was stuck with it. I watched Colin Bannatyne creakily approach his ball, pause, calmly hit it with his corkscrew swing over the grassy mound in the general direction of the hidden green. I called, 'Good shot!' but my words were whipped away. I could have sworn I saw a hint of a smile.

He was right, of course. Can't change the course, so adjust to the conditions. Can't out-hit this gale, so play with it. It's absurd to get angry at rain, or old age for that matter. Mr Bannatyne seemed possessed of unshakeable equanimity as he addressed his putt on the first green, the ball quivering in the wind

As we both holed out for 6, he handed me back my ball and murmured, 'Grand day.'

As we tacked towards the next tee, I was picturing the annoyance, the air of being put-upon, of many major golfers when the wind really blows in a British Open. In a wet gale, yardage becomes irrelevant, it's all down to instinct and feel – who can best adjust, improvise, who really has golf in their bones.

My boyhood hero worship of Arnold Palmer stemmed from a photo of him on the way to winning the Open in a Force 8 gale at Birkdale, 1961. He's in full foul-weather gear, windcheater dark with rain, trousers whipped tight round his legs by the wind as he crouches at the top of his back swing, the light of battle in his eye, and the caption read: *Arnold Palmer about to drill another 1 iron into the gale.* Who would not warm to such a man?

As we negotiated our way through 'Twa Burns', then lofted

onto the 'Crow's Nest' where the rain quit but the wind redoubled, Mr Bannatyne told me stories of the course, its history, its characters. How it had originally been a conventional nine holes laid out by the magnificently moustached Willie Fearnie in 1896; then Willie Park of Musselburgh redesigned and extended it into a conventional eighteen holes; then during the Great War the six new holes further up on the hill fell into disuse; how the attempt to restore it to eighteen holes again, on the basis of a design by the ubiquitous James Braid – how much of the history of Scottish golf has passed through this corner! – fell through after disagreement over securing the ground.

'Then in time folk came to see it was just the right length.'

It wasn't just the fatigue of battling wind and rain that made me agree. It would be pointless to dilute the intensity and variety of golf here, just to make it the same length as everywhere else. It's not a 'real course' truncated, nor a mere oddity. Shiskine is a real golf course and you take it on its own terms.

There is nothing sacred about eighteen holes. It wasn't laid down by the Almighty as a footnote to the Ten Commandments (though *Keep yer heid still, and dinna press* would have been a handy postscript.) The early courses had varying numbers of holes according to local conditions. By pure chance, a restructuring of St Andrews' twenty-two holes in 1764 reduced them to eighteen just at a time when the Society of St Andrews Golfers began to take over from the Honourable Company of Edinburgh Golfers as the dominant body of the game.

Thinking of my own experiences, and listening to Colin Bannatyne's carefully chosen words, I've come to think twelve holes is a very good length. When golfers expected to go round in two and a half hours maximum, eighteen holes was acceptable. But now four hours to five hours is normal. Everyone complains about it, but there's no sign of it going away. And that's a long time to be on your feet, a big chunk out of your day. Often by the 15th hole I'm full up, I've had enough. I've got a wife and life to go back to.

Nine holes is a snack. Eighteen is a lengthy banquet. Twelve is a balanced meal. Twelve holes allow our hotel's waiter to get a round in before he starts work at lunch; the catering manager can play in her afternoon break; lets the family golfer play regularly without abandoning that family. It means you can have a morning round without feeling weary the rest of the day, or go out alone at half past eight on a May evening and play a complete round.

As Colin Bannatyne points out the different tees used when medals are played over eighteen holes (visitors converting their eighteen-hole handicap into a local one involves hyper-mathematics), talks about former greenkeepers, players, office holders, incidents and arguments, the ebb and flow of the course's size and fortunes, he personalises the whole course. He points out the great hill of 'The Himalayas', recalls when it was mostly a gigantic sand dune, being chased off it as a laddie by the head greenkeeper. He recalls locals who emigrated then returned forty years later to resume playing the course. He talks about – and this made my head spin – the founding fathers of the club (remember: 1896) he remembers as the stalwarts of his youth.

For him, the course is personal, a nexus of local history. More than most courses, it is part of the community and social story, rather than an opt-out from it. The club is also unusual in that the great majority of its members live elsewhere, on the mainland, mainly in Glasgow or its surroundings. Arran has been a Glasgow holiday place for generations, is part of so many families' stories, memories, meetings and marriages. 'Bunties' the locals call these visitors, I was told at the hotel, because they come at the time the summer bunting is put up, and think it's for them. 'They don't like being called that,' the catering manager said wryly.

Under those gale-force conditions, 'The Himalayas' was interesting. Colin wisely prodded his ball round the side of the great peak; I hit mine over, and never saw it again. I think it sleeps with the fishes.

As we negotiated our way round 'Hades', then were blown

sideways the length of 'Drumadoon', Mr Bannatyne (I can't bring myself to think of him as Colin: respect) explained that for regular visitors it's worth paying the annual membership (£112!) for the three or four weeks they might spend here. 'The course is right busy then – we have a ballot for tee-off places, like the Old Course.' For many years these mainland members held all the senior positions; at one time the tearooms, which were used by them for summer dances several times a week, were closed to local residents' use in the rest of the year. He pulled a face, tugged his cap down into the wind as we climbed up 'The Hollows'.

'I'm glad to say that's all by wi noo.' I started and shivered, and it wasn't just the damp and wind. It was my father's phrase in old age, in his deliberate throaty voice, acknowledging the passing of everything he had seen. *All by wi noo.*

We shook hands on 'Kilmory'. 'A grand wee outing,' he said. 'I hope it might help in your book.'

Afterwards he quietly, almost shyly, gave me a copy of his *The Shiskine Golf & Tennis Club: A History*. It's a labour of love and a rather special document, a reflection on local history and cultural changes; many of the photos and stories in it are of people he talked about or is related to. In the end it is almost an accidental memoir from someone too modest to ever write directly of himself, and a moving one.

Before we parted, I asked The Question: 'So why do you think you've kept playing golf for seventy years, and still go out on days like this?'

He seemed taken aback, gave my question due consideration then said, 'Oh, I suppose I enjoy the game.'

I've heard and read many different answers to the great question of *Why golf?*, but this one's mischievous simplicity was worthy of a Zen master.

I dropped Colin Bannatyne off by his house and watched a very damp old man walk through the cross-wind a little wearily to his door. There he turned, raised his hand in salutation – a brief, delighted, boyish grin – then went inside.

I never saw him again. I think of him now, as I do of Shiskine, with gratitude and pleasure.

A ghost hole,
and other ploys

There is a ghost hole at Shiskine that only three people in the world have played. I went back there in autumn with my friends Vin Harris (of whom more later) and David Hares. As part of their mission to lighten up golf and let a bit of playfulness into what can become overly serious, every so often they spot and play a new hole on a course.

It must feel like a proper golf hole, one that could exist but happens not to, yet. This isn't sacrilege so much as creativity. Golf courses aren't set in stone, they evolve, just as the original Shiskine nine holes laid out by Willie Fearnie were later turned inside out by Willie Park.

This ghost hole, the phantom 13th, runs from the 8th tee, played across to the 5th green. It's an interesting, natural par 4, played directly towards the sea. A complex tee shot, challenging second. There was no one around, so we played it.

There was no card we could check for distance, no lore-established line to take. Like the first golfers we had to look, come to our own conclusions, then play. It was a novel sensation. When David took a photo of me playing my second with the Drumadoon hill in the background, he pointed out that probably no one had ever stood there, playing that shot in that direction. I'm proud to say that to date my par 4 is the course record for the ghost hole.

Though greens committees might be horrified, I hope this practice catches on, because it seems to me it's close to the essence of the game. After all, we're here to be playful, to explore and create, not just spend all our time grimly trying to whittle a few strokes off the same course played over and over. Since then I keep alert for phantom holes. We're not stuck here in a grid; we're moving through a field of possibilities.

David and Vin are not so much golfing gurus as golfing guerrillas, here to bring some liberation and light to those oppressed by golf. They are not the only ones. After a long and wonderful autumn day at Machrihanish that remains unrecorded and unforgotten, they introduced me to the practice of *club throwing*.

Apparently they'd come across it in Pete Shoemaker's *Extraordinary Golf*. While waiting for the ferry back from Kintyre to Arran, we took a few old clubs to an open field. Vin demonstrated: he took some easy short swings with an 8 iron, then on the next swing simply – let go. The club went flying forward, bounced end over end, stopped about 50 yards off.

'It's about release,' David explained as Vin retrieved the club. 'You're teaching your arms and wrists to let go. And somehow the knowledge you're going to let go the club frees everything up.'

I tried it. The first time I hung on too long and nearly decapitated Vin as the club flew backwards over my shoulder. The next time I loosened my grip just past the bottom of the swing, just past where a ball would have been. The club flew forward, accompanied by a strong sense of release and a desire to laugh.

I did it half a dozen times, just taking a three-quarter swing and letting go the club just past impact. It felt, well, extraordinary. Forearms, wrists, fingers, all the muscles softened. It was a most delightful sensation.

Then David lined up a few balls at my feet.

'Now do just the same, but this time don't let go.'

I did just that. The same soft looseness, the same muscle memory. The ball flew off dead straight and much further than I would have expected. I shook my head. It felt like I'd done nothing at all, just swung the club back then down again and through. Suddenly the golf swing felt the simplest and most natural thing on earth. Maybe it had been like this for brother David as a boy.

We all did some more club throwing, then hit balls across the field, laughing and giggling, it was so delightful. Then the ferry came and we sailed back to Arran.

Machrihanish was wonderful and special, but the club throwing has stayed with me more. Of all the suggestions, tips and exercises I've been offered, this is the one that stays with me most and has made the most difference.

Once in a while I leave the shed and go into the park at the end of our street in Sheffield and throw a few clubs just for the pleasure of it. And when I stand on the golf course and the timing just isn't there, I remember what that felt like, that letting-go, and then the stiffness and the tightness go, and the ball flies and we're back in the realm of pure kinaesthetic pleasure, thanks to Mr Shoemaker.

It was also at Shiskine that Vin and David showed me another kind of letting-go. It was at the 6th tee – something about the course makes it particularly suitable for these rites – that they went about 'setting the ball free'.

Take an old ball. Write on it a word, something you would like to be rid of, set free or be free from. Think of it as an exorcism. Then tee the ball up near the sea and hit it way out there.

It's just a game, a joke, a gesture. But by God it feels good. The first time I wrote 'pressure'. The second time, as we played Machrihanish together, I wrote on an old ball the name of someone I should have forgiven and forgiven myself for a long time ago. 'My God, Andrew!' David said. 'You hit that a bloody mile – completely straight!'

It's true. I've seldom hit a ball with such freedom. With no expectations and nothing to aim at, the body relaxes; what the coaches call *release* comes into play. It does indeed go a bloody mile, and straight. If you could hit all shots with that outlook you would be an extraordinary player.

So write that one word; tee the ball up and set it free into the sea.

It's so big, you can't miss.

7TH

'Initiation'

(ST ANDREWS OLD COURSE)

It was shortly after my sixteenth birthday, so it must have been October 1967, when I came back from school that lunchtime.

'You get changed out of yon gear,' Dad said. I looked at him, then at Mum. Some flicker had just passed between them. 'You'll take the afternoon off – we're booked for 2.15. Unless you've some lessons you don't want to miss?'

My father wasn't in the way of taking me off school. Optician? Dentist? 'It's time you played the Old Course.'

When I turned thirteen, he'd produced his .22 rifle and said, 'I think you're ready to learn to use this.' His expression then had been very similar, and I still can't read it. All I know is he believed that life had stages and they needed to be marked.

Our infrequent moments of closeness were always enacted like this, over ways of *doing*. With the rifle I had to demonstrate I had the maturity to handle what he stressed was a lethal weapon, before he ever put a bullet in the chamber. Which meant thinking about consequences, being heedful, doing things properly. It was that, not numerical age, which earned the right to use it.

Golf was the same. The teaching he gave us was about more than grip, stance, swing. He was passing on the ethos and etiquette of the game, which expressed his own deepest values.

They were iron laws. Never to talk or move when someone else is playing. Attend the flag for your partners. Don't hold people up. Watch your partner's ball, mark where it's gone, help search for it. Win without gloating; lose without sulking. Don't show off – but feel inferior to no one.

There was one lesson even more elemental than these.

'Bobby Jones several times called penalties on himself for infringements no one but himself had seen. He nearly lost the US Open because of it. And when he was congratulated for his honesty, you ken what he said?'

My father glanced at me as we drove over the hill to St Andrews that bright, breezy afternoon. I think even then I was aware days like this wouldn't come that often. I shook my head.

'He said, "*You might as well praise a man for not robbing a bank.*"'

I knew the Old was special, of course I did. It was in the intonation of those simple words, *the Old*. Like the way climbers refer to Ben Nevis simply as *the Ben*. The respect is such it needs no elaboration.

The Old was special, but it was also quite normal. It wasn't on another planet. I knew Dad had played on it as a student in St Andrews in the twenties. We were in St Andrews once a week or so – it's the nearest market town to Anstruther – and we'd lean on the rail by the Old Course and watch people drive off the 1st tee. My brother David was at the university then, and had the run of the Old, the New, the Eden and the Jubilee, for three guineas a year. The Royal and Ancient club might be extremely posh, and it was said people even came from the United States to play on the links, but the students and ordinary residents of St Andrews played on the Old Course as their right. Which it was. The town owned the links, my father explained, not the R & A.

He'd also reminded me, as we drove over the hill, that though golf had been played here for 500 years, the R & A was not the oldest golf club in the world, and the links at Leith and

Musselburgh were at least as old. Bobby Jones, James Braid and Harry Vardon apart, my father didn't do idolatry – he was, as I say, a very Presbyterian atheist. And even Jones and Vardon he admired not just for their achievements.

'I saw Vardon and J. H. Taylor play an exhibition match in the twenties, along with Alex Herd,' he remarked as we put on our golf shoes by the car. 'Vardon never took his pipe from his mouth, even when he drove off. Hands like hams. The man had the most wonderful *balance* I've ever seen.'

I understood that this balance was a more than physical quality.

Born in 1899, enlisted in the last year of the Great War, a student through the General Strike, my father's life seemed to extend back into pre-history. A private, wary man, but once in a while he'd come out with these snippets. They were all I'd get of him – any direct questioning and he'd stuff his pipe in his mouth and clam up.

'Then again,' he said thoughtfully, 'the most ferocious hitter of the ball I ever saw was James Braid. He was a big lang streak of a man, and he gave it one hell of a lick.' Then, as I was still gaping at this casual revelation – Braid had seemed more myth than history – Dad picked up his clubs, slung them over his shoulder and pulled down his cap. 'Right, let's get started.'

The 1st tee on the Old is big. Standing by it, aged sixteen, it seemed the size of a bowling green. My father, in his usual tweed plus-fours and heavy green woollen socks, was chatting with the starter, whom he seemed to know. I stood swishing my spoon – playing safe, naturally, and I didn't need a long drive to be able to reach the green in two – and watched the couple ahead preparing to drive off. I wished we'd had the chance to hit a few warm-up shots, but as with the majority of Scottish courses, there was no such facility nearby. A couple of practice swings then away you go.

I'd been trying not to be impressed by the Old Course. It was only a golf course, and a very bare and open one at that. I'd walked by it often enough, and it didn't look as bonnie as Balcomie or in as good a setting as Elie. In fact, this opening fairway was a bit of a flat paddock, albeit a very historic one.

But now standing here by this huge tee, with a row of casual spectators at the rails, and more golfers waiting behind, and the gigantic austere windows of the R & A clubhouse staring down at me, my neck felt thick with blood, there was a faint roar in my ears, and I believed I might faint.

There was the road, Granny Clark's Wynd, running right across the fairway, maybe 150 yards away. I watched a couple of women slowly push prams along it, each absorbed in her own new game.

God, please let me carry the road at least. If I pulled the ball, at worst it would end up on the 18th fairway. It would take a big slice to go out of bounds on the right. So it's just a matter of making good contact in front of all these people, the living and the dead.

'Old Tom Morris drove off from here,' Dad reminded me. I'd seen the old photos; the bearded patriarch who looked very like my grandfather, stern, wise, dignified, knowing exactly who he was – a man who'd won the first Open championship and three more after that. There's a haunting grainy photo of him driving off in old age, jacket, waistcoat, watch chain and all. He seemed to have a very open stance.

Though my old man never claimed to have seen Old Tom, now in the twenty-first century it's astonishing to realise he could have. Old Tom died in 1908, when my father was nine. Young Tom Morris was already long gone. 'He died on Christmas morning, aged twenty-four, of a broken heart,' Dad told me. Apparently his wife had died in childbirth, with her first baby. 'That was all tae common in those days.' He spoke with feeling, and I was very aware that for twenty-five years his profession had been to prevent such losses.

So the shades of Vardon and Taylor, Braid and Herd and

Allan Robertson – 'a very bad-tempered man' – all jostled there, along with centuries of unknown, forgotten golfers. No wonder the 1st tee had to be so big.

The pair ahead of us drove off. The first player's drive was long and strong. A small murmur of approval from the spectators. I dreaded following this. The second man had a clumsy grip and stiff legs. I was relieved to see his sliced drive hit the road, stott high in the air then dribble into the long grass.

A respectful silence, as at a funeral. I couldn't do any worse.

The golfers marched off. Suddenly I fancied tackling the Old. It was certainly much better than sitting in Double Latin, and I rather fancied my chances of beating or at least impressing my dad.

I can see him still, addressing his ball on the 1st tee. He'd have been sixty-eight, still tall and lean, but his face weathered and heavily lined. He was still a force, my old man. No starter nor the R & A intimidated him. He respected the institutions but its representatives 'are nae better than you nor me'. I can see his 'Willie Baldy' driver with its big tan head, his modest canvas bag of clubs with the ridged putter.

The big, powerful, skilled hands that had once secured scores of problematic childbirths, waggle the club head twice.

A sharp *crack* and the ball's gone. My memory senses that he pulled it a bit. As I step past him onto the tee he says quietly, almost sympathetically, 'Just keep your head still.'

The tee is very wide, the gallery seems enormous. I'm on the Old, playing with my father. Young and Old Tom Morris, Braid, Vardon and Jones are watching.

I tee up the ball, take a last practice swing. Suddenly I feel up to it. I know I've a better swing than my dad's, and recently I've begun to hit some drives past his. I am young and I can play this game. If he is Old Tom, I am Young. I'm the coming man.

My drive is OK. Not the best, slightly heavy, but fairly straight and it clears the road easily.

'Good enough,' Dad says. He doesn't do unearned compliments, and he's quite right. 'You'll be looking at a mid-iron next, to clear the Swilcan. It's a big green.'

The Swilcan Burn guarded the 1st green – only a few feet across, but for golfers the Swilcan on the Old is what the Tiber is to Rome. *Please don't let me top my second into the Swilcan.*

Again, standing at the ball, comes that late, almost angry, assurance. Still tight with nerves, I hit that iron a bit heavily, but it clears the Swilcan and runs through the back of the green. Dad's shot goes left again, a small grunt from him. I take three putts and we half the hole in 5. We're away.

The sensation I had on the 1st tee, I recognise now in Leo – at once aware of how much he doesn't know and hasn't experienced, but sustained by the necessary arrogance of youth. At sixteen – his age now, mine that day on the Old – if nothing else, you know you are the future. Time is on your side, your day is coming as your elders' day fades.

Through that afternoon with my father, I heard snippets of histories, and played the Old, and was intrigued but not overwhelmed. We kept track of who was up or down, but more as part of the custom of the game than some crucial father–son competition. My memory senses that he won by a smallish margin, maybe 2 and 1, and that I was slightly disappointed at that.

But it didn't spoil my day. Learning to play guitar was making inroads into my previously absolute commitment to golf. I also knew, with the ruthless clarity of adolescence, that in a year or two he'd be weaker and I'd be stronger, and I'd beat him regularly. The prospect saddened and pleased me.

All afternoon I was being given glimpses of things he felt I should know. Glimpses of golf's history, of the Old Course, and of his own back-story. A private and wary man, his inner life was given out in anecdotes. Nearly forty years on, twenty years after he died, I'm still trying to fill in the gaps, imaginatively recreate the hidden inner person and work out what happened to him in Penang that led to his abrupt departure.

I think it was on the 16th green that he remarked as he marked his ball so I could putt, 'I once laid my friend Alec Morrison a perfect stymie here by pure accident. No damn merit about it – but it won the hole!'

I said I'd thought stymies – one ball blocking the path to the hole of the other – had died out in the nineteenth century. Not at all! This set dad off on his story of the great struggle between Bobby Jones and Cyril Tolley during the British Amateur Championship in 1930. 'Of course, I wasna there to see it, being in Penang. The only time I saw Bob Jones was playing a warm-up here, before the Walker Cup in 1926. A small group of us went round with him while he shaped different shots into the greens. I thought at the time he was as good as Vardon, only longer off the tee. Lovely rhythm . . .'

While I was still boggling at this casual aside, he told the story of that match. Right here on this links it was. The day was an out-and-out gale. Everything was improvised. Ding-dong stuff, first Jones ahead, then Tolley, all the way round. They came to the 'Road Hole' all square . . .

My father grasped my shoulder as we stood on the 17th tee. 'See those sheds on the right? Cyril Tolley took a risk and drove right over them, which gave him a possible angle into the green. Jones went left, which meant he couldn't get onto the green with his second, because of the Road bunker. You'll see soon enough it's not a place you want to be . . .'

We drove, both down the left, the Jones line. I couldn't imagine anyone other than gods hitting over those sheds. We walked on, my father continuing the story. I could see it all – the wooden-shafted clubs, the knickerbockers and hats, the gallery following the handsome brilliantined American with his ceaseless cigarettes and Tolley the equally determined pipe-smoking Englishman.

Jones cut his second shot towards the Road bunker, which

could have been the end of the match and the Grand Slam, but it hit a spectator and bounced clear. (I left my second shot short of the bunker, which looked vicious.) Tolley left his second short of the green, but hit a fine chip shot to 2 feet from the hole. Jones pitched his to 8 feet – and holed it for the half.

I looked at my pitch shot. It had to clear the evil little bunker without running over the green onto the dirt road the hole was named after. A tricky shot, even with the 9 iron that came with the new set of clubs Dad had bought me after I won at Elie. A wedge would have helped, but he didn't really approve of them.

I opened the face of the club. The main thing was to clear the bunker. I wasn't that afraid of a dirt road – which was as well, because that's where my ball finished.

As we played out the hole, my father took a swerve out of the Jones story. 'Joyce Wethered – you'll maybe no have heard of her but she was the best lady golfer of her generation – had a putt for the match on this green. As she was lining it up, a steam train went by on those lines just over there. She holed the putt, and someone said, *"You must have been put off by that train."* And she replied, *"What train?"* Concentration, you see . . .'

If I remember rightly, he won our little match on that green, with a five to my poor six, and I have to wonder now if those interwoven stories were a piece of gamesmanship. But I doubt it. I think he just felt these were things I ought to know.

My education continued on the 18th. I wanted to finish the round well. I also wanted to hear the rest of the Jones–Tolley epic.

My father teed up and looked down the 18th fairway. We were playing back towards the clubhouse and the Scores Hotel, I could see casual spectators leaning on the rails like carrion crows on a fence. The Swilcan Burn was not a problem, but I took my spoon to play short of Grannie Clark's Wynd that ran across the fairway. I thought it strange but rather great that anyone, and even the occasional car, could use it to cross the course from the town to the beach. Public land, public access. Dad told me they didn't even have green fees here till 1913, shortly before he first played the Old Course.

'You mean it was free?'

'Just so. I missed out on that. But it was still awfy cheap to us students when I first came here in 1919.' He swished his spoon, dismissed the thought. 'A man named Ted Blackwell once drove the green here – with a guttie ball.'

I contemplated this feat. The man must have been a giant. I knew the old gutta-percha balls flew not nearly as far as the succeeding rubber-wound ones.

'Did you play with gutties?'

'There were a few still around when I was a laddie. They were hard to hit right – made your hands sting if you topped it! The new balls were much better, though some of the older folk disapproved of them.' He laughed. 'Just as I expect their fathers disapproved of the gutties replacing the feathery ball! There's aye changes, you see, and aye a generation that doesn't like them and one that does.'

I knew what he meant. His reaction to The Who playing 'My Generation' on *Top of the Pops*: stony-faced silence, then he left the room without comment. For me, it was savage joy, my liberation music, the sound that succeeded all others. My music, my hair length (the Cliff quiff now replaced by a combed-forward fringe, hair over my ears at the sides), my general outlook – the generation gap was becoming a chasm. Over the following years, I didn't rebel against my old man so much as move to a different planet.

But about golf – the use of the wedge and the sand wedge apart – we could agree.

'Keep your drive a bit left, and don't worry about the road or the Valley of Sin,' was his advice, and it seemed sound, so I followed it. Then as we walked after our drives, he continued the Jones–Tolley story. Though he'd have denied it, my old man had a certain dramatic flair.

'Well, at this hole they both hit their tee shots just short of the green. I think they must have had the wind behind them. I'd suggest you run your ball in low, through the Valley. That's what Jones did, only from much closer in.'

I used a mid-iron, choked well down, to play my shot. It went off well enough, but I was disappointed to see it dragged left by the Valley of Sin, finishing on the green but a long way from the hole. Apparently Jones overhit his approach, and ended up 25 feet past the hole. My dad judged his better, ended up maybe 20 feet away. Tolley had chipped to about 12 feet.

'So he had that for the match,' Dad concluded. 'But put that out of your mind and get this down in two.'

Neither instruction was easy, especially with a dozen or so casual onlookers. I've seen a picture of Jones putting right here, in the Walker Cup. No stands, no cameras, just a couple of hundred men and women, every one wearing a hat. He has just stroked the ball, his putter extended towards the hole, waiting to see if it'll go in. These frozen moments, these energies, these ghosts on this very green . . .

I laid my approach putt to about three feet. 'There's no borrow on a three-foot putt,' Dad instructed. It's not always true, of course, but it does simplify things. I managed to run the ball in, felt pleasure and relief equally. I'd not played very well – that was only my fourth or fifth par of the round – but it was good to finish respectably.

Dad had his putt for a birdie 3. He inspected it from both sides, so he must have wanted it badly. He missed it, grunted, tapped in.

We didn't shake hands but he briefly clapped me on the back as we walked off the green.

'Tolley missed his putt too, of course,' he said. 'Then on the sudden-death hole, Jones laid him a stymie and won the match – and that led to his Grand Slam. What did you think of the Old Course?'

'A lot of sloping lies!' I said. 'And I'm not used to greens that size or bunkers that steep-sided.'

'Better than Latin and Chemistry, then?'

'A bittie,' I replied, then remembered my manners. 'Thank you very much for taking me.'

He nodded briefly.

'Mind you keep working hard at the school,' he said as we loaded our clubs into the car, then drove home for our tea.

On golf, sex, and
the joy of timing

I often think of sex, or its more mysterious, alluring and joyous cousin, making love, when seeking comparisons for the profound satisfaction of a drive sweetly hit, a pitch shot that soars and falls just right, a long iron clipped off a downhill lie.

But let's be clear: golf isn't sexy. It's a cool game, not a hot one. It's about self-possession, not self-surrender. It has a painstaking, considered, inner-directed quality that embodies the culture in which it first evolved. Believe me, though they took both very seriously, the Scots never confused golf and sex.

But in sex and golf we know ourselves as embodied beings. Both can yield up moments of absolute sweetness, known through the whole body as it connects into the world.

It's the joyous mystery of *timing*. Timing of wrist, arm, shoulder, hips, legs; when all becomes clear, harmonious, right; when the whole thing fits. There is no effort then, no jolt or jar. It must happen in other sports, say tennis, football, sailing, horse-riding, archery – these moments of sweetness that are the heart of the activity, that keeps us coming back for more. Moments when the same body that weds us to pain, ageing, loss, death, becomes also our delight in this world.

Any child knows it. A tin can on a rock, a small stone in the hand, flick – clang! Pleasure. Joy. Satisfaction. We're wired for it, for the pleasure in coordination, timing, physical skill of hand and eye. It's not a small thing.

A calm river pool, early on in my time with stepson Leo – a bright and witty ten-year-old who it turns out has never skimmed a stone. Unbelievable. So I select a small flat stone, show him how it snugs into the crook of the index finger. Wrist cocked, crouch low, arm back, eyeing at once the water and the far bank . . . I count fifteen brief shining flirts of water, then the stone clatters into the far bank. It feels terrific.

One of the pleasures of inheriting Lesley's children with our marriage has been these occasions for revisiting long-neglected physical skills. All those hundreds of childhood hours spent skimming stones, aiming at cans, flying kites, throwing and catching tennis balls, are suddenly restored as valid, valuable, useful enough to bring a gleam of approval to a ten-year-old's eyes.

The passing on of physical skills is a bond never quite forgotten. It can come back to ambush me with a lurch of the heart when I knock the cap off a beer bottle on a wall as one long-lost friend taught me. Or when I cast a line over a Highland loch as another, now dead, showed me. I iron shirts the way my mother once demonstrated before I left home – I taught it in turn to Leo the other week – and I seldom do it without thinking on her. And most of what I do with a golf club, that's my father of course. As long as I live and breathe, he is resurrected in me every time I step onto a golf course.

No, it's not small stuff. And as for those who taught me sex, and the few who taught me to make love – I don't forget them.

So: golf. My full 8 iron soars into the sky over Scapa Flow, drops then kicks left as anticipated, runs down onto the heart of the difficult sloping green at the 4th at Stromness. Though I'm alone I grin like an idiot, find my lips utter *Thank you*, and feel my heart lift. I won't apologise for that. For it's a joy, pure joy. There are many of them in this life, joys, and for all my Protestant heritage I totally approve.

On golf, sex, and the joy of timing

We know now Yeats (like most poets) was extremely interested in sex, but at times I wonder if he was a golfer too. For surely only a man who has watched a smartly struck long putt run across the green, swerve then clatter into the hole, could write:

> So great a sweetness flows
> I shake from head to foot.

Maybe he was thinking about the magi, or maybe of Maud Gonne. The lie I prefer is that he was recollecting the drive he'd hit that morning, clean across the dog-leg on the long 16th.

8TH

'Good Isle'

(GIGHA)

Gigha (Gaelic) = Gudey (Norse) = Good Isle, probably owing to its fertility

Clubs in the roof-coffin, clothes stuffed in the suitcase; the back seat a slew of notebooks, cameras, damp waterproofs, flask, maps, fragments of biscuits, chocolate wrappers, golf tees and loose balls; sand, mud and dried grass cuttings filling the footwell below the pedals . . .

Where's it going, this ploy that teed off on the wind-swept links of North Ronaldsay? I don't even know what it is I'm after. What I do know is this flush of departure, the freedom and lightness that comes from shaking hands with company you have enjoyed, then heading down the road.

What's up ahead, the heart of golf, the mystery of living and dying, how my father is in me and more present than when he was alive, how my mother really feels day to day when we're not there, why I sometimes pull my tee shots hard left – there's so much I don't know. But I do know the wheel turning to the winding road's prompting, late May pouring in through the open window, the little kestrel hovering over the road junction as I turn off for the Lochranza ferry. I'm on the loose in my beloved Western Highlands and Islands.

Leaning at the rail, the sun is full on my face as the boat crosses the Kilbrannan Sound between Arran and the Kintyre peninsula. Rising and dissolving in the wake behind are days on Bathgate with Al, Aberdour with Liz, North Berwick and Musselburgh with Patrick, then Shiskine twice, that first impulsive solitary round into the gloaming, then with Colin Bannatyne in the rainy gale. Beauchief and Stromness . . . So many holes, shots, themes, faces and conversations.

A memory flash of Mohammed Ali Changezi on the Mustagh Tower trip in 1984, his cowboy hat raised as he stood and whooped when our jeep pulled out of Skardu on the dirt road into the Karakoram Himalaya. 'Forward going!' he cried. 'This is my home – forward going!'

I was young then, on my first Himalayan expedition. As the ferry bumps ashore, I feel young still, for forward going is always home, always young.

For me there will always be special words like *Kintyre, Tayinloan, Assynt, Achmelvich,* and possibly the most mysterious and thus most potent of them all, *Gigha*. An aspiration, a sigh in Gaelic.

As the narrow B8001 twists over the neck of the Kintyre peninsula through floods of green woods, fields, roadside ditches thick with flowers, I'm driving into the imaginative heart of my childhood. The road dips down and on my right is West Loch Tarbert, opening out into the Sound of Gigha. Across the alternating blue-platinum sea, stapled to the horizon are islands: Islay of the whisky distilleries, Jura of the Paps, Colinsay behind.

Something about islands seen across water, any islands, makes me yearn to be there. Yet when you land it's not an island any more; it's solid ground, the centre. I've learned this in Orkney, where the main island is quite rightly called Mainland. In a way islands with their built-in otherness are the ideal objects of yearning, like a lover, attainable yet always just out of reach. Land there and they're changed.

I drive down to the village of Tayinloan like my father did

before me. Same road, only now it's wide and smooth and fast. In the 1950s it was a juddering single track, took us many hours to get this far from Stirling in the old fawn-coloured Humber Hawk. The journey was long: to Balloch, then grinding up the single-track Loch Lomond road, stuck fuming behind caravans, Tarbet for lunch. Then the long haul to Inveraray, down Loch Fyne to Lochgilphead on the old A83 (why should only Americans romance their road numbers?) that runs to Tarbert (plenty of Tarbets and Tarberts in the West, means 'a neck of land a boat can be hauled across'), then right down Kintyre to the Mull (and I really *must* get that song out of my head).

It planted something in my soul, coming here as a child from rural inland Stirlingshire, for the first time encountering mountains, lochs, inlets, the Atlantic, the astonishing white sand of the West; getting out of the car to a softer, moister air, heavy with bog myrtle. And those names, those words so deeply foreign yet sounding like coming home: *Ardrishaig, Machrihanish, Hebrides, Lochinver, Gigha*. We had five summers here in the latter fifties, staying at Kilzean Farm, through Tayinloan a mile or two, past some trees, just off the road on the left.

A little bridge, I had forgotten that. But this ruined chapel, yes. The tractor shed has gone, and the byre where I milked the cow. The old road still curves to the farm, but the new one goes straight on by.

I get out of the car, walk slowly past the farmhouse. It's as well Lesley isn't here. I'd have too much to say about these flickering memories, the sensations of childhood, the faces, toys, games and voices. The McLarty family owned this. One of the sons played the accordion; both took part in the tug-of-war at the Games. Jim and Bill seemed giants of men with their huge boots, bulging hairy calves, red hands the size of hens. For a moment the very taste and texture of Mrs McLarty's ginger biscuits dissolves in hot milk in my mouth. And somewhere, my father laughing uproariously. I'd forgotten how he did that on holiday.

Kilzean Farm doesn't look the same, of course. The house and the yard are the wrong size and shape. The stone is much too flat and clean. But across the road, the track still leads through rough pasture towards the shore, and across the Sound is the low, unforgotten island.

Though only a mile or so offshore, with so much light bouncing off the water it was often hard to see Gigha in detail. It was more a silhouette shape, a mystery, than a real place. Extraordinary sunsets burned behind it. Some evenings the McLartys would drag their heavy rowboat to the water, jump on board and row out a net. I saw them once, carbon-black against a crimson western sky, two rowing, one paying out net. The black striving shapes, the angles of oars and arms, the soft elongated vowels of the tongue they never spoke in front of us drifting back across the water as they went about their work – they seemed more myth than men.

I have no memory of us ever going to Gigha. The ferry service was limited; the island was owned by Sir James Horlicks, said to not be keen on visitors. Even aged six, it was puzzling that one person could own an island, all the farms, houses, livelihoods, lochs and hills of it. Certainly my father, who still voted Labour in those days, communicated a deep, personal anger against the largely absentee landlords of Assynt, Knoydart, Eigg. Perhaps that's why we didn't go.

He'd have smiled at the Gigha community buy-out of 2001, when the people finally bought back their own island. Assynt, Eigg and Knoydart had already gone the same way. When I start thinking the world has entirely gone to pot – which says more about being a certain age than the world itself – I remember that.

A twenty minute crossing on the regular ro-ro ferry, another boon. Gigha starts becoming real and particular as we approach Ardminish, a scattering of houses above the dazzling white shell-sand of the Western Isles. I drive off, park the car by the beach, get out and sniff. It's so hot, the light is pouring down. It's like being on Delos in the Aegean, sacred to Apollo, except this place is green. The same stunned, living silence that is not silence yet feels like it.

I sit on the machair, take off shoes and socks then lean back against an old beached boat, and just take in the day. A lobster boat putters faintly down the Sound. The post-office van goes up the only road, towards the north end. Hot rubber smell from the car; the sand soft and fine between my toes. The ferry churns briefly then dwindles back to Tayinloan.

People on islands can look at the mainland just as the mainland looks at the island, perhaps with the same wild longing to be elsewhere. But today I have no desire to be elsewhere; today I have arrived.

The Gigha Hotel looks just fine. Jean at reception confirms it is now owned by the Community Trust, and run on their behalf. Behind her shoulder, I see heads in the bar, hear laughter. It's open all day, seems to be the unofficial community centre. Things sound pretty lively in there.

And the golf course? Is that owned by the community?

'I suppose it is,' Jean says. 'If you want someone who knows more, you should see Plumber Brown – he and John Wright the gamie made it.'

In an island with a population of 110, everything is personal. I love the idea of two ordinary local men making a golf course. It seems to fit with the spirit of the buy-out. In fact this is the *second* golf course they've made on Gigha. The first was laid out on Tarbert Farm in 1986. Then they let it go, and laid out a new one at Drumeonbeg Farm. According to the sheet Jean has given me, the first ball was driven off there two months after work started. More names: Jim Alexander became the next greenkeeper; now John Bannatyne and Bill Legge are doing it.

It's a far and happy cry from the millions of pounds of design, investment, earth-moving machinery, greenkeeping, upkeep and promotion that lies behind the new courses recently appeared all over the country (and across the globe, from Brazil to Borneo to

China: we're in a new global growth phase of golf). This is do-it-yourself golf course creation. It's here not as a colossal leisure-industry investment, but for the personal enjoyment of the creator-members, the residents, any visitors. It's there because they like to play golf on their own island.

'Our hope is with the golf course, more people will want to stay the night,' Jean says. She nods towards my clubs. 'Is that what's brought you here?'

'That's my excuse.'

'You don't need an excuse to be on Gigha.' She smiles. 'You'll find the course a mile or two up the road, on your left. Have a grand day.'

The 'clubhouse' marked on my map is a sturdy shed, empty and unlocked, in good condition compared to the one on North Ronaldsay. I can see flags dotted around the green slopes, but no one's on the course. The 'car park' is empty. Inside the shed, I flick through the book, count forty-seven paying visitors in May so far. That makes £470 income, put towards petrol for the tractor and the £5 an hour paid to the part-time greenkeepers.

There's an honesty box. I put my tenner in, pick up a scorecard, then step back out into the shimmering light.

Hamish Todd could walk into *Taggart*. A strong, powerfully built, fit-looking man in his sixties, short iron-grey hair, affable and funny and very Glasgow; those ironed black trousers and that pressed white shirt shout it loud as he stands on the 1st tee: retired police inspector, Glasgow CID.

'Aye, saw a lot of bad things. Attacked often – knives and that – but never shot at, thank God.'

He swishes his hollow-headed driver, whacks the ball well up the sloping first hole. He's capable, not absolutely fluent, but unforced. We've already had the handicap conversation. He plays off 18, but that's on a championship course; in Stromness or Beauchief, he'd be more like 12.

My drive is all right, but not great. I'm tired: this is my eighth consecutive day of golf, and last night in the bar of the Gigha Hotel after my first round was – well, the kind of night that happens when you sit down in a bar in the West. A lot of very friendly people, lot of laughter, lot of whisky. It was Rhona Grant introduced me to Hamish during the fourth round of drinks, gave me Plumber Brown's phone number . . .

So I'm not quite with it today. My first round here yesterday, happy and empty-headed in the shimmering heat, may have left me with mild sunstroke. My judgement of distance is even worse than usual in the different West Coast air. The greens are mossy, lumpy and slow after the lightning-fast, shaved-to-the-bone greens of links courses. I've changed back to Dad's heavy hickory shafted 'Benny' putter, but it doesn't help much.

But it's another gorgeous day, with a bit of breeze this time, so I concentrate mostly on Hamish and let the golf be as it will. I'm impressed he's this competent after taking up the game at fifty. A natural athlete?

'No really,' he replies. 'I was once a semi-pro footballer. Played for Morton.' Even allowing for the standards of Scottish football, and the position of Morton, that does suggest some athletic ability. 'Then my boss suggested I decide if I was a policeman or a footballer. And I asked myself, *Which can I see myself doing at forty?*

Some days it's about the course and the golf you play, some days it's the people you meet. Still, a few golfing moments linger. The pretty short downhill 2nd, wafting a 9 iron straight towards the Sound of Gigha, losing the ball in the dazzle then spotting it lying doucely on the green. Then the 3rd, with a demanding, pleasing drive over the burn; the 5th a bonnie uphill par 3, with a challenging tee shot to a raised green that I made a mess of every time. A towering full 7 iron, can't remember the hole but remember the shot, to four feet of the pin. Bit of respect there from Hamish.

On our second time round the nine holes, we are stopped by a camera crew. Would we mind taking part in a bit of filming they're doing for the R & A? There's no one else on the course but Hamish, me and the two film-makers as they ask us about how we feel about the course, playing here, its condition. It seems the R & A donated a couple of green-mowers to the course, and the film aims to emphasise not just St Andrews and the administrative capacity of the R & A, but also its good works.

When interviewed, we skirt politely round the iffy condition of the course. Despite being on a small island, this isn't a links course. Instead of short dry sandy turf, they have long lush farmland where soft grass grows fast. Despite the small number of paid hours and the many voluntary hours put in by members, it's very hard to keep up. And the greens – well, it seems there's been a problem there. Hamish is being slightly evasive. On a small island, you have to be careful what you say and how you say it.

So we say nice things for the mic, then hit our tee shots for the camera. 'Good shot!' Hamish cries sportingly for the microphone as my drive veers right and off-camera.

They pack up, drive off. Silence sweeps in like the wake after a boat has passed. Then the sounds return: a lark fizzles; terns peep down by the shore; a dog barks on the next farm then thinks better of it.

The sky is so blue and high and wide. Streaks of cloud drift in the light breeze. Across the water lies the length of the Kintyre peninsula, all the way to the hazy mound of the Mull and the legendary Machrihanish golf course I remember from childhood. Brushed by the breeze, the sea shifts from powder-blue to deepest cobalt; another ruffle, and it's gleaming pewter.

'No bad, eh?'

'No bad at all, Hamish.'

'You see what keeps bringing me back here? That and pals. Good people here, maist of them.'

As we play on, he mentions casually that as a lad he'd wanted to be an astronomer. Now that's the kind of human quirk you don't get in *Taggart*. But he hadn't the maths, so he worked in forestry, then the police. Now that he's retired, golf is a big part of his life. He caddies out of interest, has met some of the big pros. Also plays in some pro-ams. Golf takes him many places, meeting lots of people. He likes that. That's what he liked about the police: meeting people.

We agree there's a buzz and an energy to Gigha now, and it's not confined to the bar. Even as a child, I could feel a sadness and passivity behind the other-worldly beauty of the Western Highlands and Islands. It was in all those mounds and rickles of stones on the hillsides and shores, where crofts, runrigs and shielings had been; in the emptiness and silence; in the dying language heard in shops, falling silent when you entered; in the Gaelic songs that seemed only to convey loss; in the failed projects of regeneration my father told me about, Lord Leverhul-me's, Gavin Maxwell's.

The sorrow and loss are part of the beauty, but that doesn't make them good. One of the reasons I've never lived in the West, despite it being part of what I must call my soul, is it's too damn sad. And then there's the rain and the midges. I chose instead Orkney, busy, pragmatic, practical, more Norse than part of Gaeldom.

But now the Gigha people have bought back their island and are no longer at the mercy of feudal superiors. There are problems, antagonisms, strains and uncertainties come from taking responsibility for the future, but it's unleashed an energy, I can feel it.

As we finish our round, I reflect the course is so new that its character hasn't fully emerged; without the inbuilt undulations, mounds, sand-scrapes of the links, or the trees and water of many inland courses, it will take time to evolve. Right now it is a plain home-made course in a stunning setting, part of the common wealth of Gigha. Some of the historic courses I've been playing seem to dwarf in significance the people that play on them. But Gigha golf course *is* the people that made it, play it, keep it up.

Hamish and I shake hands at the end of our round. I'm tired and *drouthy*, ready for lunch and a beer.

'It's been a pleasure,' he says. 'Mind and look us up next time you're back.'

At the very north end of Gigha, the only road stops. A yellowed track threads down through heather towards a little headland, Eilean Garbh. It must have once been an islet; now a narrow strip of land connects it to the island. On either side curve the most dazzling white sand and clear-water beaches this side of paradise.

The afternoon is still and hot, the water chilly at first as I wander up and down first one beach, then cross over to the other. There is no one in sight or sound. Down at sea level I see nothing but the sand, the water, the headland. It feels I'm in a little world that has detached and drifted off on its own. I try to think of Sheffield; it seems implausible. Arran is unreal. Even the rest of Gigha is too distant to take seriously.

I sit a long time in the sand with wavelets breaking over my feet. I become aware of lots of tiny fish moving in the clear water. I wish intensely that Lesley were here to share this, and then I forget even her.

I wander across a few yards to the other beach, and sit there. More blue sky, white sand, clear water, air sweet with salt, seaweed, myrtle. Perhaps I was here as a child, for the sense of return is overwhelming.

For the rest of the afternoon I do nothing. At my feet tiny ripples write, white on white, pages of my secret life.

I met Alastair 'Plumber' Brown in the bar, early evening. He admitted setting up two golf courses gave him 'a certain satisfaction, aye'. But he doesn't play there much now. Can't be bothered. He stopped; I sensed there'd been some parting of the ways, some small-island ruction.

Most of his life and golf were spent at Machrihanish, one of the truly great Scottish courses, a championship course excluded only by its remoteness. My dad played on it during our Kintyre holidays while we played on the beach. Now I think on it, Machrihanish may well have been one reason why we kept going back to Kintyre, and why he seemed so much more relaxed in those precious weeks.

Plumber Brown had clearly been a good golfer, and his vision of golf is competitive, even combatative. 'It's easy to play well on your own,' he said dismissively. 'It's no real test. I never did like practising – waste of time.'

He produced some old newspaper clippings. Despite playing off 6, he'd won selection for Scotland in an amateur international championship, played between Scotland, England, Ireland and Wales at the Belfry.

'What was it like, the Belfry?' I asked, frankly impressed.

'Och, pretty straightforward after Machrihanish. The greens were a bit slow.'

So much for the great Ryder Cup course. I looked again at the team photos. There he was, in his thirties, rather handsome, staring pugnaciously at the camera in the full confidence of his prime. I glanced at the elderly, vaguely resentful and tired man next to me.

'That must have been so exciting.'

He shrugged. 'We lost.'

American Kimberly, the efficient restaurant manager at the Gigha Hotel: 'I hear you're visiting Orkney after this?'

'Not visiting. I live there.'

Her eyes open wide as she stands by my table with the coffee.

'Oh my God! Take me with you!'

'You'd rather be there than here?'

'You kidding? I've been reading about it all year.'

'George Mackay Brown?'

'Yes! I want to write children's books, full of myths and history. It just sounds so much . . . *more*.'

I drink my coffee thoughtfully, watching the sun go down in midgie heaven.

Next morning was the other side of West Highland life: drizzle gradually thickening over breakfast to steady rain.

'How long do you think this will last?' I asked Kimberly.

She glanced out the window.

'About a week. Are you going to Orkney today?'

'I had planned playing Machrihanish.' I considered the weather, the hangover from another gaudy night in good company in the bar, the growing pain in my lower back from eight consecutive days of golf and driving. I was suddenly wearied of golf, of travelling, of being away from home. 'If you really want to live in Orkney,' I said, 'you should just go and take it from there. I'm heading south.'

I was leaning over the rail of the ro-ro, watching the Good Isle recede, when there was a shout. I looked up to see someone waving at me from the wheelhouse.

The island telegraph had been busy. John Bannatyne – no relation of Colin in Arran – had heard about my projected book. He was a burly, relaxed man with a heavy handshake, more chatty Glaswegian than reserved Gael. He called one of the crew to do us coffees, then as he adjusted the wheel and kept an eye ahead, he gave me his take on the Gigha golf course.

He told me about the money crisis of 1998, how he himself had paid Jim Alexander for the first month's greenkeeping; Jim then stayed on for a couple of years. 'And "Plumber"?' I asked neutrally.

He glanced at me, then forward towards the Kintyre shore. 'Mmm . . .'

Now Bill Legge and Neil Bannatyne work part-time at £5 an hour, cutting greens and mowing fairways. John himself tries to put in ten hours a week voluntary. It's quite a job, keeping up. The R & A mowers helped. Then came the gang mowers, bought with Lottery and local-enterprise company money. But the fairways grow so fast . . .

I drank scalding coffee, watching Kintyre come closer. This is the reality of it, the meetings, frictions, struggles for time and money, the unglamorous effort it takes to set up a golf course, to buy back an island, to make it work. I'm a terrible romantic and Gigha isn't Tir na n-Og. It's just a very good place to be.

John went on to apologise for the state of the greens, and I conceded they were mossy, patchy, lumpy, with rabbit scrapes where I was allowed to prefer my lie.

'They suffered in April,' he said. 'It's a crucial time, and it was my mother's final illness, in Glasgow . . .' He put his big hand on a book on the ledge by the wheel. 'I'm reading *Practical Greenkeeping* in my spare time. I can tell you more than you want to know about "thatch", scarifying and aeration. And now my second bairn is due in a few weeks . . .'

He smiled to himself. There's more to life than golf courses.

'Tell folk to come and play our course,' he concluded. 'More the better.' He held out his hand. 'Good tae meet you – now I'd better dock this boat.'

I thanked him and left the wheelhouse, feeling cheered again despite the rain, my aching head, my back. It was the image of John Bannatyne making the Tayinloan–Gigha crossing with his charts on one side and *Practical Greenkeeping* on the other that cheered me; his mother's death balanced with his child's birth.

It can seem hard work sometimes, making room for play. Hard work and so many meetings, conflicts, decisions, uncertainties when a community tries to run its own life. Island life is close, intimate, interfering, intense, *personal*. It's a problematic gift, a mixed blessing, like golf itself.

The ferry bumped ashore, the ramp came down, John waved goodbye from the wheelhouse. I drove off, heading south, going home. The rain had set in, Machrihanish would have to wait.

I left Gigha and Kintyre behind, but some things came with me on the journey. Among them, the shadow of a buzzard drifting cool over my neck as I bent over a chip shot at the 9th, the wavelets making white scribbles over my feet on the beach at Eilean Garbh.

The secret life isn't what we choose not to share, but what we cannot: unspoken and unspeakable, the way it feels, the good isle magical and real as water running over feet, or another's hand in your hair.

Golf heaven, no caddy-carts admitted

Golf is a walking game. The walk between shots is not an interlude, non-golf. If it were, most of a round of golf would be non-golf and a great waste of time.

Having gone through a phase where it seemed to me only the shots mattered, I have returned to this much earlier notion: a round of golf is a brisk walking, a thread with little knots of activity along its length. Its essence is moving across a terrain on foot, connecting to it with senses and mind alert; evaluating, deciding, accepting outcomes, weighing up new situations. All the time, through these streams of mental and emotional activity, there is this walking, this seeing, the sensations of this body meeting the world. Take away the walking and something essential is gone.

I used an electric caddy-cart just once, in Bermuda, on a course where it was mandatory. At first it seemed great fun, a laugh, like being a kid set loose on the dodgems. Nice too in the heat to have no weight of clubs, and carry loads of food and drink, suncream, change of clothes, the mobile phone.

After a while, a number of things became apparent. First, far from speeding things up, it slowed down the round. Instead of each player walking directly to their own ball, the cart zipped back and forward, player got off, played, got back on, then the cart zipped sideways to the next player's ball. It was anything but direct. Also they're rubbish in the rough, can't go through heather, whins or woods.

Above all, it cuts you off from physically experiencing the course. Because you're no longer walking over it, feeling the contours and distances directly, it becomes inert scenery. It becomes virtual, just a stage for setting a series of problems. And I don't come to a golf course for virtual, no matter how air-brushed perfect the grass, the greens, the butterflies, the flowers, white bunkers and blue water. There's enough virtual in my world; golfing is an antidote to that, not an extension of it.

The Bermuda golf became reduced to the shots played and the results. All the stuff in between was just transport, guzzling and badinage. That round took four and three-quarter hours. The course was almost surreally pretty, heavy with scented air, so watered and green it appeared dyed. It was fun of a sort, a lark, a new experience.

It was not golfing.

In the final holes, climbing down yet again off the cart, swigging water in the heat then pulling a club from my bag and surveying a shot onto another perfect manicured green, I realised I was bored. This was just *playing at golf*.

I was heavy bored – a terrible thing to feel on a golf course. It was so *slow*, this foursome of zigzagging carts and snacks, repartee, side-betting calculations and arguments about yardages. Up ahead, an even slower foursome were doing the same; behind us, another set of guzzling babies in oversized white shorts and tee-shirts, looking as if they were wandering around in nappies, whooping, cursing, triumphing 'I *crushed* that drive!'

It's not a wild-boar hunt, guys.

Choking on that beautiful golf course, as everyone moved around the perfect greens as though wading through sun-drenched treacle, I ached to be out of there. To be gone far from this place of indulgence and decadence, to another place, part-remembered, part-imagined.

I yearned for the cool air and stripped landscape of a Scottish golf course – any course, but preferably by a cool grey sea. I wanted to be moving briskly, on foot, with a lightweight bag and set of clubs, in old trousers, a sweater and windcheater, with friends or alone, up an uneven faded yellow fairway lined with scraggy gorse, heather, whin. There would be no distance markers or refreshments stops. No electric carts, no bullish shouting, raucous laughter or screamed curses. No one would come by on another cart selling drinks or snacks of any kind. A chocolate bar, quickly shared round on the tee, or a snatched cigarette while friends holed out, that would be enough.

At this point my Scottish Presbyterian genes rise to the surface as I affirm golf is not a game of indulgence. It's not for swanning about on a cart, stuffing yourself with food, drink and figures, emoting your ego to the four winds. Golfing should be brisk, wry, simple and direct. You are there not to indulge but to control yourself. To accept outcomes, not rail against them. To accept the role of approximation, instinct, guesswork and chance. Walk to the ball, pause, play it and walk on. Take it seriously but only as a game is taken seriously, as recreation, as an extended shaggy-dog story.

This is not war, gambling, business meeting or rocket science we're practising here. It isn't even Buddhism (though it could be regarded as a form of walking meditation). This is golf. That's all. That's enough.

I've come to realise my golfing heaven is not the colour-saturated, flawlessly maintained, designed and sculpted master-pieces on the covers of golfing holiday brochures. Make my heaven a bare, undulating, problematic links with a hint of rain in the wind off the grey sea. No carts and no distance markers there. (It is of course beyond the range of mobile phones.) No calculator or stroke-saver will determine what to do; only your eyes, wrists and legs will know what's going on. There will be no bawling or whooping, curses or screams of triumph, though there will certainly be quiet chuckles, groans, and murmurs of satisfaction, sarcasm or commiseration. There will be no inept slow-motion foursome up in front, pacing out the yardage to a green they can never reach. There will be no pushy, bullish pair behind, hitting drives over your head.

There will be other players on this course, but not so many. They will wear old gardening trousers, grey windcheaters and flat bunnets. They will sport no logos. As they go round, they will know pain and pleasure, satisfaction and disappointment, but they will do it quietly and with forbearance, for they are grown-ups playing Scottish golf on a Scottish golf course.

An odd sort of heaven, I know, I know. So it won't be overcrowded. Yet people do come from all over the world, leaving warm dry countries and perfectly equipped, fully resourced courses, to search for that heaven in Scotland, because they know there lies the font, the mother-lode, the true source. In the course of this golfing year I met on windy links men and women from Canada, Australia, the United States, Germany, Ireland, Japan, Korea, Nepal, France, and I salute their taste and integrity.

And they're right: that heaven can still be found here. You may find it in the well-advertised heavenly high-spots of St Andrews, Gleneagles, Muirfield, North Berwick, Royal Dornoch, that litany of sacred sites. They are magical places, and I've played on a fair number and written up a few here. But it will cost you, and there will be many other heaven-seekers there in what passes for our Scottish summer.

The true pilgrim wanders off to the outlying, the more humble and obscure courses. (I've written up here ones that happened to fall my way; this is a personal wander, not a survey.) For it is on those unsung courses, on a damp morning in April or a blustery afternoon towards the end of October, that you may look around at your friends, the pulsing light on the grey sea, the undulating fairway, the club in your still singing hands and the distant green, and know yourself in earthly heaven.

9TH

'Brothers'

(GLENBERVIE)

That shot, not mine, hangs there still.

At the 9th hole, 'Bluebell Woods', at Glenbervie, my elder brother David tugged his drive into the rough along the left of the fairway. I had a chance to win a hole back, not that we were counting. Over-eager, I sliced my drive into the woods, and the ball vanished for ever among the blue haze. 'Bet there's hundreds of balls in there,' younger brother Sandy commented. 'I'm going to find some – there's not much golf being played here.' He set off towards the woods, and I teed up a second ball, which I banged smartly into a big lone tree on the left.

So I'd rather lost enthusiasm for the game as I watched David select a wood. Ambitious, I thought, taking a 5 wood from the rough. The green was distant, on a slight rise, encircled by bunkers; maybe 250 yards off, he couldn't possibly reach it. Smarter to have played safe.

He took a practice swing with that effortless tempo I'd admired since I was a child: no hurry, no jerking, just one smooth balanced flow. Then he stepped to the ball and hit it with just the same swing. A light *crack!*, a flash of white. His ball flew low at first, rose, then dropped gently as a swallow onto the middle of the green. I never saw a cleaner shot.

'The ball was sitting up nicely and we're not playing a medal,' he said calmly as he joined me. He seemed quietly pleased. 'So I thought I'd try the driver.'

What?

God knows where David got his swing from. My father's was functional, studied, effortful: his character note. He took David as a boy to John Panton, the leading Scottish pro based at Glenbervie. Panton watched him hit a number of shots, adjusted his grip slightly then refused to do more, remarking, 'I don't want to spoil this boy.'

'Dad had showed me the basics,' David said. 'Then I just did what seemed natural.'

A golf handicap is a fairly accurate indication of how many strokes a player is likely to take to get round a course. But it says little about shot-making, and nothing about the beauty of a swing.

Some people have it from the start. There's a trueness of hand and eye; a balance; an inbuilt physical understanding. In a senior schoolboy match at Dollar I once saw David, batting on a hard pitch against a truly fast bowler, casually flick a leg glance that landed just a yard inside the boundary. For me it was a moment of revelation, like the first time I *got* 'Subterranean Homesick Blues' or 'The Love Song of J. Alfred Prufrock'. It was in the use made of the ball's speed, the minimal movement, the balance and split-second coordination it took to flick that ball with the turning blade; the near-invisible effort and the extraordinary result. I do not remember the result of that schoolboy cricket match, but the shot lives with me still.

Even allowing for a ten-year old boy's impression of his four-years-older brother, David's swing was special. Had it been less willowy and graceful, a bit stiffer and more constrained, above all, had he played more regularly, he might have been more effective and become a scratch player instead of a 5 handicap. But as far as I'm concerned, golf would be poorer for it.

And so: to use a driver from the fairway, let alone from the rough, is a piece of breathtaking chutzpah. The kind of thing Ballesteros might have done in his pomp. I've never seen a club golfer attempt it. But to try it in one's late fifties, and hit that ball without effort dead straight 250 yards onto the centre of the green – well, that is something else.

Life is not golf, and love for an ageing parent isn't trying to play a tricky shot out of the rough. There's no good news, no miraculous recovery, no driver onto the heart of the green. My father had prepared me for this as a child: *You maun thole it, laddie.* You must bear it. Most of my generation are doing a lot of tholing these days; it comes with the territory of entering one's fifties. In conversation with friends these days, it seems all our parents are dead, dying or demented.

David had come over from Australia to spend a couple of weeks at our mother's. He'd been trying to fix what needed to be fixed, assess what couldn't, and clarify her finances. I drove up from Sheffield on more golf quests, and to see him and Mum.

My God he looks trim and fit, I thought. Must be the orienteering. He quietly told me Sandy's partner Michele's mother had died this morning, after prolonged Alzheimer's. Our eyes met briefly. Mum has 'multiple cerebral infarcts', but the effect isn't so different.

As David and Mum bonded over the crossword, I cooked the tea. The house seemed very quiet without the recently departed bouncy young dog. The doorbell and the phone used to go all the time; now nothing happens for hours on end.

At the end of the meal, David asked casually, 'So who is this book aimed at, Andy – golfers or non-golfers?'

'I don't know yet,' I replied awkwardly. 'Both, I hope.'

'Can you do that?'

'I don't know.'

Our mother looked up. Her short-term memory had been erratic all day, but discussion she could handle.

'Surely you must know your market before you begin,' she said.

'No, I just write what interests me then hope for the best,' I said defensively.

'Isn't that rather precious?'

David nodded, and I was suddenly angry. I worry about this myself.

His daughter Fionna spoke up. 'It's the same with music,' she said. 'There's the manufactured pop bands made to market research, then there's real music.'

'What's that?' Mum asked.

'People playing what they want because they believe in it.'

I too want things I can trust precisely because they're not calculated to please me.

'I heard a joke the other week,' I said. 'Mouse meets an elephant in the jungle. Elephant looks down its trunk and says, 'You are the smallest, most insignificant thing I've ever seen!' And the mouse looks up and squeaks, 'I'm not always this small – I've been sick!'

'What has that to do with your golf book?'

'That's what I want to know.'

It wasn't so much the golf that mattered, more that we were playing together at all. With David living in Australia, I hadn't played with him in twenty years. Sandy lives near Cambridge and in Dublin, a couple of summers back, we'd gone round Stromness together. Sister Judith lives in Italy. Our family are on good terms, but geographically challenged.

So the three Greig brothers hadn't played together since the early seventies. And we'd certainly never had a round together on Glenbervie.

It was my first golf course, my father's club. While he played the course, as children Sandy and I sometimes came too and were left to potter up and down the practice fairway with our cut-down clubs. Our main excitement was finding balls in the rough, which we could sell back to my dad. Meanwhile the colossi that were adult golfers stood on the elevated prow of the first tee and hit the ball miles down the endless fairway. One day David stood there beside them – he'd be nearly fifteen – and though smaller than the men, he swung that swing so smooth and easy his drive went further than any of them. I was awestruck and proud.

From the beginning, Sandy was a cheery, extrovert slugger: Arnold Palmer to David's Sam Snead. He used a baseball grip and hit the ball as far as he could. He was also a very bold putter who believed he could hole everything and sometimes did. While David quietly did his best to win, Sandy openly relished competition, enjoyed the banter and the wind-up.

Three brothers triangulated and defined by their approach to golf. If David was calm and naturally talented, and Sandy the swashbuckler, I was always intense and cautious in my game. I didn't relish competition, but hated losing. My main aim was to avoid making mistakes: don't miss the fairway, don't miss the green, don't three-putt.

It sounds rather negative. The fact is that if you avoid making mistakes you will never be an outstanding golfer, but you will score well and win your share of youth tournaments.

For all our very different temperaments, swings and approaches, at our best we probably played to a very similar standard, and won and lost a similar number of competitions. When I first proposed Glenbervie, Sandy was keen to find out just who was the best these days. 'The great shoot-out,' he called it. 'Last man standing wins!'

As the time came closer, the excuses and caveats started to come by e-mail. From David, saying poor weather and his orienteering had restricted his golf. From Sandy, explaining he'd developed a muscular problem with his wrists that sometimes made him incapable of squaring up the clubface at impact; in addition his knee-cartilage problem was getting worse. I replied to them, stressing that despite the golf book I'd scarcely played these last months; I was struggling with new glasses; had a painful lower back and a wrenched neck. David then escalated to a frozen shoulder. A couple of weeks before the Big Match,

Sandy topped us all by falling off his bike in Prague and cracking a couple of ribs.

He was out of it. Which was a pity, but at least that would tone down the level of naked competition. He still insisted on coming, to walk round with us, add his commentary and tell us where we were going wrong.

With competition diminished, what we were left with was curiosity and comparison. Of course I wanted to see how I measured up with David these days. I also wanted to see if he still had that swing.

Walking up from the car park to the low, rather ugly clubhouse, going in through those heavy doors, made me feel a foot smaller and forty years younger. This was my father's clubhouse, the mysterious place where adult men went through the door and disappeared into their unknowable world. It seemed improbable David and I could sit in the bar by the big windows looking over the course, order coffee and pay for it without anyone questioning our right to be there.

'Hey, look at this, Andy.'

I joined him in front of a little glass display box. Inside was an old, slightly yellowed golf ball. A Spalding, I noticed, dingy, battered and small – the old British size. I'd forgotten just how small and difficult to use they were. This was the ball Bobby Jones played when he won the British Amateur leg of his Grand Slam. He'd given it to Tommy Armour, the 'silver Scot', who had given it to a friend, whose widow had handed the sacred relic on to a former captain of Glenbervie.

I stared at that somehow forlorn ball, feeling a long-gone day stir inside me. Heard my father's voice, throaty and amused, replaying the Jones–Tolley match as we played out the 17th and 18th on the Old. I wondered if it was this very ball that had blocked Tolley's path to the hole on the 19th green . . .

Then Sandy arrived – 'So who is feeling a winner today?' – and we went outside to loosen up in the nets and then finally stand on that high first tee, look out over the green expanse, over the big mature trees from our childhood, and all the younger ones that had been planted since. The new ones were implausibly tall; even in the life of a tree, forty years is a fair while.

The June morning was milky, mild and still. The course gleamed green and lush; through the trees, sunlight glittered on one of the burns. Glenbervie is an inland course, so fertile it could be in England.

'On you go, Andy.'

For the younger brother, it's not a matter of proving you're better, just that you're on equal terms. Which you can never be. Whatever intimate family exchanges there would be between us wouldn't be conducted in words; that would make David uneasy and Sandy laugh. It would be done through sport, as it always had been.

It's a bonnie and golfer-friendly outlook from that 1st tee. The ground falls smoothly and steeply away to a wide, tree-lined expanse of fairway. However poorly the ball is hit, it's going to go some distance.

I could feel the artery pumping in my neck, and a slight shake in my wrists. Sandy stood behind me with the camera ready. I wished he wouldn't; took a deep, slow breath, slackened my grip. This is nothing special; just hit an easy one. Here we go . . .

'Well hit, Andy,' David said quietly. 'That's long.'

And it is, pure and straight down the left side. Such a relief not to have a repeat of Bathgate. Whatever happens in between, it's often the first and last shot of a round – like the first and last sentence of a book, which is why we put so much work into them – that you remember it by.

'It felt OK.'

David's effortless drive – he said he's holding back because of his shoulder – was well struck but pushed slightly out to the right.

'And they're off!' Sandy cried. 'Big Dan has been outdriven!'

And, yes, I was absurdly gratified to note when we got there that my drive was some 10 yards longer than his.

My second shot, misjudged, flew right over the green. David's was slightly short and finished on the side-slope of a bunker. He chipped dead, holed the putt. I thinned my chip to the back of the green and took two to get down.

'It seems the pressure is telling on Greig junior,' Sandy murmured in hushed commentator voice.

Things went downhill after that. As my short game fell apart in a welter of misjudged pitches, weak chips and three-putting, David carried on imperturbably. Despite his painful frozen shoulder, which had him mostly using an iron off the tee, his easy rhythm never altered. Whatever the shot, he walked up to the ball, stood upright and relaxed over it for a second, then went into the leisurely backswing that started the effortless arc that flicked the club head through the ball to a full follow-through. Driver, iron or putter, it was all the same tempo.

I noticed unworthy and depressing emotions in me. A flush of pleasure or at least relief when he finally pulled a drive in behind a massive tree. Is there any golfer who doesn't know this *Schadenfreude*, this malicious glee? I noticed my satisfaction that my drives outdistanced his, then the surge of irritation as I surrendered this advantage to poor finishing.

A round of golf often doesn't tell us what we'd like to be told. Golf remorselessly shows up our pettiness and failures of character. Our impatience, anxiety, childish grumpiness – they're all there. Playing with Liz at Aberdour, I'd begun to suspect that enforced, painful self-knowledge is not a drawback to the game but part of its essential nature, even its virtue. At Glenbervie, knowing this didn't help at all.

After the opening nine holes, even Sandy took pity on me, and stopped his animated running commentary on the state of play. David and I weren't formally playing against each other, but you notice, you notice. I see from the scorecard Sandy kept meticulously – including my various lost balls and out of bounds – that after being all square after the first four holes, I 'lost' four of the next five.

I tried to stay cheerful and not sulk as I thinned another chip, misjudged another easy approach after a fine drive, muffed another short putt, but the effort that took was dismaying. It wasn't so much that I was four holes down to my elder brother – he was playing rather well and I was playing poorly and these things happen – but how rotten playing badly with him and Sandy watching made me feel, that was the real disappointment. It seemed I hadn't learned anything at all.

When we're still too young to have much to base our self-worth on, we over-invest in something trivial – like golf, or having the right trainers, or knowing the capitals of all the countries in the world. When we're older, with luck we'll have done something and become someone enough to know these things are not that important, and to fail at them is not to fail as a human being. While the twelve-year-old part of me was sliding into dark sullenness, the supposed adult was trying to keep a cheerful mien, and that struggle between child and adult was much more demanding than playing golf.

As we sat and had sandwiches at the 10th, David recalled Dad once coming home bitterly disappointed from playing in a medal here. He'd been leading by a mile, then taken ten shots on the last hole to lose by one stroke. I remembered Dad speaking of it a year before he died, still annoyed at himself. The wound may stop bleeding, but the scar remains.

David suggested we play our best ball against par for the remaining nine holes. The brothers would play together against the course. I had to smile, remembering the one time Sandy and I had played together at Stromness. I'd insisted we wouldn't play against each other. 'I really mean it, Sandy. Win or lose, it just stops me enjoying it.'

He'd looked taken aback. Finally he'd agreed, then suggested we at least took on the course by playing our best ball against par. So we did, and gave the course a fair run, lost narrowly at the last hole. It was really enjoyable playing with him, conferring and cooperating rather than competing.

Maybe it was this joining of forces against the course, or the inspirational effect of David's magical shot, but I began playing less badly. I let go any vestigial notions of keeping up with him, and started to enjoy what was there to be enjoyed. Glenbervie was stunningly lush and green, with its mature trees and saplings, threaded through with burns; the day was warm now, birds sang on cue and bluebells bloomed. And I had the all too rare company of my brothers; Sandy being Sandy, David being David, me being me, and all that known, accepted, understood in a way possible only between people who have shared childhood.

Every so often I'd have flashbacks from my early youth. This dog-leg round the woods: I'd once lost a ball in there, gone in after it and found three others. I still felt the pleasure of that – in those early days, Sandy and I measured the success of an outing by the number of balls we found. Then that interesting par 3 with the green flanked by trees: I'd hit my spoon onto that green, playing with Dad, and won my first ever hole against him. Mal Duff was with me too, alternately hacking and enthusing about the pleasures of Upper Nepal, about drinking hot *chang*, the beauty of the Sherpanis and the line he'd selected up Lhotse Shar.

I see from Sandy's scorecard that David and I scored the same for the second nine. Not that I was counting. Unfortunately David's golf, after going out in one over par, deteriorated with the pain in his shoulder, so we lost quite heavily to the course.

So we came to the last hole. I hit a good drive, followed by a good 8 iron onto the upper tier of that elevated green cut into the slope below the clubhouse windows. How often Dad would have sat there, watching the other golfers finish. He must have sat there smarting from that horrendous 10 at the last.

For his shade, I wanted a good par finish. Twenty-foot uphill putt. Mustn't be short again. So I hit it 5 feet past, leaving an awkward down-and-across putt. Then missed it, on the low side, as I'd somehow known I would.

We all shook hands and walked together up the brae to the clubhouse. 'Lucky for you two I was crocked,' Sandy said as he handed over the scorecard. 'You were rubbish.'

My mother pauses by the hall cupboard.

'Andy, what am I looking for?'

'Your credit card, Mum.'

'Is it lost?'

'You said it was.'

'Oh. Then we should look for it.'

Pause.

'I'll look in the sideboard.'

'It won't be there. It'll be in my purse.'

'We've looked there twice.'

'Nonsense!' She goes through to the kitchen to the purse-drawer, then hesitates. 'What am I looking for?'

I tell David about this exchange as we drive back after playing Glenbervie. He glances at me.

'You've got to see the funny side of it.'

'I do. But it's still painful.'

'Andy, it's better not to think too much about things.' His smothered laugh is a quick intake of breath. 'I'm sure the good golfers aren't too emotional or imaginative. They just believe in themselves and want to win, and that's enough.'

In the back of the car, Sandy agrees. 'I'm sure most golfers don't feel as badly as you did when you took four putts at Aberdour.'

I turn round and stare at him. Unlike David, he likes a good argument. 'Have you never seen a grown man sulk for the rest of the round after missing a short putt? Shout, complain about the greens, the wind, the rules, that bloody bunker? Heard the language people use on a golf course? Where have you been, Sandy?'

He shrugs. 'I still think you feel it more than most.'

I stare ahead. It's a recurring debate. We've had it about marriage, divorce, golf, music, life in general. Apparently I think and feel too much within. 'Look, I've the same stuff inside me as everyone else. The only difference is it's my nature – and my work – to pay attention to it!'

'Hey, it's not worth getting upset about,' David says.

'Life is worth getting upset about,' I say defiantly. 'Because it's also worth getting happy about. What's the point of getting to the end, and all you can say is: Well, at least it hasn't bothered me much?'

Bit of a silence then, even from Sandy. Truth is, I'm in an edgy mood because I've played poorly with David on our first golf course, and am upset that it upsets me. And of course behind that, Mum. When David's wife Sue had asked last year what was our Plan B, we'd just looked at each other. There is still no Plan B.

'Tell you what bothers me,' David says at last, 'is getting in a pint at the Dreel before we get back to Mum.'

'Sandy's done nothing all day, so he's buying.'

'I agree.'

'Hey! You mean sods!'

That time Sandy and I played together on Stromness, competing against the course and not each other – how enjoyable his company and our solidarity had been. As we came off the course we agreed it had been great just to play round together without getting distracted by competition. Then as we changed our shoes he said casually, 'You've got better, Andy   I think you beat me two up and one to play.'

I shook my head. 'Actually, it was 3 and 2, Sandy.'

Brothers.

A 6 iron to the green

There are times on a golf course – that evening gloaming at
Shiskine, or the second nine holes on gleaming North Berwick,
and all day on North Ronaldsay – when I play in a state I've called
a dwam. Which suggests drowsiness and absent-mindedness, but
that's not it at all.

Sometimes, playing golf, I'm enchanted awake. And if I say
'dreamy', I mean the particular clarity of some dreams. Playing
golf, over and over I am awoken.

Awoken to my physical being. Body is my ground, my reality,
my sanity. I love and trust its appetites, its movement, the five
senses that like eager messengers bring the world to me. I'll never
entirely adjust to its inevitable demise. I can almost accept it, but
by God I regret it. When life, physical life, is so good – how can I
not hate leaving it?

I trundle my trolley up to the little white ball, look at it sitting
there on the turf, dimpled white on coarse green background. It's
in a slight hollow, a depression a few inches across, which will
make this shot more difficult. Though I've played this hole – the
5th on Stromness – dozens of times, I've never seen this exact
spot on the fairway before. Had I just been walking over the
course, I'd never have attended to it. Now I see it clearly because
it's relevant.

I look up to the green. The cool, grassy wind is blowing into
and a bit across me, right to left. This is not the usual airt of the

wind here, it will alter the shot I have to make. Other factors run, half-announced, across my mind into my hands. The pin's near the front, the fairway is damp from last night's rain, but drying; the ground before this green tends to be soft. Keep away from that bunker on the left, but don't let it intimidate.

It's not a conscious decision to pull out the 6 iron, it's just the body's memory taking over. I swing the club slowly a couple of times, remembering club-throwing with Vin and David: that sensation of release in shoulders, wrists, forearms, hands, going *through the ball*. That's all we're trying to do here: release and go through it.

I stand to the ball, rock slightly on my feet, feel the ground firm, my weight, the reality of this body. Flex wrists once. Look up at the green. Now the thinking stops. There's just the ball and where it's going, forth from this shallow depression.

Something happens, the body flows, club arcs, the ball departs – a bit pushed, though the wind drifts it back, and right distance. Against the pewtery light above the old army camp, I can just see my ball finish maybe 20 feet from the pin.

I slot the iron back in the bag, grasp the trolley handle and walk on, body still singing quietly to itself that click through the wrists seconds ago; mind awake to the cool, fragrant breeze, the clouds moving over Hoy, the tide race scouring through the Sound. A memory of playing with my friend Eddie Farrell here, the time he hit a terrible tee shot at the short 8th, and we crested the rise just in time to see his ball dribble across the green, hit the pin and drop in. I smile, remembering Eddie, our friendship, our laughter.

As I approach the green, watching the contours, eyes already sizing up the putt, I'm thinking of that remark attributed to Mark Twain that non-golfers always toss at me: *Golf is a good walk spoiled.* From which we can only conclude either he'd had a bad day on the course or, more likely, had never played the game.

I crouch to the putt, taking in the slope down and the slope across, the slight grit between the grass blades, the faint pearl of moisture at the tip.

This is where golfing takes place, at this intersection of calculating brain, the body awake to itself, a calm that highlights the thoughts, memories, emotions that drift through the mind, and the physical planet known in this moment.

When I take a walk by the course – as I regularly do on the way to the graveyard – there's pleasure, interest, relaxation, an opportunity to think, or to leave thinking behind. But there is not this little drama of intention, hope, execution and outcome. There is not this heightening of the body. Above all, simply looking at the world, there is not the same clarity and knowledge that comes from engagement. I'd have missed that little depression in the fairway, the pale sandy divot scuff beside it, the darker flat green of a daisy's leaves.

The putt bobbles past the right rim of the cup. Pity, but I gave it a chance and it's still a steady par. I knock the ball into the hole with the back of Dad's putter, and walking off the green, thoughts already turning to the next hole, the short 7th down the hill towards the sea, it comes clear to me.

A walk is a missed opportunity for golf.

'Gilders'

(ELIE)

Michael Gilderdale gave me the only 'real' job I've ever had. I mean the kind where wages ('salary') go into a bank account monthly, invisibly, rather than the little brown envelope with folding money ('pay') at the week's end, or the short-term contract paid by long-overdue cheque. He later said he gave me the job because he liked my poetry, and reckoned I could do things with words. He is a man of an optimistic, idealistic temperament.

I've always been grateful for that vote of confidence, however misguided. At twenty-four I felt almost grown up, catching the bus up from Leith then walking with the rest of the rush-hour crowd through the West End, turning into the doorway off Shandwick Place, up the stairs and into the Creative Department of McCallum's Advertising.

My desk! My files! My own stained coffee mug next to my ashtray! My co-worker Andy Beale is already hunched over his typewriter, clutching his hair in one hand and a Gauloise in the other.

'Good morning, Andy!' He dredges up an awful smile that conveys an insomnia-tormented night followed by the banal horrors of another day.

'You'll get over it.'

Then Mike breezes in, wearing his blue blazer with shiny buttons, striped shirt and cravat. Mike Gilderdale is a cravat man; his jocular voice, gleaming brushed-back hair, the faint whiff of anxiety beneath his aftershave and boyish urbanity – is all cravat.

'And a jolly good morning to you, Andrew! There is just a teeny bit of a rush on for the industrial workwear copy, so if you could be so good ... By noon, do you think, possibly?'

I glance at the photos of boiler suits and shiny plastic jackets, and the few hesitant lines I typed up yesterday, all trying for catchy variations on 'economical', 'multiple zips' and 'fur-lined around the wrists and collar'. It's a long way from the stoned lyric poetry and philosophical essays of my student days. This is real life, what people do after they've had their fun. That's what my girlfriend says, and as a teacher in the tough Leith Fort primary school, she should know. She seems very sure about this, as she is about it being time to get married.

'Do my best, Mike.'

He claps me on the shoulder. 'That's the spirit, laddie! Just sprinkle on a wee bittie of yon creative magic!'

He knows his attempts at a Scottish accent are appalling, but I appreciate that he tries to bring a bit of levity into a serious business. That's Mike's job: to keep things jollying along, to take clients out to lunch and schmooze them with drinks, jokes, talk of golf, so they won't move their accounts elsewhere. Because there's no doubt about it, this agency is springing leaks, the smarter crew are deserting, while Mike's role is to move among the deckchairs assuring the passengers everything is top-hole, spiffing, jolly fine. In fact, now I think of it, a bit like Sunny Jim Callaghan in that year of 1975, trying to avert our gaze from the rocks and man-eating crocodiles up ahead.

I make the first of many mugs of coffee, light my first Gitane of the day, and sit down to the workwear brochure. After this, I'll move on to the Rexco Smokeless Coal campaign; there may be a jingle needed for that, and even a chance to go to the studio to hear them record my snappy lyric: *Get the Rexco rabbit habit / And keep your burrow warm.*

It's not rock and roll, but as near as I'll get. There's the first stab of headache as I pick up the thesaurus to find other words for 'smart', 'practical' and 'cheap'. This is known as creativity; it's what we do in the Creative Department. It's why we don't have to wear ties.

Andy Beale utters a deep groan, then shakes his head in a way that suggests nothing can be done, ever, about anything.

'My God, this is piffle. Do you think I could still make a career in music?'

'You've got the talent.' Indeed he is a very fine jazz pianist, in the more far-out and painful reaches of that idiom. 'It probably depends on how much do you want it.'

He considers, then groans again as he goes back to honing the fifteen to twenty words he's allowed to add below the photo of Bonnie Prince Charlie's Own Secret Recipe Drambuie. It's his misfortune to have a mother who is a director of this company; his job is secure, but he hates it.

I guess if it were possible to make a living from writing poetry, I wouldn't be here. But it isn't, so I am. I glance out the window. From up here I can see across Edinburgh to the Forth and Fife. It's a stunning October morning, windless, with a pale, pure-blue sky. It would be great to phone in sick and go down to Cramond, walk along the shore to South Queensferry. Or drive back across to Fife – a flash of standing on the first tee at Anstruther with the fairway ahead of me . . .

I'll do it. If it's like this tomorrow morning, I'll phone in sick. It's a crime to be stuck inside on a day like this. But I have to; that's my life now.

And then – I remember the moment still – the treacherous, subversive thought came: *My life's too important to live for weekends and three weeks holiday a year.* Not important in the world's terms, of course, just important to me.

I can see now that those months of copywriting for McCallum's were a possible life. The job was demanding, pointless but interesting. Most folk had it much harder, I knew that. And after the student years, it was good to run a car, be able to buy records and a good stereo, and afford wine or hash to unwind from work in the evenings. It was good to have a regular life, to feel a part of the mainstream, to be normal.

It so nearly could have worked. But it was such a fine autumn that year, and the hills, coastline and even occasionally the golf course were calling, and one sickie led to another, and another. It's not so much phoning in sick that is the rebellion; it's the principle that is subversive: *My life is more important than this job.* Once that notion gets into your head, it stays there, quietly muttering insurrection as you head for the workplace, until one day you stop and say, *Sod this for a game of marbles*, then go off in another direction.

Mike Gilderdale did me a big favour, giving me that job. And he did me an even bigger favour when, some six months later, he took me into his office and, with much embarrassment and many apologies, told me the company was having to shed jobs and I was being made redundant.

I walked out of the office a free man. From now on, I'd be making up my life as it went along. I'd tried 'the real world'; it was OK, but no more or less real than what I'd been doing before.

From time to time, writing alone without guidance, support, colleagues or deadlines, I missed the office, having a place to go, people to see and set work to do. I missed those regular payments into my bank account. I missed Andy Beale's sardonic despair that masked his real despair; I thought affectionately of Mike and his cravats, the almost music-hall impression he gave of a jolly nice chap. If it hadn't been for the involuntary redundancy, I could be there still, trying to find a snappy rhyme for Rexco Smokeless Coal, or thumbing through the thesaurus for another way of saying 'smart', 'sturdy' or 'fur-lined fly with reversible cuffs'.

Instead, nearly thirty years on, I'm driving to Elie to meet up with Mike Gilderdale and his wife Jenny, to play a round of golf for the new book I'm on. It's early June, the Firth quivers under a light breeze; clouds like fleets of white ducks drift over the Pentlands; the day is full of promise, and I think, *What a great day for a sickie.*

When Mike retired, he and his wife Jenny bought a large cottage on the outskirts of Elie. Following his directions, I drive through that genteel town of Edwardian villas and bungalows, turn up the single-track road that cuts across the links. Though I'd thought of him from time to time, I never expected to meet Mike Gilderdale again till my mother ran into him at her Quaker meeting in St Andrews.

Mike a Quaker. It made sense. I'd always sensed a humility, balance and sincerity behind his bonhomie. When we met again I thanked him for giving me the job and later making me redundant. He looked relieved, said he'd always felt bad about it. 'Best thing that could have happened to me,' I assured him. Apparently the firm had continued to decline despite my departure, and finally folded.

'My wife's really the golfer,' he said. 'I'm a decrepit old stick, what with my hip.'

I assured him it was important he played with us. It would bring not so much a closure as a pleasing circularity: playing with the man who gave me my first and only job, on this course of my adolescent competitive tournaments, for the first time in thirty years.

The cottage is smashing, looking over those undulating, windswept links, out across to the wide Firth and the distant Lothian hills. The arthritic limp apart, at eighty-two he's sprightly as ever. Still the boyish gleam, the jovial kindliness, the self-deprecation. 'Old Gilders is a bit of a duffer on the course,' he reminds me. Getting past the dog, I shake hands with Jenny. I remind her we met last in 1975, when she and Mike asked me and Irene to Sunday lunch at her mother's house in Elie.

'I remember,' she says. 'Mother really enjoyed that day.'

'She's –?'

She nods. 'Still,' she says briskly, 'it's a lovely day for it. I've booked our tee time, so we'd better get off.'

As Mike sets up his electric buggy – special dispensation from the club, which doesn't normally allow them – Jenny and I talk as we walk over the course. She first played golf here when she was eight, on long summer holidays, has loved the game ever since. Though born in Gerrards Cross, at the age of nine she went to St Leonard's, the smart St Andrews school.

Though she must be in her early sixties, it's impossible not to use the word 'willowy' of Jenny. She's tall, slim, athletic; with her curly fair hair and open expression, I had her down as the popular vice-captain of the girls' hockey team.

'I was house captain of games,' she admits. 'We also played a lot of lacrosse, cricket and fives.'

'What's "fives"?' It sounded straight from the school annual.

'A bit like squash, except without a racket. But I liked golf best because it got me away from the school.'

She's a stalwart of the Elie and Earlsferry Ladies Golf Club here, and for some years has been Secretary of the Handicap Committee. 'Rather a demanding position,' she admits. 'A lot of complicated calculations, and some very touchy players!' She plays regularly through the week, mostly with women friends; also in the monthly medals. Much of her and Mike's social life is through golf and the club. I'm interested in lives so unlike my own, this world of comfortable retirement, golf and bridge, dogs and gardening and holidays in Portugal.

'The club really is just that,' she says. 'It's our meeting place. We have dances, raffles, fund-raising dinners – and play a lot of golf in summer.'

'And in the winter?'

'The women play bridge.'

'What do the men do?'

Mike has shoogled up in his dashing electric steed as she pauses.

'Drink, mostly,' she replies, and he hoots with laughter.

I warm to the affection with which she looks at him, the open appreciation with which he looks at her. They're alive to each other. They have no children.

Whenever I meet someone who has played on the Elie links, what we share is always the same: *That periscope! The hill!*

The 1st tee is right in front of the extensive Edwardian clubhouse with its big bay windows, billiard table, dining room, flagpole and all. The starter's hut is on your right, and through its roof rises – yes! – a giant periscope. It's there so that the starter can see over the hill that swells up across the 1st fairway. With members watching from the clubhouse, as well as the queueing golfers, and the sadistic casual onlookers drawn by the prospect of humiliation, that hill looms like a green tidal wave over the frail open boat of your self-belief.

When I first encountered it at nearly fourteen, standing there with my cut-down spoon, it seemed truly enormous. The periscope added to that intimidation, rotating as the starter followed the progress of the players on the other side of the hill. Then he formally called Dad and me to the tee. There's a lot of history here; generations of golfers have stood on this tee, heard the silence of anticipation, and felt their knees quiver. I'd seen the photo of Harry Vardon and A. H. Scott teeing off here in their exhibition match in August 1899; Vardon looks relaxed ('The finest little course I have ever played over,' he remarked), Scott and the spectators less so.

My dad, who still seemed a giant then, hit his drive fair and square over the hill. Then it was my turn. I had left the long misery of Dollar Academy just weeks before. I hadn't done much with my father for years. I wanted to impress.

Standing on that tee, looking up at that ever-mounting hill, I doubted myself. The golfers and spectators had fallen silent; the starter stood impassively in the doorway of his hut. This wasn't homely Anstruther's nine-hole stroll; nor was it Dollar's quirky, short, side-sloping course. This was a links course, one of the true early ones. The 18th green had seemed vast as we'd walked by it, hard and bare as concrete when I'd tested it with my thumb. This was a beast.

There can be several moments of truth in a round of golf; there is always one on the 1st tee. *Please God let me clear the hill*. That was all I asked: not to top or duff my drive. Get the ball over the hill and out of sight of starters and spectators, and then maybe I could breathe again.

My fervent adolescent prayer was answered ambiguously, as such prayers tend to be. I caught the ball well enough; it cleared the hill but sliced off to the right, towards the stone wall. It could well be out of bounds.

My father, who had his compassionate moments, suggested I didn't play a second ball from the tee because he was pretty sure my first wasn't out of bounds. It was; now out of sight of all but the starter's periscope I dropped a ball into the light rough by the wall. I feel still the keen pleasure of that clean-struck wood from the rough, the ball running towards the distant green, the sea breeze cooling the sweat in my shirt.

My East Fife school friend George Boyter recently told me how he'd introduced a pal to the course. Lots of joking, bending and stretching beside the 1st tee; then the joking stopped as it was their turn to play. To his great relief, George cleared the hill ('I felt like a wee boy again; it just looked enormous!'). His friend took a mighty swipe; the ball shot sideways right off the toe of the club, just missed the ducking specators and the clubhouse windows, bounced off the dining-room wall and ended back on the tee.

After the laughter had exhausted itself, and the friend had managed to regain his self-esteem from the far corners of the globe, then hit a second tee shot over the hill, George paused to apologise to the starter. 'That's naithin, son. I've seen golf balls rattling aroon inside this hut like bullets, and me leaping about dodging them!'

No such fireworks today. I seem to have controlled my inner thirteen-year-old, though he's still there, of course. My drive clears the hill, which isn't that big after all. Mike cracks a joke or two, settles over the ball. 'Let's see Gilders make a hash of it!' Then he's still, briefly serious and concentrating. His swing is scarcely graceful but his ball wobbles heavily over the hill like a wounded partridge. I hear the involuntary puff of relief.

Jenny relies on a long, full swing to generate distance. At the top of her backswing, the club is past horizontal; her follow-through is equally full. There's no great snap of the wrists, it's just the flow of the swing, and the ball climbs high and pretty straight over the hill. It's the unforced shot of someone who plays regularly, knows their game's strengths and limitations – yet still I hear her relieved *Ah!*

Mike hirples into his electric cart and zooms off up the hill, waving. I find my drive in the little bunker on the right I'd forgotten about. But it's OK, I cleared the hill, and a youth spent golfing in the East Neuk of Fife has left me laid-back about bunkers. In fact I rather enjoy them – easier than playing off a very tight lie, and with lower expectations there's less pressure and more likelihood of a pleasing result. I hit a decent iron most of the way to the green, and follow Jenny and Mike down the fairway with sun on my shoulders.

When all analysis is done, it's a simple thing. It happens most often when the breeze blends warm grass with seaweed, when the turf is short and springy, and the fairway rolls and tilts among gorse, whin and rough. Walking over a links course with a club in my hand and the next shot up ahead, I know myself to be happy.

Mike struggles through the opening holes. However laid back, he still wants to do well. He tells me he took up the game at forty, when he met Jenny. 'I thought, if I'm going to spend my life with this lovely girl, I'd better learn her game!' He'd played a lot of competitive tennis at school in York, then at Manchester School of Art, then the Slade. Art school? This was a side of Mike I knew nothing about.

While Jenny prepares for a long downhill putt, he says his father had been a director at Rowntrees. That made sense of the Quaker part.

'I'm proud to say my father was involved in the development of the Aero bar. I always thought that was a worthwhile achievement.'

'It certainly is!' There's something about the texture of those collapsing bubbles.

Mike must have been good at tennis because he was entered for Junior Wimbledon, then the Second World War broke out.

'I'm not a very good Quaker,' he says, 'but I couldn't be in the business of killing anyone. So after I'd finished at the Slade, I was drafted into agriculture. But I wanted to do something more useful, so on my second application I got into the Friends' Ambulance Corps, in Germany towards the end of the war. Hamburg in ruins, I saw that.' He paused, then awkwardly got down from his buggy. 'Young Gilders rushing pregnant women to the only working hospital through streets of rubble, it was quite exciting. And then, well . . .'

He tails off, and for a moment I glimpse a different man. I've had a hint from my mum what he's thinking of, but this isn't the time.

I remember the second hole from my boyhood. 'High Hole' was always tricky: an awkward bunker to catch the drive, and then the narrow green perched high at the top of an angled ramp, surrounded by more bunkers and steep drop-offs. It's a classic links problem. I lost this hole in each round of the first boys' tournament I played here, and it still gives me a sinking feeling.

I stumble through it with another bogey, then step with pleasure onto the 3rd tee. This is the high outlook point of the course, and today it looks fantastic. Out on the white-crinkled blue Firth of Forth are a scattering of islands – the May like a giant black sperm whale; the fortress-like hump of the Bass Rock; little Fidra that R.L.S. never forgot. Mike waves at it all, exultantly, and his sombre mood of five minutes before is gone. 'Isn't it wonderful!' he enthuses.

I peel off my sweater, drink some water. The sun is high and downright hot. Down the Forth I'm looking at Edinburgh, Arthur's Seat, the Pentland hills purple-brown, the gasometers above Granton, the Forth Bridges, South Queensferry. Nearly twenty years of my life went by there, years of studying, writing, playing, climbing; adventures, escapades, loves and losses. Trying to grow up. There's very little to show for it now, just seven books. I seemed to spend much of that time waiting for my life to begin, as though this were some sort of rehearsal.

But we're here, now, which is all we'll ever be as Jenny runs her tee shot right onto the green, looks delighted then embarrassed as we congratulate her. Mike tops his into horrible rough; I drag mine into a greenside bunker, and we all set off in pursuit of the consequences of our actions. Golf is a Scottish Presbyterian karma game. You pay for what you get, and what you get is what you did. It's also somehow finally God's Will and out of your control, so don't rail against it.

Mike zips up in his buggy as I'm raking the bunker after my explosion shot, points out the building by the road that is the Earlsferry Thistle Golf Club headquarters. 'Used to be called "the Artisans' Club" because that's what it was, but we're not meant to call it that any more.'

It is one of the oddities of golf, especially in Scotland, that on many courses, particularly the old ones, quite different clubs play over the same course, for quite different subscriptions. When we step over the road to the 4th tee, we cross over one of the reasons why this is so. We're now on the original nine-hole links course where the game was played for several centuries, for free. I love this part of the course; the air over the fairways, rough and grassed-over dunes, quivers with the shades of departed golfers (or maybe it's just the heat-haze). This is a place where hickory-shafted clubs were once a new-fangled, American innovation regarded with suspicion; where the old feathery balls were clouted till the stuffing leaked from them to join the seagull feathers that littered the fairways.

Because the early links were usually common ground, or leased by the burgh from a landowner, access to them was free. Golf had been played for a few hundred years before the first members' clubs were formed. They were just that: clubs. Places where members could meet, change, eat, drink, shelter and compete. They didn't own the course.

So the members of the elegant clubhouse of the posh Elie Golf House Club, and those of the more restrained functional building of the Earlsferry Thistle Golf Club aka 'the Artisans'' (which lots of local folk, including its own members, still call it – these are not people who apologise for who they are) both play on this course, usually keeping to themselves. There's an annual match between the clubs for the Liberty Cup; it is, you might say, keenly contested.

As I hit a poor drive way right into the rough – Mike connected with a good one and trundled off gaily into the distance, while Jenny was straight as usual – I'm thinking of another school pal, Alec Morris. His dad was a plumber and dedicated player of golf and, of course, an Artisans' member. Alec told me that throughout the six summery months of the year his dad would come home from work, strip off his overalls, wash his hands, pick up a sandwich and his clubs, and meet his pals for a round.

According to Alec, for years his dad did this three times through the week, every week while the light permitted, always in the same foursome. Alec wasn't allowed to join them. On Saturday, his father would play in the medal if there was one. On Sunday morning, he would play with Alec.

This dedication and consistency is almost disturbing. How much the game must have meant to him, that he'd go out to play eighteen holes after a full day's – presumably tiring – work. The same people, the same course. Oddest of all, and perhaps most perturbing, he was not alone in this, and this was thought quite reasonable, almost admirable, behaviour.

Then again, we seldom question spending our evenings watching television, which would have seemed a waste of good daylight to Alec's dad, and totally aberrant to my grandfather's generation.

I eventually find my ball, deep in those long scrawny grasses that wrap themselves round the club head. As Jenny points out, she can't afford to get into rough like that, because her wrists simply don't have the strength to force the ball out. Liz Duff said much the same. Not surprisingly, women golfers tend to focus on keeping the ball on the fairway rather than on distance.

That was very much my game in my mid-teens. I didn't even have a driver, just kept hitting the spoon some 190 yards up the fairway. If you keep doing that, seldom get into the rough, never go out of bounds, lose a ball once in a blue moon, and get reasonably good at the short game, you can score surprisingly well. At fifteen, I'd have expected to go round here in under 80. At Anstruther, I'd be looking for 70 or less.

Watching Jenny calmly play the 4th after I've hacked from the rough then cajoled my next onto the edge of the warped green, it strikes me that women golfers and lads like myself in my early teens, we have the best of it. We get to play the course the way it was made to be played, with all its challenges, decisions and pleasures intact.

An example: for Jenny, and myself aged 14–15, 'Provost' at 378 yards is a good full-length par 4 hole. The second shot will be a challenging long iron, maybe a fairway wood. It's a skilful, interesting shot, where you must feel the lie of the fairway to get the ball to run in and trundle onto the green as she just did. A delightful shot, a real golf shot. I rather envy her as I congratulate her.

(My 1899 guidebook by J. More Dall notes here: 'A well-struck second brassy or cleek shot should see the ball on the green.' How much lost golfing experience there is wrapped up in those words! *A well-struck second brassy.* I had one my father gave me, though I seldom used it, regarding it as too risky. It was roughly a 2 wood, with a brass plate screwed into the sole. And my dad would still refer to a 'cleek' sometimes, meaning a long iron, and the golf-club factory still in operation when I moved to Anstruther in 1963 was known simply as 'the cleek factory'.)

Even Harry Vardon or James Braid (that great pro of golf's golden age was Earlsferry born, and a member of the Artisans') would have played this hole in much the same way, with their hickory-shafted clubs and the new guttie ball. They had the challenge and pleasure of skilfully manoeuvring their way round these links courses. There was no question of crushing the course into submission. A 420-yard hole was a complex challenge to them, as it is to Jenny and was to me. Back then, I didn't find Elie a short course at all, and needed my trusty spoon off the fairway hole after hole on the back nine.

Then again, it's quite long enough for me still, as I fumble my way to another bogey.

Then, almost inadvertently, I start to play golf. A par 4 at 'Doctor' – always one of my favourite holes, with a deep rolling trench on the fairway, rising up to a green that then runs away – is followed by a sweet birdie at 'Quarries'. Which both bears out and gives the lie to the above elegiac thoughts of the lost integrity of golf. This 316-yard hole, played blind over a ridge, then sloping away towards the sea, even into the breeze becomes a 3 wood followed by a running chip shot which emerges somehow from my lost youth: a 7 iron held down the grip, hands well forward, clip it low and let it follow the contours. A pleasure watching it actually work, the ball running to four feet, hole the putt on the quality green.

It's even more marked at 'Peggy's', 252 yards. Though it's down as a par 4, with the breeze behind and the fairway hard from weeks of sun without rain, my 3 wood runs right over the green, and the tee behind it. Under these conditions, with modern clubs and balls, it's not really a par 4.

Yet, of course, I'm dead pleased with a run of four pars and a birdie. Only part of me wishes the course was harder. The other part is really enjoying cutting the holes down to size, reducing 382-yard 'Neuk' (which had always been an interesting problem, with a raised dirt road running at an oblique angle by the green) to a decent drive and a lofted iron that can clear the road and still stop on the green. Two putts, and I'm quite glad to be the age I am with the clubs I have.

Let's say the game is not reduced or destroyed, just altered as it's altered many times over the last five hundred years. Something is lost, that's for sure, and it's most apparent on these classic links courses. But much is gained; there's an unalloyed pleasure for men, women and children hitting the ball good distances, and modern clubs, the metal woods and cavity-backed irons and specialist wedges, are frankly much easier to use.

(Something similar happened to winter climbing in the 1970s, when the angled twin ice-axe, the front-point crampon, and far better clothing, changed snow and ice climbing from a highly specialised, uncomfortable sport with a long, arduous apprenticeship, to something anyone could take up and with application after a couple of seasons do routes which had been regarded as strictly for the leading practitioners. There's something lost here, no doubt, but a heck of a lot more people can enjoy it.)

We take a break after the 9th hole, to eat sandwiches, drink water, and let through the faster pair behind. It's good to take time out during a round, especially here with the beach nearby, the thousands of points of light smoothing to one broad blaze as the breeze fails. At the end of the bay are the twisted cliffs of Kincraig. On the beach there in the last two years of our school life we had summer bonfires; classmates would walk over the course in the gloaming carrying food, guitars, cans of Tennent's lager, bottles of cheap cider and Don Cortez wine, even the odd half-bottle of vodka bought from the friendly grocer's.

I stare along the beach where we once sprawled and partied. I planned my first trip abroad on one such summer night, walking with Tommy Reekie, the Elie pro's son, zillions of sand bugs whispering over our shoes as we decided on the fish lorry to London, then don kilts and hitch to Paris, then Marseilles, then the Camargue.

We did it too, and it was great as first times are, but the biggest buzz was in the planning; as we walked up and down the beach under the faint summer stars, passing the bottle back and forth, both just turned seventeen, the world lay open before us.

And there were girls too on those barbecue nights, those intense or merely accidental summer romances that lasted a long week or three. I remember lying on damp sand near the heat of the bonfire, the dizzying proximity of a firelit mouth and unfathomable, shadowed eyes.

It, sex (or as near as we came to it in those comparatively innocent days), boys and girls getting up to good in the open privacy of the this coastal strip, must have been going on here even longer than golf. It's common ground; that's what it's for: recreation and procreation.

Golf is a painstaking game of patience, balance, self-control and self-possession – qualities essential in a marriage, but having little place in the spontaneous self-surrender of making love. And yet a golf course, particularly a links course, has a vaguely erotic charge for me.

I take a last look down that beach of my adolescence, think too of summer nights in the long grass above the 6th green in Anstruther, and for the first time understand why that might be.

The 288-yard 10th at Elie is another memorable hole – a blind drive right over a big rise onto the downslope that in summer hurries the ball down and right over the green into light rough or the sea. Luckily I mishit my 3 wood, because I find it inches short of the beach.

There's always a strange atmosphere in this corner of the

course. Instead of sand, there's wildly twisted igneous and composite rock. It's a place for fossils and garnets, old volcanic vents and curious schists.

I remark on this to Jenny as Mike tees up on the short 11th.

She smiles, nods. 'I'm going to have my ashes scattered here. Isn't that so, Mike?'

'Absolutely, old girl,' Mike says happily. 'Jolly nice place for it too.'

'Have you any plans for yours?' I ask.

He glances at Jenny; something flickers between them. For all his boyish fizz and bubble, he is nineteen years older than her. 'I think we said something about the lawn at the back of the house,' he says, then wafts his tee shot neatly over the raised ridge of rock that hides the green. He smiles, pleased. 'Now I can only hope for the best!'

I tee up my ball, wondering which outcome he was referring to.

It's an indication of the changing times and technology of golf that the next hole was once 410 yards long, and Mr J. More Dall gave it as a par 5. Now my card says it's 466 yards, but it's a par 4. Certainly as a laddie, this was two full shots then a fair bit more. I've a notion that in my first tournament match here, I uncharacteristically pulled my drive into the grassy dunes on the left, and then had the deep, shameful joy of seeing my opponent hook his right onto the beach.

Now, nearly forty years on, I pull my drive into those same dunes. Mike makes heavy weather of it too, and had we been keeping score against each other, Jenny would certainly have won that hole outright. Her wood off the fairway, low, straight and easy, makes all of us smile with pleasure.

It's so good to not play competitions any more. Win or lose, they took so much out of me there was little room left for pleasure in the game itself. I had wanted to win that first year of the Elie Boys Spring Open with all the desperate fervour of a fourteen-year-old.

Dad dropped me off in the morning with sandwiches, a bottle of juice, and half a crown for emergencies. 'Good luck,' he said briefly. He may have touched me on the shoulder before driving away. Some fathers would accompany their children as a caddy, to encourage and advise; Dad believed in leaving us to get on with it alone. He thought this was good for us, and would better prepare us for life.

I won my first match quite easily, then sat and had my sandwiches on the grass outside the pavilion. Then the afternoon match, which I just squeezed through. I was now in the quarter-finals, so I treated myself to a Vimto till Dad picked me up.

Next morning he drove me through to Elie again. 'Keep your head down,' he said, then left. I kept my head down and sweated out another win. Now I was in the semi-final; already I could see the final glittering ahead, a win, Dad's expression then.

I supposed he cared how I did, though I couldn't be sure. I think that, along with his generation's distaste for emotional display, he kept well back from most aspects of our lives because he didn't want to interfere. He hated being coralled, and granted us the same independence. If we wanted to work hard on our golf, that was up to us.

Playing the closing holes with Mike and Jenny, I keep having flashbacks of how it felt back then. My semi-final opponent had his father to carry his clubs, to advise and encourage him, read the line of his putts. I carried my own clubs and felt outnumbered. It was close, that match. Coming up the 17th, I was one hole down but ahead on the hole. Then my opponent laid a very long approach putt dead; I hit a weak chip and took three putts, and it was all over.

That trudge back up the last fairway to the clubhouse was long. I saw Dad standing waiting behind the 18th green. He made no comment, just nodded. Back in my room, I cried a few bitter tears of frustration then lay on my bed hating golf.

Maybe it's because I'm remembering all this, or because I'm tiring out here in the June heat, the last five holes go by in regulation par. The game can sometimes seem very simple and straightforward: hit the drive; next shot onto the green; two putts. That's all you have to do.

Back then I was an emotional wee soul – still am, I guess, only I've more to fall back on now. I always say defensively that I'm not competitive, I'm just depressed by losing. Golf makes you look into yourself, and what's there isn't always pretty. Adolescent dreams of glory, certainly, but also a dread of failure. That fear could have limited my life – as a writer you sign up for criticism and rejection from the start.

But I've probably the old man's thrawnness, the stubbornness that I seem to have got from him, to thank. Next week I got down to serious practising, especially the chip shots. Some mornings I got up early enough to cycle to Anstruther golf course and hit balls for an hour before school; then more golf after school; then out one more time after my tea. I seem to remember a Bullworker muscle exerciser, and taking spring hand-grips to school, squeezing throughout Double Chemistry.

That summer, still fourteen, I entered the Gay Memorial Trophy for Boys under Sixteen (now, due to much sniggering at the back, renamed the Crail Junior Open). It was one round of stroke play. By not making any significant mistakes, I won with a 73 against the par of 70. Even with the new clubs and balls, and all my extra weight and strength, I couldn't score that now. I earned a nod and a rare smile from Dad. 'Well played,' he may have said.

But the one that mattered more, I'm thinking as Jenny hits a canny second shot to the 18th green, was the next year's Elie Spring Tournament. Through two windy days I made it through to the final. Next morning the wind had dropped; I remember the course was dew-damp as I stuffed my sandwiches in the golf bag and Dad drove off. 'Don't press,' he'd said.

Well I didn't press, but it was an emotionally exhausted laddie that managed to tap in a short putt on the 16th to win 3 and 2. Once again my opponent had his father caddying; I felt for the boy, silent and head down, as we walked in the remaining holes. After that I remember only holding a cup briefly in a room full of people and, hugely embarrassed and gratified, glanced up and saw Dad at the back. I can see him still, his face flushed, his big hands clapping.

'So did you go in for the Senior Boys the next year?' Mike asks.

I shake my head. 'Girls and guitars,' I reply. It's what I always say, but it's as true that I'd just burnt out. That summer I played poorly in the Gay Trophy and the Fife Boys, and the game was losing its savour for me. Far more interesting was learning to play 'Don't Think Twice, It's Alright' to please myself and impress a girl at the school Folk Club.

Now I can play dozens of Dylan songs and am absolutely married, I shake hands warmly with Mike and Jenny on the 18th green and go with them for lunch at the café. We sit outside in the hot sun, just a few yards from where I'd once sat to eat my sandwiches and juice after the morning matches. I'm talking about the golf book, and say in part it's about dead people. Mike volunteers he's always been very aware of death, and more so these days. I lean back and look at two high contrails inscribing a saltire cross in the blue sky.

'Some might say thinking about your mortality is just being morbid.'

'At eighty-three, it's just being realistic!' Mike replies, then laughs. He relates how, at seventy-nine, his father had his morning's golf foursome and won it; then home for lunch and gardening; then bridge in the evening, a few drinks; finally felt tired, went to bed and died in his sleep.

'He was a lovely man who had a great last day,' Mike says simply. 'I felt he'd earned it.'

'Anyone who helped invent the Aero bar deserves the best possible end.'

It's unexpected, sitting with these two, talking like this. Sometimes I realise I'm not the only one with living and dying on my mind. Then Jenny tells of playing with a good friend at the ladies' golf club here. Her friend won her foursomes at the 16th, hit a cracking drive down the 17th, then dropped dead. A shock for one's partners, but a good way to go, we all agree. Much better than lingering on way past closing time.

But I have to get back to my mother's. In the last few weeks her failing memory, which used to just irritate and frustrate her, has been leaving her confused and distressed. Then she feels all right, and forgets earlier she'd felt all wrong.

Mike asks me to tell her he won't be able to take her to the Quakers on Sunday. 'Got a gig in Ayr, you know.'

For at eighty-three, he's the drummer with the Auld Reekie Scottish Dance Band, who play country dance music with some jazz – his first love. Apparently these gigs can go on past two in the morning.

'I like to think I'm the oldest working drummer in Scotland. I keep telling the band they should get themselves some sprightly sixty-year-old, not this old codger, but they're a charitable bunch!'

And he laughs, this elderly happy man who often thinks of death. Then his voice changes.

'You know, a friend in the Ambulance Corps phoned me in Germany at the end of the war and told me there was something important I had to come and help with.' His voice changes, and I sense what's coming now. 'He was right, of course, though often I wish I hadn't.'

'Was it Dachau?'

'Belsen.' He pauses, passes his fingertips across his forehead, just above his eyes. 'We were among the first in. I still can't . . .'

He tails off and we sit there in silence with the hot and lovely day all around us. Then Jenny puts her hand on his arm, and I can see he's done in.

'Come on, darling. Home!'

He nods, gets awkwardly to his feet.

'Stiffening up,' he grimaces. 'Must get Gilders' old bones into a bath. We've people coming this evening, drinks and so forth.'

We shake hands again, and they leave. I sit in my car for a few minutes, thinking again about dead people. Then about the living, who continue to surprise. My damp hands are minutely grained with sand, soil, sweat and grass. The lines are high-lighted; the heart line, the life line, the ridiculous lines that say I'll have four children. I put them to my face and inhale.

A round with Rilke

What was real in that All?
Nothing. Just the ball. Its glorious arc.

Don Paterson,
from *Sonnets to Orpheus*

Ten or so years ago, the putting green in Princes Sreet Gardens, Edinburgh, shimmered before us in the heat. We had a couple of hours before we caught our trains, saw some kids playing and fancied a go. I'd already mentioned my adolescent passion for golf, how it had been the focus of my existence in those years that Don had spent speaking in tongues then becoming extremely good on the guitar. Don had said he hadn't really played golf, but had gone putting once in a while.

'Were you any good?' he enquired casually as we paid our money and selected our putters.

The choice was between some very nasty tinny blade putters and a centre-shaft. I tapped it, searching for the sweet spot. There wasn't one but I took it anyway.

'I suppose so.'

Don grunted, tapped the blade of his putter. As often, he looked like he was fighting a headache at once physical (hangover) and metaphysical (Don has issues with the presence of an absent God).

'We'll toss for who plays off first.'

Ah, right. And I'd thought we'd just have a light-hearted

round of putting as the backdrop for roasting that old chestnut 'Romantic Love: miracle or psychosis?' – as well as the latest gossip from the small but exceedingly virulent world of poetry.

I tossed a coin. He called it and won.

'You first,' he said, and then I knew this was going to be serious.

A couple of practice putts each, to get the feel of the speed of the dry, scuffed grass. I regretted the centre-shaft putter already. They'd suddenly become the rage when I was in my teens. I lost the semi-final of the Under-15s Boys Tournament at Elie to a lad who had a new shiny one with a little fitted tartan cover. Afterwards, I'd borrowed a centre-shaft from a pal but it never worked for me.

I stood over that long opening putt below Edinburgh Castle. Ten years on, I can still feel the heat of that stalled afternoon, see the uneven faded turf, the sunbathing girls who so painfully distracted us not with sex so much as with all the lives we'd never live. The ridge suggested a left-to-right borrow. I gave it a good clip: right distance, wrong line.

Don had been standing slightly behind me, in the position to get the line.

'No bad,' he said.

He stood over the ball for quite a time. Looked up, down, up, down, gave it a brisk firm knock. Both balls finished a few feet from the hole.

We walked towards our balls in near silence. In a casual round of putting one would often just leave the pin in. If the ball hits the pin going not too fast, count it as in.

Don removed the pin. 'You first, I think.'

There's a history. I first met Don Paterson in London when we were both shortlisted in the *Observer*/Arvon Poetry Competition. I'd recently read his first collection *Nil Nil* and been completely won over. It was brilliant, severe, profound, hilarious. So it was good to meet him, and also to be in London with a fellow Scot, even a spiritually afflicted Dundonian.

'Your poem ought to win,' I said, just before the announcements started.

He looked at me suspiciously. 'Why?'

'It's a better poem.'

'A Private Bottling' was a better poem than my 'The Green Places', or any others on the shortlist. It was and remains one of his finest, deep and complex and slow-burning as the best malt.

'How can you say that?'

I shrugged. 'Because it is.'

After the usual blethers, the winner was announced: 'A Private Bottling'. I patted him on the back as he went up to read it. Justice had been done.

'Told you,' I said.

The second time I met Don was before a reading in Edinburgh. We had an hour to kill, he suggested the pub across the road. There was a pool table, he suggested a game. Doing nothing isn't one of his talents. He has a dread of inactivity – in case, he says, the full horror of existence sneaks up on him.

'Sure,' I said. 'But I'm telling you now you'll win.'

Again, that quick, suspicious glance. *What's this fella up to? What's his game?*

'Oh sure,' he said. 'Right.'

'I mean it,' I said. 'I'm good enough at some things, but pool isn't one.'

A quick half-laugh I'd come to know, quickly smothered as though he were entertained and amused, then had to quash it.

'You're not supposed to say that.'

'So?'

Another quick appraising look as he picked up his cue. Don has pale-blue eyes that burn like dry ice. I think it was in that moment we connected. Then he scattered the balls and thrashed me, as I'd predicted.

Which I didn't have a problem with. I don't mind acknowledging when someone is far better than me at something. That old Adam, the fevered competitor, only rears up when it's a close call. Especially when – oh ego, ego! – I believe I'm slightly better but have to put it to the test.

The first time I stayed with Don in Dundee in his freezing, chaotic, comfortless flat, I discovered he was a ferociously good guitarist. I play competent guitar and know a lot of songs. Music is my therapy, joy, relaxation. But Don is a jazzer, one of those musos who play an awful lot of notes and complicated chords, very quickly.

Because of the wine, whisky and beer we'd had earlier, I played a couple of songs in front of him, then handed back his Spanish guitar and asked him to do something useful with it. Once again, no question, no competition. He is so much better a guitarist and musician that we're not on the same planet, so I can be quite happy with mine.

The point of this digression being that though – or because – Don became a friend of my heart, there is a history. Poetry, pool, guitar. Now we were playing something I'd claimed I really *could* do, it became important to deliver. Otherwise I was just a big-mouth humiliation freak.

I played off for our second hole.

As the round progressed there was less and less talk. Less discussion of the fatal one who leaves her mark so early on; her reality and the unreality we project on her and her successors; our complicity in the whole sorry, gorgeous, self-defeating, addictive endeavour of misaimed passion. Even literary gossip dried to a trickle as I went two up, then one up, then all square after missing a very short putt.

I was amused and regretful at this unspoken tussle. I didn't wish it, and I certainly disapproved of it, but there it was. Most dismayingly, I knew I had to win. To lose to a person who had scarcely played real golf at all! Humility is certainly a virtue, but so is self-respect, and I seemed to have pinned mine on a duff centre-shafted putter.

By halfway round we weren't conceding any putts over a few inches from the hole – the ground being so worn, there were no certainties. I remember the sun smacking hot on my neck as I bent over the ball. Everything else – the backdrop of the Castle above us, the array of girls sunning themselves wearing alarmingly little, each one a possible life we would never know, the real or imaginary symbiosis of Suffering and Art – all had blurred to insignificance.

Ah well. After a close-fought, silent struggle, Don faded a little towards the end. I think I won 2 up. I remember our handshake, at once ironic, amused, and shamefaced. Then we handed back our hired putters and balls, went for a drink then parted for Orkney and London, each to his own.

I spent long intervals on the A1, on my way back to Sheffield from playing Glenbervie and Elie, thinking on that round of putting with Don. It was a distillation of a certain time, full of painful intensity, hollow riches and restlessness, loves, confessions and friendships. There were delights, and moments of peace before the yearning and the incompleteness returned. Those girls, those women in their summer clothes, it wasn't even about sex but some deeper, more unanswerable loss.

Like mine, Don's life has changed since then – though the word 'change' is a bit mild for suddenly becoming the father of twins, living in Kirriemuir. We don't see each other enough now. His poems get better and better. Though these days I mostly write prose, we have always been putting round the same course.

Heading south from Scotch Corner, above the shimmering tarmac lanes, the faces of that time come back to me. I think on them, thank them, let them go.

I twirl my fingers to uncramp. For a moment, the reflex to touch my temple, but I resist it. I know what's there. Of late I'm almost getting used to it. I keep both hands on the wheel, blink and drive on. In two hours I'll be home.

> All these are at rest:
> Darkness and light;
> The book and the bloom.
>> Don Paterson,
>>> from *Sonnets to Orpheu*s

'Colum Cille'

(IONA)

You must remember this

Lesley and I walk along the Oban waterfront, checking timetables
for the Western Isles. We could sail to Barra, lovely microcosm of
the Hebrides. Or South Uist, that haunting fragment of planet
Gaeltacht. To the Treshnish islands; Staffa and Fingal's Cave . . .

Talking about all the places still out there, her hand finds mine,
warm and perishable. In the long term there's only one place
we're going, and we are sworn to keep each other company on
that journey, but for today our destination is Mull. And from
Tobermory, we'll drive right down the island which is always
bigger than I expect, to Fionnphort, and from there the short
crossing to our destination. This is a holiday, but like the best
holidays it's also a pilgrimage of sorts.

As well as being one of the earliest Christian settlements in
Britain and a spiritual hotspot, Iona has a free 18-hole golf
course.

People stare, smile, look away as we hurry onto the little ferry
from Fionnphort to Iona. We hadn't realised this wasn't a car
ferry so we had to hastily prioritise, and finally board carrying two
cases, walking boots, two budgies chirruping loudly in their cage,

and my dad's putter. My pockets are stuffed with balls and tees, and I'm trying to follow the test match on the radio clutched to my ear. We may look a trifle eccentric.

As the ferry casts off, I stand at the rail watching someone: a fifteen-year-old boy in tight jeans and chisel-toed boots with Cuban heels and elastic gussets (an effect spoiled slightly by his Arran cardigan with chunky buttons), with Brylcreemed hair in a Cliff Richard lick, sits on the jetty wall working out 'It's All Over Now' on his first guitar. He is earnest, intensely absorbed, buoyed up with converging excitements: crossing to this mythic island, and discovering he can sort of play the Rolling Stones.

He is absurd, ridiculous, and alive in a way I can never be. Yet if that boy had been offered a future that held this, a life with a true mate, wife, lover, improbably making a living by writing books of his own choosing, with a putter and a couple of budgies, I think he'd have chosen it gladly.

The only difference between him and me is I know the price of these blessings.

Along the rail, Lesley is looking forward, her characteristic orientation. Her eyes are shining, an intense blue one shade paler than the sky here. She is humming to herself. I move closer, she leans into me. As Colum's Isle comes clearer, I recognise the melody that will cling to me throughout our stay: 'As Time Goes By'.

The Iona Hotel is full of pilgrims, mostly Church-connected as well as a few New Age seekers. The little island of Iona is one of the most historic and resonant Christian sites in the world. The Irish-born monk Colum Cille arrived here (though probably not in a stone boat), and in AD 563 founded the church from which he would begin to spread the News. He seems to have been extraordinarily vigorous, almost combative; a great sailor, criss-crossing the waters, founding dozens of churches before dying in Iona in AD 597.

On the walk to the hotel, we pass the burial place of a few

centuries of Scottish kings. Rows of weathered effigies and slabs bake in the sun. Kenneth Mac Alpin is there, also MacBeth. But the most visited tomb is from 1994 and the man was not royal: John Smith, the leader of the Labour Party before Blair; a much-loved man, socialist, devolutionist, lover of hill-walking and whisky; died abruptly one morning after a massive heart attack in his bath. One of those deaths where people suddenly realise what they once had.

His slab is clean and new; in a few hundred years in this lovely small island it will be indecipherable as the others. *As time goes by . . .*

The budgies sing their little heads off as we walk on, leaving a trail of bright little blue feathers on the breeze.

The fundamental things apply

Though a small island, it's easy to visit Iona without being aware of the golf course. It's on the western shore, the opposite side of the island from most of the sacred sites. Next morning in the hotel I'm offered the manager's set of clubs, add my putter to it, and we're given a lift to the course. The Land Rover drives off, and we're alone.

The day is improbably bright, warm, with a steady breeze off a shimmering pointillist sea. It bears the other-worldly sweetness of the Western Isles, a blend of myrtle, heather, turf, sea pinks and seaweed. I'd say it was intoxicating but that's lazy. Something about the scent, the light and the openness – the next land west is North America – makes my senses feel utterly true, miraculously sober.

And the light! The whole island is hung with it today. It's not the thin, pale, clear, rational northern light of North Ronaldsay. This feels like the deeper light of another world, another time, a radiant dream.

This is the West, for God's sake! There must be weeks of murk and drizzle, of gales and horizontal rain. But on our one family day here nearly forty years ago, it was like this. I'd wandered off by myself while the others looked round the works at the Abbey, found a little nook among the rocks, and fell into a long teenage dream of love and Art and glory. I woke, groggy and sunburned, with the beginnings of sunstroke, spots dancing in front of my eyes . . .

'Can I have a go?' Lesley asks.

It's her first – and probably her last – golf lesson. The course is free but, unlike North Ronaldsay, it has tee boxes. I roll out some balls, hand her the 6 iron. Show her the grip, the stance, bend her knees and straighten her back. I find myself repeating the ancient orthodoxies: keep your head still, your left arm straight, let the club do the work. *The fundamental things apply.* Doubtless St Columba would agree.

'It's a simple thing,' I tell her. 'You're just making an arc, with the ball at the bottom of it.'

She swings and hits the ball. It runs fifty yards or so across the short turf. She hits another, and another – all along the ground, but all straight. She seems quite pleased.

'Think of it like a dance,' I say. Sometimes she'll do little silly dances, a kind of mock Isadora Duncan, just for the fun of it. Few things touch me more than a serious person being light-hearted. 'Or faster t'ai chi. This is the move known as *The club bids farewell to the ball.*'

This time she swings with less effort and more rotation. For the first time the ball takes off and flies. She laughs and turns to me. 'That's good, isn't it?'

'It certainly is. You've got timing.'

She's flushed, exhilarated. It's a simple, enduring human thing, this pleasure at making a ball take off. She hits another, to the same effect. The ball lands and rolls across the sandy track that winds down to the sea. The next she takes a great swipe at, and misses completely.

She hands me back the club. 'For a moment there, I could almost see the point in this. I'm going to take my walk.'

She sets off down the sandy track on her exploration and leaves me to mine.

Unlike agricultural Gigha, this course is spread across true links land, common grazing, that short, dry, cropped turf that golf invented itself upon. My course guide informs me I play here 'as a guest of the local crofters' Grazings Committee', which is as it should be.

A few sheep and a few walkers drift about as I tee up, but this is a stage on from North Ronaldsay. There's this numbered tee box, a clear flattish area that is the tee, and according to my course handout, that pin is 320 yards away. It's in the middle of a flattish disk of paler ground, which must be the 'green'.

This is just wonderful. The manager's 3 wood feels good enough. I loosen up, tee up a ball, watch Lesley's tiny figure move along the beach. Some people go to church, some wander along beaches, I play golf alone. All ways of connecting.

My drive sings off into the blue. With some difficulty, I find it among the daisies and feathers, sitting up in a patch of clover. Shading eyes against the light, I guess at an 8 iron. The brief silly dance of the swing – the ball rises, falls a bit short. Pitch and two putts. The green is much the same as the fairway but has been cut fairly recently.

However basic the golf course, the fundamental things apply. Still have to keep your head down, allow for the wind, judge distance. A good tee shot is still that. My pulled second is still a bad pull; the following duff chip still disappoints. My next chip-and-run is five feet, and the holed putt reminds me the joy is still the joy.

It doesn't have to be Gleneagles or the Old or Pebble Beach. The game is wherever you play. I look for Lesley but she's out of sight, on her own adventure.

The 3rd hole looks great. I can see the green up on the hill, on some kind of raised outcrop, with natural sand erosion protecting it. But a pull is still a pull – it finishes on a sandy track. My recovery runs into a big sand hole. Next shot onto the 'green', two putts.

I've taken a 5 at a bonnie par 3, but looking back over the 'course', I feel only joy. It's gorgeous from up here. The links is a pale-green sprawl – there's no fairway or rough as such – settled around the curving white-sand bay. What's striking are all these outcrops and rises where bare rock, at once dark and pale, breaks the surface. The course seems to use these as obstacles, features, challenges. There's a lot more contours than on North Ronaldsay; in that respect, it's more like the gem of Shiskine.

From up here I can see a pair of golfers have just arrived, and a threesome is out at the far end of the course. It seems a number of residents play, as well as the occasional visitor who knows about it. This course is semi-evolved. All the fundamental things are in place – links, tees, greens, obstacles, contours. I imagine golf was pretty much like this for its first four hundred years.

From up on that high point, a sliced drive is still a sliced drive, and a crosswind still carries it wider. But the following 4 iron into the wind when truly hit still holds its own, though the whereabouts of the green is a mystery. A run-in shot over the rise to near the pin still brings the quiet satisfaction it did to Scottish artisans on Elie and Musselburgh in the seventeenth century; the holed putt for my first par brings the same pleasure.

This is my church. There is nowhere I'd rather be. I play on, entranced yet excited, dreamy but wide awake.

The 9th is a strange and wonderful short hole. Though according to my piece of photocopied card it's only 90 yards, there's no sign of the pin. No hurry, so I walk on, find it cupped in an abrupt pocket, the kind that will collect any approximate ball and gather it in to the pin.

I walk back to the tee, and drift a 9 iron down the wind. Walk over the rise and look down to see my ball 2 feet from the pin. A quick rap with Dad's putter, and it's in. Saint Columba might have felt as good after a particularly nifty conversion.

As time goes by

I take a break for a flask and biscuits, recline on a bank of warm turf. Some curious bullocks drift my way then lose interest. I'm looking at these rock outcrops the course makes use of so well.

If, crossing from Mull, Iona looks as if it's come from some other place and time, that's because it has. These worn outcrops are formed of Lewisian gneiss, as is the whole island. Mull is volcanic and comes an awful lot later. When I was a lad Lewisian gneiss was the oldest known rock in the world, the first formed on the solidifying planet. I was inordinately proud that it was first found and identified in Scotland, on – yes – the island of Lewis. Many years later, walking among the rocks of Peggy's Cove in Nova Scotia, I felt at home among the same geology.

Iona is a little shining chip off the original block.

Some of today's intensity and clarity is probably to do with playing by myself again. Yet it's been an education, playing with other people this last while. Reclining on Iona, I can see this golf research has become a reconnection with family, childhood, adolescence, family, old and new friends, aspects of my culture and my country. It's a catching-up with what has been, and where I am now. Every decade or so in one's life it's necessary to look around and take stock.

I'd thought this book would be a holiday, a lark, something to relax in before getting on with my real work. But it's not turned out like that. Like this round today, I've set a process going, and the only way to find out where it's going is to play it to the end.

I screw on my flask top and get, slightly dizzily, to my feet.

This course just gets better.

The 10th needs a full driver into the sweet-smelling wind off the sea. I walk on past my ball to find the green hiding in a hollow over and behind another rock outcrop. A true, unusual golf hole. Pick up another par there and, encouraged, move on to the 11th. This is the most rocky end of the course, and a great outlook from the tee past outcrops to a rock stack and the sea dazzling beyond it.

My drive cracks off, blind over the ridge. I walk up and down for ages, trying to find it. It should be on the fairway, or maybe just dribbled down onto the shore. I poke around in the low dune, in seaweed, in the light rough. There's a beautiful little cove here, brilliant white sand, clear turquoise water − I've a strong sense Lesley will have found it and stopped here, engaged in her own contemplation. Perhaps it's this winding of absolute intimacy around a core of distance that forms the armature of a marriage and makes our life's current flow . . .

I give up my ball, drop a second and pitch towards the green sunk ingeniously under the rock stack, walk forward and find my first ball on the edge of the green. Check my card: 285 yards. Saint Columba has just converted, first to Sin and then Redemption, another couple of Pictish tribes.

Two putts bobble along, another birdie. Hallelujah.

At the 13th, I meet and chat with a couple of women golfers. Both Iona residents, they play regularly. I say how much I'm enjoying their course, for its stunning setting and the holes themselves. 'Lucky for you the greens were cut recently!' Apparently a couple of school lads took out the lawnmower the other day and had a quick whiz round. Unpaid, of course.

'A labour of love,' I comment.

'That is what it is.'

After they've gone, I run the ball to 6 feet. The putt holds its line and drops for another birdie, and I bless those lads and their mower.

I pick up three more pars in the closing holes. Somehow putting is easier on these unrolled greens than on 'proper' ones − less pressure, I guess − and the ball keeps dropping. By now, stunned with sunshine and wind, mild fatigue and sustained happiness, there is no effort. Shots just occur. New holes come up, I play each, move on. Things are almost entirely silent in my head. I'm just here. On Iona. Playing golf.

I see from my score 'card' that the second nine holes went by in 35, one over par. Total 74 for the day, one of the most radiant I've ever had on a golf course. I hitch a ride back to the Iona Hotel, see through the plate glass Lesley absorbed in a book, having afternoon tea and scones in the lounge.

I walk into the lounge and she looks up and smiles.

Some days it's not the score but being there to receive it.

My father avoided ministers whenever possible, but he had a great admiration for the Reverend George MacLeod. He thought the man had guts, charisma and integrity. From an orthodox ecclesiastical family, after being decorated from fighting in the Great War, MacLeod moved steadily towards socialism and pacifism. He believed the Church had to be practical, political, returned to the difficult lives of working-class people, or else be irrelevant.

He created, as we say in Scotland, a great *stushie*. A fuss, a furore. He decided on a landmark project to enact his ecumenical vision: rebuilding the long-ruined Abbey on Iona. With very little money, in 1938 his group of unemployed Clydeside craftsmen plus trainee ministers as labourers, started work. It took nearly thirty years to complete, an act of persistence, faith and sheer bloody-mindedness of the sort my dad admired.

As we leave next morning to catch the ferry, there is music, human voices, coming faintly from the Abbey. We deposit our cases and the budgies by the entrance, pull open the great door. A swell of sound rolls over us. A visiting Canadian choir is rehearsing, and they're not singing dreary hymns but complex choral music.

We stand transfixed as the voices raise then rearrange great blocks of sound. The acoustics are good; the sounds resonate in the chest and belly, and do strange things high in the head. Lesley is no more a believer than I am, but this is the real thing.

We stay at the back of the near-empty Abbey – this is a rehearsal, not a service – until the choir takes a break. A few exit for a cigarette. I'm still clutching my putter as we emerge blinking into the sun-flooded day.

We say little, just a look exchanged and an experience shared, before we pick up the cases and the birdcage and head for the ferry.

It's still the same old story
A fight for love and glory . . .

Interlude: on Friendship Bridge

'There's something about Tibet nothing can prepare you for. The people I met, the places, the friendships, the landscape, Mount Kylash . . . It wrenched me open.' In the foyer of the Old Manor House Hotel in Lundin Links, Vin glances at me, blue eyes wide and candid. 'I've been home a week now, so this isn't jet-lag I've got. It's something else.'

He hesitates, a neat, self-possessed man in his middle years, unremarkable, and yet from the moment I saw him sitting in the foyer I knew this had to be Vin Harris, early member of the Samye Ling Tibetan Buddhist monastery in Dumfriesshire, who had helped build the place. He looked ordinary enough; the difference is in the eyes – so much innerness opening out.

'When I had to say goodbye to my Tibetan friends, I didn't think I could bear it. They'd come with me to the Friendship Bridge – that's a joke, eh? The Chinese friendship with Tibet . . . Anyway, they couldn't go further and I had to go on. It hurt so much as we shook hands, hugged and made silly jokes. At the far side of the bridge I stopped and looked back at them, waving, and it was then . . .'

His voice falters, his tanned face alters. Edie Irwin, former therapist and now friend, had phoned me last night in Anstruther, just as I finally located Mum's purse in the fridge. 'Andrew, I've a friend I think you should meet. He combines your main interests – golf, mindfulness, and death!' Her big laugh down the phone. 'Vin is a golfing Tibetan Buddhist undertaker.'

An irresistible combination! So I'd phoned the number, talked to Vin, who said he was just along the road at Lundin Links on a 'Fairway to Heaven' course – would I care to come by?

Sometimes you go with the grain. I was free, Mum had her purse and seemed settled. I'd put my clubs in the car just in case, and went to meet him.

'There's a river, a big glacier-melt river that thunders down under the bridge like an express train. I looked down into the roar and spray, and at the friends I was leaving, and it hit me then. That it's really, really, really true, the core of the teaching – *there is no permanence*. Nothing solid, nothing to hang on to. And there's nothing we can do about it. We just have to let go, let it all go . . .'

He picks up his coffee cup and drinks with an entirely steady hand. I sit and wait. I know when I'm being offered something. Colin Bannatyne had done it at Shiskine; Mike Gilderdale at Elie; Al McLeish after our round at Bathgate; Mark the pro at Beauchief holding a new club and casually saying, 'Whatever the manufacturers say, nothing on Earth can enlarge the sweet spot – but we can *enlarge the area of forgiveness*.'

So many people, so many teachings.

I read the badge on Vin's red sweater: 'Moffat Golf Club'. This is a practical, competent, socialised man. He runs a joinery business, making sash windows, and coffins on the side. He has a wife who helps with the undertaking, and a grown-up son; he's a businessman and skilled tradesman. After taking up golf at forty, he's a single-figure handicap player. He's in the world, not in flight from it. He's also been deeply involved in Tibetan Buddhism for thirty years.

Vin looks up, grins ruefully. 'You'd think I'd be pleased to have it confirmed and know the teaching really is true. In fact I'm still dazed and shocked. If you'd seen that river, Andrew, so unstoppable, charging under the bridge, the roar and the spray

. . . On Balcomie today I found I couldn't care what happened to my shots.'

'And if you're indifferent, should you be playing golf at all?'

Vin nods vehemently. 'But if you care too much about golf,' he says, 'you've lost the point of it. That's what we're trying to do on our "Fairway to Heaven" course. Let go the seriousness, the competing and the tension, and just play mindfully.'

So there are other people in the world who think about golf the way I do. I may be a crank but I'm not a lone one.

Vin glances at his watch. 'I may have to give up golf, though I hope not. Caring and not caring, that's the riddle, isn't it? And now I've to meet Graeme Lennie, the Balcomie pro who's coming to talk to us tonight after dinner. I hope you'll stay and play with us tomorrow at Lundin Links – I'm sure we've lots more to talk about.'

'I rather think we do.'

Graeme Lennie gives the lie to anyone who believes golf is an elitist, exclusive pursuit. He is a strongly built, humorous, down-to-earth Glaswegian, a natural member of the Artisans' Club. He also cares about golf; it's more than his living. After the dinner he gave a wonderful talk, at once personal and historical. He'd brought a selection of antique clubs which he passed round – hickory shafts, and even pre hickory, when willow was used. Strange curved club heads like clogs; some 'guttie' balls, even their precursor, the 'feathery'.

'There are far tae many medals and competitions at our club,' he said. 'It's aa getting completely out of hand. Folk are taking golf way too seriously. I think you fellas have the right idea here – it's meant tae be a *game*.'

Somebody asked him his idea of a great shot. Without hesitation he replied, 'Ben Hogan said, "A great golf shot starts in my hands and finishes in my heart." I wouldnae argue wi that.'

Someone else, happily flushed with drink and the deep happiness known only to someone who has that day gone round a golf course for the first time in less than 90, asked him what was the best round he'd ever had.

His reply sticks with me yet. For it wasn't about when he won this tournament or that, or his lowest score ever. Instead he told us that four years back he'd been driving through St Andrews shortly after the New Year. It was one of those cold, sunny, windless winter mornings we get once in a while. He glanced at the Old Course as he went by, noticed there was no one on it.

On impulse, he went to the starter, introduced himself. Aye, sure he could get on. Now would be fine. There was one American fella out on the course.

So Graeme Lennie laced on his golf shoes, took his clubs from the car, and played the Old Course on his own. Passed the American and his caddy as they putted on the 15th. He never saw or met anyone else. He just played golf by himself, on a cool, sunlit winter's morning, over the most famous course in the world.

'I went roon in two hours five minutes,' he concluded. His voice was slightly choked. 'It wis the most enjoyable round I've ever played.'

He never mentioned his score. It was not the point. That was his point.

A group of us sat up late watching 'The Masters' final round, live on TV. Saw Phil Mickelson take a fatal three putts from no distance on those lightning greens, and lose by a shot. For these pros, each shot represented an awful lot of money; more than money, lasting reputation. Winning a Major would be like winning the Booker Prize in literature – whatever happens after, they can't take it away from you.

The Augusta course looked, as always, improbably perfect, all lush green and blue, banks of flowers, limitless sunshine, breathtaking manufactured holes, green sand for the fairway divots and surely blue dye in the ponds – a TV executive's dream and, in the end, just as kitsch. But when I tottered bedwards to get some sleep before the round on Lundin Links I'd impulsively agreed to play with the 'Fairway' group next morning, it wasn't a vision of Augusta and shooting great scores and winning Majors that glowed in my mind. It was Graeme Lennie playing alone round the bare austerity of the Old on a January morning, in two hours five minutes, having the best round of his life.

As I finish this in the shed in Sheffield, heater on and raindrops forking like icy lightning down the windows, Vin Harris's leaving-Tibet moment comes back to me: that irresistible torrent rushing under Friendship Bridge, the parting friends, his mind aching at the certainty that there is nothing anywhere to hang on to. Just the roar and spray of the world, impersonally arriving and departing in the instant.

Like the river itself, it's a vision of things too overwhelming to live with long and too awesome to forget.

But here's one last lie I'll let myself prefer: that headlong river is bound for the sea, and along the shore there is a golf links. And we can play there awhile, hearing the distant roar of the surf as we settle over our opening drive, still moistened by its spray as we stroke the last putt home, following down the line.

12TH

'The Shot'

(LUNDIN LINKS)

Remember the name Bob Beamon? One afternoon at the 1968 Mexico Olympics, after struggling to get into the long-jump finals, he sprinted to the mark, hit the take-off board and flew, breaking through the 28- *and* the 29-foot barriers. He never came near repeating it – in fact he never cleared 27 feet again – and the record stood for over twenty years. 'Everything came right,' he said simply.

When I think of 'The Shot', I think also of St Paul's conversion on the road to Damascus: a blinding light and a change of heart.

Certainly the light was very strong, that afternoon on midsummer day when Tim stopped, gestured, then silently handed me his trophy driver.

It was the 18th hole at Lundin Links, the end of my round with the 'Fairway to Heaven' people. Tim had said nothing when he offered me his driver because this was our elected Silent Hole, where no one would speak from stepping onto the tee till we left the green.

I noticed how silence intensified awareness – of my partners, of the light, the course gleaming like a reflective surface, so dried out it was, lying under a vast sky, by an impossibly bright Firth of Forth. Despite being brought up only ten miles away, I'd not played Lundin Links before. It had been a revelation, a true championship course. I knew again the sheer spacious naturalness of a links course, and the release and uplift that arises there.

The 18th green shimmered palely in the distance by the clubhouse as I took out my driver for the last time. Tired now, sore back, knees, legs, but I'd entered that happy, near-vacant state where there are no nerves and few thoughts left, and the golf flows easily. A pleasing run of a birdie and four pars; I wanted just one more, then into the cool dim clubhouse to rest and talk with these interesting people.

I swung slowly, the drive was sweet and timed, the ball disappeared − as they do for me these days as my eyes get older − dissolving into the light. Silent thumbs-up from Maria.

Tim next, our group's alpha male. He'd begun well, swinging fast, hitting the ball long with his new driver. Inevitably he began to swing faster; a few wayward shots, and he swung faster still; these last few holes had gone badly for him, and he wasn't very happy. 'Just because you're on "Fairway to Heaven" doesn't make you a saint,' Vin had remarked. 'If you ever think life's easy − try golf!'

Again Tim mashed into his drive, pulled the ball into the rough and silently pushed the club back into his bag. Its head was ionised scarlet, huge, bulging with titanium and testosterone. I'd seen and heard of these hollow-headed drivers; apparently they hit the ball great distances. They looked freakish to me, and unbelievably expensive: trophy clubs, the golfer's equivalent of a new penis-extension sports car. I'd always said, and believed it, that length didn't matter, only being straight. Still, I was mildly curious, not wanting to resist and condemn all change. My body is the age it is, but I don't have to get old in the head too.

Dutch Paul drove next. Tall, thin, gawky with big horn-rimmed glasses, he had broken 90 the previous day on Balcomie, ten shots better than he'd ever played. I'd never met a more radiant golfer; no pro scorching round in 62 could have been happier than this man. But today had been an anti-climax, typical of golf: one day you've got it, next day it's gone. He was disappointed but hanging in there, dutifully marking his full score for every hole, getting into three figures now.

He went through his long, slow, painstaking routine, and finally settled to his drive. It would be misleading to call it a swing, more a tentative, flurried jab at the ball. Still, it was on the fairway and 170 yards or so nearer the hole. We signed approval; he adjusted his glasses, shrugged.

Silently, we all moved forward to the ladies' tee. Maria had been a pleasure to watch all round, easily the best woman golfer I'd played with. She had a long, rhythmical swing, natural timing and a good short game. Her handicap was 8, and she'd played to it. It was her first time on 'Fairway', her first experience of Scottish links courses, and she was exulting in it.

She stood up, and her long slow swing sent the ball off through the light breeze into the near-white light above the fairway. Smiles and thumbs-up all round.

It was then that Tim stopped, gestured to us to wait, and silently offered me his scarlet Big Bertha driver.

It felt very . . . odd. So light, despite the engorged head. And the shaft unusually long. I'd have to swing this very slowly to have any chance of getting the club head through the ball. I stuck my hand into my bag and pulled out a ball: one of the new Titleists I'd bought back in March at Beauchief in Sheffield and never used in case I lost one.

I'd read somewhere the idea with these drivers was to hit the ball on the up, sweep it off that high tee with a hint of top spin that would make it run – a radically different technique.

No time to hang about, I didn't want to keep my partners waiting. So a couple of easy swishes, getting the feel of this, then I stood up to the ball. My last thought was: *A bit extra shoulder-turn.*

A faint *click*, sweet and easy on the wrists, pleasure running through my tired body. The ball takes off at a velocity and height I've seen only on television. It goes up, and it goes on. And it keeps going up. And on. Still climbing, it dissolves into the dazzle.

I damn near drop the club. Maria looks at me, mouth open, lifts both her arms with a huge grin. I mime back utter astonishment. It was as if the club had held an explosive charge. I hadn't done anything except swing it fully and very slowly, without expectation, in a spirit of free enquiry. I must have hit the sweet spot, that point on the club face so small as to be almost theoretical, for that ball had climbed and vanished like a tiny white Sputnik. It was almost supernatural.

We move down the fairway and the bleached-out rough, bound together by silence, pausing to watch each shot, to encourage and support. That's the ethos of 'Fairway': we're here to *play*, be mindful, buoy each other up and bring some innocence back to the game. I find my first drive, contemplate a 4 iron down an undulating faded fairway of mounds and hollows, rising to a slightly elevated, sloping green: a real golf shot.

I hit a real golf shot, watch the ball kick and run on this baked fairway, climb onto the green and finish in easy putting distance. Very pleased. But my new Titleist?

I wander on and on, looking from side to side. Paul catches my eye, shakes his head, points another 50 yards down the fairway. And there it is. Impossible, but here it is.

Tim jerks his thumb back at what I've learned is a distance marker, then points to his illustrated booklet I've discovered is called a 'stroke-saver'. Among other things, it shows the features of each hole, the principal bunkers, mounds, dykes, and their distance from tee and green. He's spent a lot of time consulting it as we've gone round; I felt it cluttered up my head, so just relied on my eyes.

According to this stroke-saver, I have hit this ball, without any effort and into a light headwind, slightly over 300 yards. A good 25 yards further than I've ever hit a drive.

I glance back at the distance marker. Yes, I've allowed for the ladies' tee. And this next shot looks like a gentle 9 iron. It can't be, but it is.

Still reeling inwardly – perhaps it's the heat and dehydration that has made everything slightly hyper-real – I hit that simple approach to about 15 feet. And as I walk towards the green, floating a couple of inches off the turf like a figure in one of 'Le Douanier' Rousseau's paintings, I reflect that though the pitch shot was pleasing and closer to the hole, the 4 iron was a much better and more interesting golf shot. In some ways, with that freakish drive I have destroyed a very good golf hole.

God, but it feels *sweet*.

Back in Sheffield a week later, I went to Mark's pro shop and bought a second-hand hollow-headed driver for forty quid. It's shiny blue, with bits of paint missing. I carry it in my bag, and use it from time to time instead of my regular driver. It's useful when the fairway is wide and I'm tiring. Swing slowly and the club seems to do the work. It is also extraordinarily forgiving. Yet though the trajectory is still utterly different from my regular driver, I've come to realise the ball doesn't go significantly further – five or ten yards, maybe – and with rather less directional control.

I've hit some poor and some good drives with hollow-headed drivers, but I've never repeated that first time on the 18th at Lundin Links. I've stopped trying, because it's counter-productive.

Also I've stopped being sanctimonious about length off the tee not being of interest. The fact is it feels wonderful when you really catch one; a pure, unarguable physical pleasure fizzes like sherbet through the veins. Holing putts makes a score; a delicate chip-and-run shot harvests years of experience; to my mind, the long iron or 3 wood off the fairway is the measure of a golfer – but bloody belting a ball out of sight is a deep, legitimate primal joy, known to all the forefathers of golf. (Saintly James Braid was one hell of a hitter, on occasion driving over 300 yards with his extra-long hickory-shafted brassie.)

I've come to accept with gratitude there was that one time on that one course on that one hot midsummer afternoon in good company when everything went utterly, effortlessly, right. All golfers have known it, it's part of the mystery of the game. It's like a visitation from another world.

Somewhere that shot sails on still, further through blue sky stretched above pale turf next to the dazzling sea, flying beyond all likelihood.

Why golf is unnecessary

As we drive north for our Orkney summer – car and roof-coffin stuffed with clubs, fishing gear, computer, budgies, teenager nodding in his private sound world – Lesley suddenly says, 'I hope you'll not be so obsessed with golf when this book is over.'

'I'll not be away as much once the book is done,' I reassure her. 'But I do expect to keep playing. Surely you're glad I'm enjoying myself.'

'Of course I am!' she says. 'It's just . . .'

As we drive past Tain, she admits she's not just baffled by and indifferent to golf, she vaguely feels it's an unworthy, unnecessary activity. She remembers her father played a lot, largely to get away from his family, staying on late at the clubhouse. When she thinks of golf, she still detects her resentment from those days.

'Golf seems really . . . unnecessary,' she says eventually. 'Superfluous. It has no practical value. Why suffer from doing something so unnecessary?'

There are times when I agree, especially on those days I've played badly. And it's true, golf is not necessary. We could turn that heresy around and affirm that's precisely its value. It is *play*, non-practical activity.

As we pass the Dornoch turn-off – I hope to play that course some day – Les admits that in societies where children work all day, when they finish working, if they can still move, they play. It's hard-wired in them.

Now we're having a discussion rather than an argument. I suggest play isn't a childish thing we put behind; it's a big part of our being fully human, balanced, realised. Pat Kane has written a fine book about it: *The Play Ethic*. I like that.

As a child Lesley had a rich fantasy life. Her games were in her head, imagining stories, people, events, conversations. She didn't play physical games if she could avoid them. Hockey is her idea of hell. So, she wonders, was it that she didn't need physical games because she had mental ones, or did she turn to mental ones because she didn't like the physical?

In the same way, I admit I'm baffled and slightly irritated by people spending hours doing crosswords or Sudoku. Seems entirely unnecessary. They're just made-up problems, they don't mean anything. It's not Enigma.

As we drive and talk, and the budgies gabble quietly and Leo emits low cries to his inaudible music, I'm remembering body-boarding at St Ives last year. I tasted then (along with a deal of salt water) the joy of doing, of play, absorbed in pure physicality. Maybe golf is more akin to surfing than to football, tennis, and all other sports constituted around *playing against*.

My physical existence makes me feel truly on the planet. Thinking is all very well, but it doesn't make me feel *connected*. Swinging a golf club does.

The other day I'd played a quick nine holes at Anstruther while Lesley and Mum did the crossword. Back on the course of my adolescence, I suddenly wondered, *Why am I doing this?*

There were many possible reasons. For the book. In order to get better at it. For the exercise. In search of some insight into the game and myself.

But right then, bumping my trolley down the hill at the last hole after a decent 4-iron tee shot, the sea dark and gurly on my right, looking across the Forth to the Bass Rock and North Berwick, the truth appeared much simpler: I play for the pleasure of playing.

For being here now, sizing up this approach to the green at the

9th with the wedge in my hand, at once a reasoning mind, a skilled body, a hopeful heart.

Golf isn't important, but there's a value in taking unimportant things seriously and serious things lightly. So let's not play golf in order to get better at it. Don't make it into yet another striving, another activity stuffed into an already overstuffed life, something else to 'work at'.

'Let's not be busy this Orkney summer,' I say.

On the gearstick her hand drops lightly on mine.

I often catch myself starting something in order to finish it so that I might get started on the next thing so I can finish it and then ... This is madness, and it's contagious. One might as well start a round of golf in order to finish it so as to get on home in order to do a few things so as to be able to go to bed.

It tells in the body – a subtle leaning forward, as though one is perpetually trying to get to *the next thing*. It tells too in a tightness in the breathing, just below where the ribs divide, as I snatch for the next breath before quite finishing this one.

Given that we don't want life to end and know it must, you'd think we'd drag every moment, move forward through time as though through glue, as though we were taking a walk to the scaffold. That and not a round of drinks in good company is what's really waiting for us at the 19th hole – so let's not hurry along the way.

Her hand moves on mine, drifting skin over warm skin.

'Shades'

(STROMNESS)

The Auld Fella

Look into any activity closely enough – golf, for instance – and you'll spot the auld fella lurking in the gorse bushes behind the 1st green, or languidly rolling a cigarette between bony fingers as he leans against the shelter hut, waiting for you.

What he has to say is predictable because, frankly, his conversation is as limited as his social skills.

He lights that cigarette, points out the people who are not with us today (you need reminding?); then indicates those who are, only to assure you they will not be for long (you could forget?). When he finally turns and looks at you, you feel blankness travel to your bones while the club in your hand is eaten up by rust, dissolves, vaporises (you think it won't?).

From up here at the shelter hut this July afternoon on the crown of the Stromness course, the golfers no longer appear solid. They are flickering shades, like passers-by in early photographs, poised on the edge of non-being. On certain days it is the same when I walk through the town – the people I see and greet, old and young alike, are semitransparent, almost not-there. And their conversation is hard to attend to on account of this companion muttering in my ear his tedious, irrefutable message.

It's been like this ever since I nearly died but didn't. One would think I'd be thankful to be reprieved. I am, but I have tasted dissolution and know, beyond all finessing, I will perish.

My pale hands tighten as I play at golf... The stray line floats in from an Iain Crichton Smith poem I read years ago. We met and talked a number of times; he was a lovely, melancholy, funny man. I see him yet though he's long gone, hear that Lewis lilt, the slight shushing of the 's' that marks the natives of that island. Mum has a photo of him with his wife Isobel and myself, and we're all laughing as we lift glasses of free wine (the best kind) at a Scottish Arts Council bash in the late eighties...

Death inhales, silently points out the shades moving on the course. My father, Mal Duff, Jimmy Gilmour, Mr Duncan, Fergie Boyter, Jimmy Hay our Latin teacher, the quiet lad who was in our class at school and in his thirties killed himself.

Death exhales and through the dispersing smoke I see some non-golfers out there today – Ingrid von Essen who made me write better, Anthea Joseph who gave my book to her friend Dylan to read ('The poetry was OK – liked the pictures'), Alex Watson the quiet fisherman who disliked the sea. Strolling by the shore in a group I see Norman MacCaig; George Mackay Brown the poet of this town; sweet, learned, haivering Sorley Maclean; disputational Chris Grieve aka Hugh MacDiarmid; funny and sad, short and round Robert Garioch; Alastair Mackie all bony, tense, honed in Doric. All those dead poets whose faces and words still remain layered like old wallpapers in the inside of my head.

But the fact is, Mr Death, you've nothing new to tell me. I've lingered too long listening to you in this shelter halfway round the course. I've holes yet to play, and I would draw your attention to the fact that the day, though indeed transitory, is gorgeous, being full of weather, water and light. It is probably so gorgeous *because* it is passing. I don't imagine immortals such as yourself have much enthusiasm for golf – or for anything. Perhaps that's why you envy us so.

It could be the golf I've been playing these last months, the people I've met and what they've offered me. Maybe it's just having plenty of regular exercise. The fact is I've come a long way from the tentative, shaken man who first stepped onto this course to try to get his life back. I feel stronger, less provisional, more rooted.

I'll be damned if I'm not going to experience and enjoy each moment here, each shot remaining in this round, as fully as possible. Then I'll leave my clubs in the locker and go into town to meet my beloved and my friends, feel my feet and wrists ache slightly as I raise a pint of Northern Light to my lips, and taste for one more summer evening the sweetness of not being dead.

Only connect

Playing golf I am connected. Connected with my body, that does more or less as I ask. And through my skin and lungs, ears and eyes, connected to this world. Playing golf over a landscape connects us to it in a completely different way from driving over it, or even just sitting looking at it. In these manoeuvres, however absurd, one knows slopes and distances, turf and sand and long grass, air and angles, with extreme intimacy.

My friend David Drever in Kirkwall delights in hunting wildfowl. It's not simply because he enjoys eating roast duck, widgeon, teal. He takes no pleasure in killing. Nor – Scot though he is – does he seek for its own sake the extreme discomfort of lying in cold mud for an hour in November drizzling dusk. What he loves is that sense of connection to earth and air and water and the life around him; the vivid truth of the world known physically.

Though I can no longer kill anything warm-blooded, this Orkney summer I still fish the Loch of Harray for wild brown trout, and the Sound of Hoy for haddock, cod, mackerel and ling. And the joy of that is not the killing; nor just in the eating. It is in that alert peace that comes with hours spent on the water, scanning light, casting and retrieving, watching weather, working and waiting.

So it is with golf, only no one and nothing (as a rule) has to get killed to enjoy it.

Sometimes this iron in my hand feels like a divining rod. At others, a lighting conductor. A wand. A staff to lean on. A probe. It connects my body and my will to the earth, the earth I believe in, from which I come and to which I will return.

One might even consider – if one were a fanciful person and not an empirical Scot – this slightly scuffed and muddy white ball to be our planet in miniature, and that we address it frowning slightly yet grinning inside, brimming with our effort, our desire, our best hope, *to make good contact.*

Golf as spiritual practice?

No sniggering on the tee as I tee up this ball, please! Let's drop the image that 'spiritual' invokes of some non-spatial yet vaguely yellow-white plasmic blob flittering inside us, which we call our 'soul', that will survive our death, with our essence intact.

I'd like to believe this, but I can't. I cannot believe this just because it would be pleasanter to do so. That would be preferring my lie knowing it a lie, giving the ball a nudge with my foot while pretending I hadn't. It may assist the shot in hand, but it's cheating and it won't do. *You might as well congratulate a man for not robbing a bank.*

Walking up the fairway at the 3rd (adequate 3 wood off the tee, pushed a bit right leaving interesting shot over the bunker), I look around this Stromness course at the other golfers, my hands, this black-backed gull that holds steady into the wind, and know again *the world is something that happens to me*. As it is for each and every golfer, also the dog-walker and the dog walked. We all have to stand somewhere, and this is where we stand, in our self at the centre of the world.

The anxiety I feel addressing this short pitch, the mix of pleasure and slight disappointment when it flips up nicely over the bunker but runs away 10 feet past the pin, the slight twinge in my dodgy right knee as I turn back to my bag – that is all mine. No one else can feel it. My secret life lives and dies with me. That round on Iona, the beaches of Eilean Garbh on Gigha, no one else can know those hours (though I write to cross that distance; messages from one secret life to another).

Yet I live in the world and am of it. Even as I remove the pin, crouch to assess the borrow on this putt which I would very much like to make, I can see other holes, other golfers. I believe in their existence. As I do in the dark swollen hills of Hoy, and the flat platinum gleam of Scapa Flow, the ferry heading south and the distant hills of Scotland, the hoodie crow wrestling with a rabbit carcass and the lark fizzling in the lift.

Their elements are mine. The air passing into my lungs as I stand over this putt contains – so we are assured – molecules not only of Caesar's last breath but presumably also that of Bobby Jones, Joyce Wethered and debonair Walter Hagen. My father's and mother's DNA runs through my body like the word *Edinburgh* in a stick of rock, surely as it's my dad's putter that clicks this ball that stutters slightly as it runs, hits the side of the hole and kicks away.

I wanted that one.

Still, as I walk to the 4th tee on the crown of the Stromness course, survey the open fairway and decide to have a good belt with the blue hollow-headed driver, I feel pretty good. Because I am connected. Connected better than any dodgy businessman, Mafia underling or networking socialite. I am connected to Lesley, and through her to a wider world, which is connected – and this is science, not wishful thinking – to everything else. Which is pretty wonderful when you think about it, as I do from time to time, especially on golf courses.

If 'spiritual' means anything it is this: inner awareness, held in balance with the outer world, and the connectedness of both and of all.

The club head accelerates, sharp *click!* and the ball flies long and high and sweet over the direction marker towards Scapa Flow, and the joy rising in my hands and head is, believe me, a physical and spiritual joy. Though I am no believer in a personal God, my spontaneous *Thank you!* rises up anyway into the morning air of one more Orkney summer.

The budgie who golfed

I'd been sent down to Billingsgate to further my quest.

The fish market had closed down but round the back I found a yard still littered with decaying fish-heads, lobster creels, fish-boxes, piles of scabby scales. I like fish and seafood – though preferably not in the raw – but this place smelled bad. Yet I'd been assured there'd be something special here for me.

Near the wall was a large cage. Inside, perched on a wooden swing, was either an unusual bird or a curious fish: featherless, translucent grey-white flesh the texture of monkfish, but chunky in build, with clawed feet gripping the perch.

I squatted down and looked more closely. Certainly a neonate of some sort, for around it dangled wooden alphabet blocks, and it sat peering absorbedly if rather stupidly at a book with large pictures and few words.

'Is he learning to read?' I wondered out loud.

'Just till he's old enough,' a grumpy, off-hand voice said. 'Then he's sent back to sea.'

I turned to see a large budgie – or was it a discreet-sized parrot? – hunched brooding over a feeder in the corner of the cage.

'Why?'

'Why not?'

The lighting was poor but I sensed the budgie was wearing a checked tartan jacket and was in a bad mood. There was nothing and no one else around in that overly-fishy yard. The bird lapsed

193

into silence. I was at a loss how to continue the conversation, so I said the first thing that came into my head.

'So, you play golf?'

The rum bird shrugged its wings. 'Used to,' it said over its shoulder. 'Life's too short.'

'How long do you live?'

The reply was muttered, evasive. It might have been 'Long enough.'

Another silence. I'd been brushed off by a bird. I nodded in the direction of the neonate on the swing, still staring blankly at its book.

'It's good of you to give him house room,' I said.

The bird shrugged again, but I sensed it was gratified. 'He'll be gone soon enough, then I'll have my cage back.'

'Look, can I ask you more about golf?'

He jumped down off the feeder and started pecking irritably at the floor of the cage while speaking rapidly. 'Very busy. Things to do.' I wouldn't be surprised, I thought, if it turned out this bird had been in the army. That tiny faded tartan jacket looks like something from one of the Highland regiments. 'Dress shirt to iron before going out.'

'Oh,' I said.

I was at a loss how to continue. I decided to find Sandy. My brother is good with people, not easily fazed – perhaps he could handle this bird, cajole it into sharing its thoughts on golf.

Sandy was round the corner. I filled him in on the situation. He said he wasn't very busy and would do what he could.

He crouched down in the dim yard, looked that cussed bird in the eye and said, 'We would be very happy if you'd read some of your poetry at the golf-club tonight.'

The bird twitched. 'Who else is reading?' it asked in a bored, off-hand tone.

'There'll be a retired major, a couple of generals, and a talented young sub-lieutenant who's won a prize for his villanelles. And yourself – as the special guest reader, of course. We're very informal.'

The bird put its head on one side and pretended to consider. 'Scratch my neck,' it said to me.

I put my finger through the bars and fluffed around among the feathers, finding the ticklish spot of its ego till it murmured 'Just a couple of poems, then.'

'Wonderful!' we enthused. 'See you there!'

As we left Billingsgate, I turned to Sandy and said, 'I think we're one step closer to understanding golf.'

I wake in Orkney thinking: *This golf thing is getting out of hand.*

Lesley shouts up: 'Isn't it your turn to clean out the budgie cage?'

'Big Easy'

(FORRES)

A personal tee-off

It is not so easy to sit in a circle in a silent room with eleven strangers, eyes wide open and linked palm to palm. For a minute or two we just look at each other. No defences, no words, no quips, nothing to do but sit and look at another person, and be looked at.

If you think that's wet, just try it.

My right palm is clasped by Nick Smith, the quiet English university librarian I'm rooming with for this week. My left is firmly gripped by Tony Hegarty, a handsome, witty Cork psychotherapist, single-figure handicap player and natural alpha male. Both have been on several 'Fairway to Heaven' courses, as have half the people here.

I'm not used to prolonged hand-holding. I'm not that good at bodily contact, except with my lover. I have a natural resistance to groups. I prefer to play golf on my own.

The silence goes on. The odd smile flickers, a nod between people who know each other from before. Opposite me is John Talbott, a neat, dark-haired chap, looks a bit younger than me. I know he was one of the creators of 'Fairway', must talk to him.

He looks back at me, gives a slight nod, and I wonder at the pain in his eyes.

Next to him is Vin Harris, my original contact with 'SpiritualGolf. com'. Joiner, undertaker, Tibetan Buddhist, golfer. He looks at me, gives a wink and quick reassuring grin.

What am I doing here, torn between curiosity, resistance and the giggles, in this big NewBold house belonging to the Findhorn Foundation, that flagship of New Age dippiness? In the centre of our circle lit candles are surrounded by a circle of 'Angel cards'. Jasmine incense sticks unwind sweet grey coils. The incongruous element, the reason why I'm here – why I hope all these people are here – is the triangle of golf balls before the largest candle.

Our folders announce, 'Fairway to Heaven: *Embracing the Mystery: Playing from your Centre*', but illustrating those cloudy aspirations is a colour photo of Nairn golf course, a magnificent evening-light stretch of bunkers, fairway, rough and trees. It's that collision of worlds, that chuckle-worthy yoking together of apparent opposites, golf and Buddhist/New Age spirituality, that tickled my fancy when I first heard of it.

I can see now I've been moving in that direction ever since I began playing golf again, enjoying the qualities that seem to descend on a golf course, noting how along with pleasure at the course, its weathers and surroundings, comes a vivid theatre of the life within, and its consequences made manifest in golf shots.

Across the circle, Bruce catches my eye. A stocky, taciturn, bearded Aussie, he looks slightly concerned and ill at ease among this gathering. All this – the candles, hand-holding, silent meditation, talk of *the Centre* – is clearly foreign to him. He looks like he'd rather be embracing a can of Fosters than the Mystery, an allegiance with which I have some sympathy. But he holds my gaze patiently, then looks round to the next person. He's hanging in, giving it a chance. (At the end of the week, he said his first thought was: *What the hell am I doing here among all these hippies?* Laughter, relieved laughter, especially from those who felt much the same. Then he added, 'I'm so glad I stuck it out. You blokes are just the greatest.')

And yes, we're here to play golf. A lot of golf. Serious golf, six rounds in seven days, on bonnie parkland Forres, monumental Cruden Bay, gorgeous tricky Nairn, vicious and beautiful Old Moray, and what would prove the most natural, noble, consummate Scottish links course I've ever known (hint of moisture behind my eyes as I write this up, remembering), Royal Dornoch.

So we're not arsing about here. These are some of the outstanding and most demanding Scottish courses going, and we're here to play them *from the Centre*, with Fun and Fearlessness. That's what brings Blair and Joan from the United States; Tony from Ireland; Bruce and John from Australia; Nick from Sutton Coldfield; Vin from Moffat; Gisela, Torsten, Rainer and Fritz from Germany. And not just once – many of them have come five times or more.

There have been very fine golfers, good golfers, adequate, poor and novice golfers on 'Fairway' courses, but what they all have in common is a passion for the game and an interest in taking that passion further.

Or as Torsten will soon say, when asked what he hopes for from the week, 'I wish to move from playing with my head, to playing from my heart,' and I will never, ever, quarrel with that.

As we drop hands and begin to move into the self-introductions, talking about who we are, what we hope for, where we are 'on the journey', I can feel both my resistance and a readiness to move beyond it.

For my 'angel card' I have drawn Obedience, something I don't consider a virtue. There are no earthly powers of State, leader, monarch, political party, Church, police, parent or wife, to which I think obedience is automatically due. I do not recognise the existence of supernatural powers to whom obedience would be possible let alone desirable. So what am I to make of this, I asked Gisela? She nodded, her long grey hair waved. I liked her eyes, soft yet direct.

'I also have a problem with this,' she said. 'I can only make sense of it as being ready to follow your own deepest orders. You know?'

'I know,' I said. 'Thanks.'

But still the card lies on my new folder and doesn't feel right. This might all be very silly. I mightn't take to some of these people, and they might not take to me. My golf may be rubbish.

Then I remember brother David after we played Glenbervie, adjusting the position of my wrists and shoulders when addressing the ball. It felt all wrong because it was different. And yet it helped, it worked, and I could see why he said it. Change is uncomfortable. Any golfer who has had any aspect of their swing adjusted by a professional will know how odd and wrong it feels at first.

It's time I moved outside my comfort zone, let go a little, risked making a fool of myself or wasting my time. It won't kill you, I tell myself. Life will kill you, that's for sure, but let there be some new ploys first.

So I sit here in this quiet, sunlit room, in a circle of strangers, before an altar of candles, angel cards and golf balls, and let it run. And when it's my turn for an introduction, the Personal Tee-off in our first group session, I take a deep breath and say something like this:

'My name is Andrew Greig, I have the good fortune to be Scottish and brought up where golf is seen as a normal activity. I nearly died a while back, but didn't, and I'm still trying to find where that leaves me. I am writing an odd book, but that's not the main reason I'm here. I'm here because I really want to play on these courses and I am willing to be . . . moved on.'

By your middle years you have probably established some comfort zones – in your marriage, work, social life, habits and relaxations. Lucky you. But comfortable though they are, they can be traps too.

My favourite golfing illustration from Tommy Armour's *How to Play Your Best Golf All the Time*, my father's only Bible, was of

Armour playing out of a bunker, almost vanished behind a spray of sand, and the white ball flying out at its centre like a white dwarf at the centre of a galaxy. Caption: *The soft explosion shot.*

Here we go: soft explosion time.

The easiest shot in golf

After lunch on the first day we assemble on the 1st tee at Forres Golf Club. After a summer of poor weather, the day is a brilliant one. Big blue sky with high wispy clouds, light breeze, sun hot in our faces. We're all keyed up, expectant, keen to get going, a little nervous. Lots of bending and stretching, clubs swishing, practice putts. And laughter, lots of laughter.

Maybe the morning meditation helps account for this sense of energy, openness and clarity I have. Everything seems very bright. The course – of parkland character, for all that it's near the coast, lots of deep-green fairway lined with birch and Scots pines – is radiant and shimmering slightly. A ripple of green light runs down the first fairway. The ground drops away encouragingly from the raised tee – even a muffed drive is going to run – then trees on the left, rough and out of bounds on the right, but ignore those because there's the two-tiered green rising some 320 yards away.

Just to show the 'Fairway to Heaven' course isn't just hippy-dippy head games, we have the Forres professional Sandy Aird accompanying us for the afternoon. He's a sturdy, powerful-looking man in his late forties, with a reassuringly down-to-earth and familiar Fife accent. He knows the 'Fairway' people, is quite at ease with what it's about. Which is bringing some insight, enjoyment and deeper pleasure to this game that so often brings frustration, annoyance and pain.

Though he will in the course of playing with us adjust a grip here, a stance there, produce thoughtful analysis of what's wrong with a swing, the biggest lessons he brings to us are mental ones.

It helps to have the core technical elements right, but that won't help if the mental stuff is askew.

So: Sandy Aird's routine. He's clearly done it before, but it's still funny and true. It goes roughly like this:

'One of the pleasures of life as a club pro is I get to stand at the window of the shop and watch the comedy. I see people arrive from work, jump out the car, change, and rush onto the tee still stuffing a Mars bar down their throat. They loosen up, have a few practice swings, argue about handicaps and bets. Sometimes their swings are quite bonnie. Then they tee up the ball, look down the fairway – and that's where the fun starts.'

Sandy pauses, driver in one big hand, ball and tee in the other, checking his audience. He stabs the tee into the ground, tees the ball up. He is transformed. He is that club golfer raring to go.

'I'm going to hit this. Boy I'm really going to hit this!' His easy address over the ball becomes a tigerish crouch. He waggles the club, stops. 'That green isn't so far away. I could get near to it.' His crouch becomes more tense, more stiffly coiled. He looks up at the green again. 'In fact, today I'm going to put this ball right on it! I'm going to amaze and impress all my pals. I'm going to drive the green!'

Sandy lashes out, a great savage off-balance heave. The ball slashes off the toe of the driver, way right, straight out of bounds into the trees. He gapes after it, baffled, shocked, dismayed. We fall about. We have all been that golfer.

Sandy Aird grins, produces another ball.

'I'll tell you a very simple secret. *The drive is the easiest shot in golf.* You think pros always hit monster drives, but the fact is their average drive off the tee is under 280 yards. What matters isn't lashing it out of sight but hitting it onto the fairway, the right part of the fairway. Right?'

He looks round, gathers our assent.

'OK, so this is easy. The tee shot is the only time you get to put your ball down where you want. You pick your spot.' He looks up at the green then hesitates. 'Oh, and to make it even easier, you get to tee it up! At any height! With any colour of tee! And you can buy them all in my shop!'

He selects a spot between the yellow markers, bends down and tees up a new ball.

'So here's what I want you to think: *This is easy*. This is a short par 4 hole. You don't have to try to drive the green. Hit a reasonable drive and you'll have a simple second shot onto the green and you'll get a par. You might even get a birdie. All you have to do is swing through this stationary teed-up ball, and hit it easily down the fairway.'

He pauses, concentrates for a moment, then a crisp, relaxed swish propels that ball a regulation 280 yards down the middle. Applause, laughter.

'Have fun,' he says by way of summary. 'That's the beginning and end of it.'

And if you tell yourself it's easy, you may even find it is.

A frickin fabulous shot

In the 'Fairway to Heaven' folder we were each given, there are two pages for each day. Each day is given a date and the name of the course we'll be playing. Then there are blank boxes: *Theme; Intentions for the Round; Review of Round; Reflections on the Day; Magic Moment; Shot of the Day 1; Shot of the Day 2.*

For Forres, I played with the Americans Blair and Cynthia (though she elected to walk round, suffering from jet-lag and having scarcely played in her life before) and our chosen theme was *Connection*. Connection to self, each other, the course, and the ball. Interesting to play with a set theme, how it colours and affects the day. I did indeed feel very connected, joyful at being here, still alive, playing on this gorgeous course on this most perfect late-summer day.

Above all it was coloured by Sandy's words. Each time I teed up, instead of being apprehensive where this drive might go, in my very Scottish way glimpsing all the possibilities for disaster that lay ahead, I thought, *Easiest shot in golf.*

Nothing to lose, nothing to prove, but aiming to play well – that's the ideal. Blair filled in his scorecard, and after an Orkney summer when I'd kept no score but simply played as few or as many holes as I felt like and Lesley could stand, I opted to keep one too. I have it in front of me, dog-eared and slightly grass-stained. I'd swear it smells still of the north-east and that long hot afternoon.

A day of light, breeze, deep shadows, yellow sunlight spread like melting butter through the deep-green trees, down sloping greens. Taking Sandy Aird's words as my mantra, I played easily, and well by my standards. Drives sang off the club and dissolved into the dazzling brightness; pitch shots clicked and ran from soft hands; the ball kept falling into the hole.

Though the Scot in me murmured it couldn't last, I enjoyed it while it did. Sandy joined our group at the 4th hole. 'Your name's familiar,' I said. 'You're frae Crail, right? You went to the Waid?'

He looked dumbfounded, asked my name.

'Are you Sandy Greig's older brother?' I nodded. 'He was in the class ahead of me at the Waid! A good golfer – him and Sandy Stephens and Ian Bolt. Thae twa turned pro, you know that?'

'Aye,' I said. I'm not a Fifer born, but it was natural to slip back into the idiom. 'Sandy Stephens was my brother's great rival. I kent Ian Bolt, played him a few times.'

'Did you no win the Gay Trophy at Balcomie?'

I nodded. 'An awful long time back. I stopped playing for thirty years after that – quit while I was ahead, ken?'

He laughed. 'Minds me of when I was called in to see the Rector. I tellt him I was leaving the school. "What for?" he says. "I'm going to be an apprentice professional golfer," I says. "That seems a waste of your abilities." "Not to me it isn't," I tellt him.'

Sandy looks around at the course, grins. 'It's been good,' he affirms. 'Now let's see how your game has lasted.'

'I'm camping in its ruins,' I say. My standard line to myself and others, but that's how I see it. Camping, fairly happily, in the ruins of a once-competitive boyhood game.

Then I tee up the ball at the 369-yard 4th, remind myself, *Easiest shot in golf*, and because it's such a bonnie day, and I've established a connection with Sandy and, now I come to think of it, with my Fife youth, it is indeed easy to birdie that hole with a 20-foot putt.

The next hole is a very appealing par 3. Tee shot onto a shapely, curved, bunker-surrounded green. I hit my iron straight into the trees on the left.

'Why did that happen?' I appeal to Sandy.

'Because that's where your shoulders were pointing.'

'You're kidding!'

'No.'

He gets me to address another ball as I would naturally. Stands alongside me, then gently twists my shoulders round.

'Now you're aligned wi the pin.'

It feels all wrong, like I'm aiming way right.

'I expect you tend to slice the ball, then once in a while hit it straight left?'

'Especially with irons.'

'Well, that's why. Now keep yon alignment and hit anither.'

To my surprise it goes right but not much, finishes 20 feet from the pin.

'Ta very much, Sandy.'

'It's easier to see frae the outside.'

Blair hits a good one, back of green left. As we all walk down the fairway, I'm in a raised state of happy alertness, thinking, *Another learning. Perhaps you do need people for this.*

In my folder, under 'Magic Moment' is simply '6th hole'. It's with me yet. I expect I'll carry it through winter to warm me through the short, dark days, like a shot of whisky going down.

The drive; brother David's words: 'Just waft through it.' With a metallic crack then whistle, the ball goes straight for an improbable distance with no effort, just a deep joy spreading from feet through wrists, from chest to head. What did Ben Hogan say? *A great shot starts in my hands and finishes in my heart.*

It's on an uphill lie on a green wave of the fairway, a few yards ahead of Sandy's.

'You hit that aboot twa eighty yairds,' he comments. 'Tellt you it wis easy.'

This hole is a 489-yard par 5. With a 3 wood I might get to the green. More likely I'll end up in one of those bunkers guarding it. So let's be sensible and strategic, like a real golfer. Take the 5 wood, lay it up short for easy par.

Waft, laddie. Head down, hit through, arms loose.

Ball vanishes in a white streak towards the green. God it's a lovely day. What a wonderful course! Heaven is right here, Eden without tricks.

I find my ball some five yards short of the green. Decide to putt it because the fairway here is short and bare. Maybe 50 feet to the pin. Give it a firm clip, follow through . . .

Sometimes you just know. It's as inevitable as it is improbable. It's almost supernatural, though to me it suggests the extraordinary calculating abilities of the human eye and mind, grasping at some pre-rational level what the conscious mind has not yet concluded.

That ball ran across the green, up the slope, curved as it should, clicked against the pin, went in. Eagle 3.

I broke the self-controlled habit of a lifetime and flipped my putter up into the air, laughing aloud at the sheer mad magic of it.

'Well,' Sandy said, 'reckon I'll move on to the other group now. Don't think you lads need me verra much.'

Another shot lingers from that day, and it wasn't one of mine. Such things are possible.

I'd been enjoying how Blair hit full short irons. Lots of go, no reservations, hit right through. (I tend to hit cautious ones, three-quarter shots prodded towards the green.) This one was a big wedge from maybe 100 yards.

'Go baby, go!' he shouted. 'In the hole!'

Which I thought merely Californian-aspirational as his ball soared into the sun, went so high I swear it reappeared *over* the sun, then plummeted down out of the blue, landed plum on the raised green, toddled sideways with the slope to 18 inches from the flag. A most beautiful shot of truly professional standard.

'Goddammit,' he cried. 'Missed!'

'Blair,' I said, 'that was a most wonderful shot.' And I swear he blushed before he murmured, 'Thank you.' Then when he walked onto the green, picked up his ball, he recovered himself.

'That was a frickin fabulous shot,' he said.

I may learn to alter my Scottish pessimism and negativity, that relentless finding of one's own shortcomings, the dismissing of one's own abilities and achievements as lucky, unmerited, or at least rare – but I don't think I'll ever learn to say: *That was a frickin fabulous shot.*

But playing with Blair every day, I came to enjoy and value his wholeness of heart, the absence of reserve or false modesty. He would enjoy and praise other people's shots with equal fervour. I'm very Scottish, perhaps even British, in mediating my responses. When you hit a good shot and your playing partner says 'Great shot!', you are supposed to murmur, 'Oh, I don't know,' or 'Lucky bounce,' or 'Well, the wind helped,' while inside every fibre silently exults: *That was a frickin fabulous shot.*

So Blair's wedge shot lingers with me still. Memorable because it was a beautiful sight. Also because of his acute and vocal joy in it. And because in that moment I – who am no less self-absorbed and un-altruistic than anyone else – discovered it really is possible to take as keen a pleasure in someone else's shot as if it were my own.

It was a beautiful thing, a magic moment.

*

Typically, at the next hole I realised what kind of score I could be heading towards, being two under par after the first six – and I got excited, keen and anxious. Then hands tightened, concentration wavered, swing got faster, and a couple of double-bogeys put an end to that fantasy.

But the day and the course were so lovely and full, and relaxed equanimity returned. It was what Patrick Rayner and I had talked about on our way to play North Berwick – that ideal admixture of concentration and happy vacancy, at once caring about the result of each shot, and happily floating above caring.

The day's happiest moment wasn't a shot at all. It came, as happiness sometimes does on a golf course as in life, for no particular reason. At the 15th Blair and I both hit decent drives, then had to wait for the group ahead to play out the hole. They looked like they'd be a while, so I sat down on the warm turf near my ball, idly turning an 8 iron in one hand, eating a melting chocolate biscuit from the other.

The raised green up ahead was in a bowl of yellow light, cupped by a stand of Scots pines of such deep, restful green. Shadows were lengthening, I was starting to think of a long pint of cool beer, I was pleasantly tired, in the late stages of a round, the end of which would bring us back to where we started but as the man remarked, *knowing the place for the first time.*

I smiled at a vision of T. S. Eliot missing a short putt and reflecting, *Between the motion / And the act / Falls the Shadow.* Had he played golf, he would have truly known the meaning of torment and transcendence. Then I blessed the keen eyes, the fabled moustache and long-departed skeely hands of James Braid frae Earlsferry who had discerned the possibilities of this very hole over a century ago. *Nobody is as wise as James Braid looks,* my father used to say. What a wonderful, noble act of vision, what a gift and challenge to leave behind, the inexhaustible poem-in-landscape of a great golf hole!

And then I thought nothing at all, but just sat there lapped by happiness that rose like early dew from the fairway and flowed onto that raised green, its high surrounding trees, the figures of my friends moving in their slow dance round the flag, transfigured into earthly heaven.

A British-sized ball

'Come closer,' the bird insisted. 'Closer.'

I put my face near the cage till the bars began to blur, still wary of this bad-tempered oracle. That beak could give a savage whack.

I was attracted to the tiny feathers along his chest. Little rectangular feathers in wonderfully varied shades of white, mauve, green, blue. In rows, like medals, they put me in mind of decorations of a senior Politburo figure at a May Day parade in the 1970s.

'Yes, medals,' the budgie whispered. 'But look at the figures.'

Figures? I blinked and peered, and the little feathers each bore two columns of numbers, written roughly by hand: 5, 4, 5, 3, 6, 4, 4, 5, 3˙ 39 OUT.

A golf scorecard. The bird was feathered with multicoloured golf scorecards.

'That was the day I won the Ladies' Scratch medal,' the parrot-budgie hissed.

'The *Ladies'* medal?' I exclaimed. I'd fallen into the old trap of assuming this bird, this supposed golfer, was male.

In reply, a large grey claw ruffled up the feathers on her head, tossed it imperiously.

'I am something of a *grande dame*.'

'I don't doubt it.'

Certainly the budgie resembled Muriel Spark in a scratchy

mood. The bird and I eyed each other. It was much closer and larger now, and there were no bars between us. I was in the cage with it. The idea was disturbing and vaguely erotic.

'There's something I have to ask,' I said. 'If you don't mind.' The budgie made no comment. 'Look – how can you possibly play golf?'

The bird began to expand. Thousands of golf-medal cards skittered on its vast chest. It was like the Angel of the North, with huge gleaming wings stretched on either side.

'With THESE!' it boomed. 'You should TRY IT.'

Dazzled and a little afraid, I looked away. Way down, on its swing near the bottom of the cage, the little neonate bird looked up from its learning-to-read book. I noticed it had some fluffy feathers now and looked less like a monkfish.

'I'd like to talk to your little friend,' I said.

'You won't get much out of *him*.'

'I don't know,' I said as I started to down-climb the bars. 'He's not as young as he was.'

'Well, who possibly could BE?' thundered from above.

I dropped onto the floor of the cage where the turf was short and springy, littered with round budgie droppings the size of black-and-white footballs.

'Look what I've got,' the young budgie said. Its voice was high and shrill, like bosun's pipes but not unpleasant.

'Yes?' I said.

It lifted one claw and revealed a golf ball.

'My advice . . .' it began. The giggles that followed ran up and down silvery treble scales. Then it pulled itself together.

'*Keep your life short and your head still*,' it said and began shrilling again.

Nothing new there, then. I might as well have stayed at home and read Philip Larkin. The adolescent bird shoved the golf ball towards me.

'You can use this, if you want.'

'It's very small,' I said, picking it up.

'It's from before we switched to the American size. Remember?'

As I stared at the ball, it cracked open like an egg. Out poured our kitchen in Anstruther in 1965: the yellow valve mains radio set on the Home Service, my budgie Mickey gabbling in his cage, my father vigorously flicking pipe-dottle onto the *Scotsman*, my mother being omni-competent with breakfast, my new copy of the Kinks' 'Tired of Waiting' waiting upstairs on the gramophone in its bright Pye sleeve.

Yes, I remember all right.

I woke in NewBold house with a joy and an ache. There is a part of us that has no sense of passing time, and another that has nothing but.

These dreams are tending somewhere. I don't yet know where but one day I will, and playing golf is part of it – a blind man's stick, a divining rod, a putter dangled from thumb and forefinger to check the true slope of the green.

15TH
'Equanimity'
(OLD MORAY)

Happiness moves on, in golf as in life. One thing is certain: you will not find it today where you found it yesterday.

The next day we played Old Moray, near Lossiemouth. Another gorgeous morning as we teed off below the clubhouse, by the ocean. The water was blue glittering fragments under the sun, the shoreline sand deep red, the air still fresh with a light breeze. The fairways today were more yellow than green, with lots of sinister gorse lurking the length of them, allied with clumps of whin, lots of heather — a downright tough, subtle, tricky championship course.

I was playing with John and Joan and Blair, and today's chosen mantra was *Fun and Fearlessness*. My 'Intention': keep my head steady, in every possible sense.

The pattern of the day was signalled by my opening drive. Strongly hit but pushed slightly, my ball ran on and on and ended up in gorse. I never found it. From then on it was a day of dropped shots. Plenty of satisfying drives, pleasing pitches, a few good fairway woods — for me the most rewarding shot in golf — but always just off the pace. One of those days when, without feeling you played significantly worse, you take a dozen shots more than the day before.

It's a harder course than Forres, more punishing (that

unforgiving, relentless and obdurately Presbyterian gorse, pricking and tearing and impenetrable as the will of God). Longer holes. Fast, true but very tricky greens. It's a fine championship course and I'm thankful we caught it on a comparatively easy day with little wind and the ball running long on the baked yellowing fairways.

Joan and I kept singing snatches of 'Perfect Day', 'Wild Thing' and 'Under the Boardwalk', which seemed to arise from the succeeding moods of the day. Happiness, disappointment, satisfaction then frustration, pleasure of the company, all drifted through under that enormous sky.

My folder entries bring back the highlights. A 3-wood tee shot (*Easiest shot in golf, right?*) at the 279-yard 9th that held dead straight into the cross-breeze, carried the feared bunkers I'd meant to play short of, ran on to the fringe of the green. Or the long 2nd hole, 465 yards of dog-legged undulation. My drive I swung at as gently as possible, the ball screamed off the club face like a shell. The next shot was a 5 wood from a tight bare lie, the kind I find scary. Told myself not to be silly, just swing through it and let the club do the work and for God's sake keep it straight. It was die-straight before vanishing into the heat haze. Even on hyper-clear days my eyes will seldom see a ball after a hundred yards – age, nothing to be done about it.

'You play lovely golf, Andy,' Joan said. I blushed with pleasure. I'd never been told this by anyone who was any good – then again, until recently I seldom played with anyone at all.

'It doesn't happen often,' I replied. 'You should see me on bad days.'

She glanced at me quizzically, shook her head. 'Have you never heard of positive thinking?'

'Sure,' I laughed. 'In Scotland we call it kidding yourself!'

'I call it unhelpful pessimism.'

'We call it realism.'

She paused at her ball, took out a fairway wood. Settled over it, gave it a firm swish down the fairway. Then we continued on together with what would be a running debate of the week.

'And maybe that's the reality you get,' she commented. 'The one you make.'

'A fair point,' I conceded. 'Personally, I blame our weather – we've learned nothing will stay good very long.'

'Like today? And yesterday?'

We laughed, and sang 'Perfect Day' as we followed our balls up the fairway. I found mine on the edge of the large kidney-shaped green.

'Bloody hell.'

'So, can you admit that was good?'

'It was nice,' I admitted, looking at the undulations ahead. 'Odds are I'll three-putt it from here.'

She shook her head in disbelief. I was winding her up to an extent, but I wasn't entirely joking. Quite dispassionately, I thought it fairly likely I'd take three putts from here. I'd try not to, of course, but I believe in saying things as they are, not how they should be.

'We're going to have to do something about your attitude, Andrew!'

I looked at her, all energy and optimism, the Californian tan, short-cropped hair, big smile and positive attitude. Someone of warmth, humour and capability. Maybe a little driven. An achiever, despite her own philosophy.

'We can try, Joan,' I replied.

'Andy, everyone loves a winner!'

'Not in my country they don't.'

And of course proceeded to take three putts.

I watched Joan and John as they played. These were the founders, the almost accidental creators of 'Fairway to Heaven', and it was interesting to see their contrasting styles and natures.

John is an easy, natural player, a neat person in unfussy slacks and polo shirt. Composed, naturally quiet where Joan is chatty.

He moved light and balanced on his feet. I wasn't surprised to discover he'd done a lot of t'ai chi. When in the Introductions/ Personal Tee-off yesterday he'd spoken of the tragedy – about the worst that can happen to an adult – that had befallen him and his wife not long ago, the emotional shock had crashed round the quiet room, and then the aftershock of empathy and shared sorrow.

No surprise then that at times, between shots, he was lost, distracted. Then he'd be back again, playing very competent, unflashy golf, sharing in the comments, laughter, snatches of song.

During the course of the round I got the story of how 'Fairway to Heaven' had started. This is roughly it:

In the early eighties, John Talbott was living in the Findhorn Foundation, exploring and committed to that movement. Then Joan Shafer arrived. They hit it off, especially when they found they shared a secret vice, a love whose name cannot be spoken in even the most broad-minded of New Age circles: *Golf.*

They kept it to themselves, and with another friend began nipping off on afternoons for what they said vaguely was *Spiritual Practice*. No one could disapprove of spiritual practice. But this spiritual practice consisted of playing golf on nearby Forres.

And gradually they realised they were not entirely joking. There really was an inner aspect to golf, a whole series of life-lessons, as much self-knowledge as you could handle, both joyous and painful, a state of play and mindfulness.

Then their friend told them they should start a course on it. Spiritual Golf. Well, why not?

After much hesitation, they put it to a Findhorn Community meeting. There was a very long pause. *Golf? That stupid game of stuffed shirts and very wrong trousers, of the country club and the businessman drowning in self-importance? The very totem of bourgeois complacency?*

But the person who was chairing said thoughtfully, 'I don't see why not. After all, we're here to try new things. If you want to set up this course, we'll see if there's any interest and take it from there.'

So Joan and John put a small notice about the proposed 'Golf as Spiritual Practice' in the Findhorn Bulletin. One of them threw in the 'Fairway to Heaven' title, the one that made me smile in recognition, that signalled a certain light-hearted awareness of the sweet ludicrousness of it all. (For let's be quite clear: golf is a ludicrous pursuit. A ludic pursuit, a game, a joke, an extended shaggy-dog story that ends with the ball rattling into the cup, then being picked out and it starts all over again.)

Then came the phone calls. First from Tom Morton, Radio Shetland, who had somehow seen the Bulletin. The interview went out. Then came the call from Radio 4 *Today* – would John do a down-the-line interview about this 'Fairway to Heaven' course? Then the *Sun* then the *Guardian*. Then it was picked up by NBC, spread to the other US TV and radio stations . . .

John shook his head, laughed. We were standing on the 17th tee, looking at a long and scary double dog-leg gleaming in the sea-light.

'All this was before we'd had a single applicant for the course, before anyone had signed up! Joan and I had thought maybe we were the only ones. We had no idea there'd be this level of interest. Part of the appeal, particularly for Americans, is the chance to play on these quite fantastic links courses with like-minded people.'

'Yeah,' Blair says. 'There's nothing like this in California. This place is just the greatest! Shock and Awe!'

He slammed his drive into the long marram grasses that cover the dunes on the left.

'Aaw! Man, I'm shocked!'

And that's how it had started. Once or twice a year they book a group of golf courses for a week, bring in a trainer or coach or pro at some point, have a range of presenters, group workshops, discussions, meditations. When Joan moved back to Oregon, Vin Harris stepped in to do more of the on-the-ground preparatory work. They agree every 'Fairway to Heaven' course comes out differently – the serious, the celebratory, the golf-centred, the hilarious.

Joan, John and Vin are always there. They play, they take part, they don't stand above it as Leaders or Organisers.

'Hey,' Joan said as we followed her drive down the fairway, 'this is my vacation, you know? I'm here to play. We don't make anything out of this – if it wasn't fun, I wouldn't be here. By the way, great drive, Andy.'

'I must be getting too tired to hit it squint.'

She stopped in her tracks, looked straight at me. 'Thank you!' she said, quite loudly.

'Eh?'

'When someone tells you you've hit a good shot and you have, you don't pretend you haven't, or make excuses for it, or say it was an accident. You say *Thank you.*'

Memory-flash of playing with my dad at fourteen. I'd driven off the 3rd tee in Anstruther with my spoon. I can see that little club yet, the inlaid face, the brass screws. 'Good shot,' he'd said. And because it was and felt so good and was nearly as far as his, I replied, 'Yes it was!' And got such a bollocking. Ever since then, I mumble something when praised, gratified but not really knowing what to say. Now nearly forty years later, I'm getting another lesson – in outlook, in manners.

I take the 5 wood – bought at Mark's shop at Beauchief just before our Orkney summer – aim across the ridge of dunes, cutting a bit off the second dog-leg. Weird-looking hole, would be a monster in wind. I must be tiring and swinging slowly, because the ball rifles off towards the green, I hope finishing short of the guardian bunkers.

'Lovely shot, Andy!' Joan says at my side.

I look at her, all tanned, purposeful, positive and grinning.

'Thank you, Joan,' I reply.

These were highlights, the magic moments. In between were the other shots: the iffy, the misjudged, the occasional say-goodbye-to-that-ball shot. The tone was set by that first hole of the day where my good opening drive ran and disappeared into gorse.

There was pleasure in the challenge, the round, the company and the stunning setting, but to be honest – and that's what we're here for, surely – there was disappointment and frustration too. I don't *like* going round any course, however tough and unknown, in 87, with a measly four pars. I certainly want to go back and play Old Moray (sounds like some oracular rural sage: *Arr, better ask Old Moray, squire!*) better next time.

A mixed day, yet in the end a rich one. The sound of the sea followed us all day, and I love playing by the ocean. The company was supportive, funny, enlightening. The fairways were bare, frightening yet flattering. The greens were so hard, so complex, so true. We all felt suddenly, contagiously, absurdly happy coming down the 18th fairway. 'A fabulous vortex of golf,' Blair remarked. Joan sang 'Wild thing, you make my heart sing!' and from John's face some of the sorrow melted.

The opening and the close at Old Moray come together near the sea, below the clubhouse where golfers sit with drinks watching players start and players finish. It's a great finish too, with a long second shot onto a complex raised green – like the whole course: beautiful, challenging, fair. I hit a decent last drive, then a 5 wood through the green, pitched and two-putted as our friends watched, then we shook hands and went to join them for the beer I'd been hallucinating for through the closing holes.

Rest after golf, long cool drink in hot sun by the sound of the sea. Weary and replete, watching our friends play out the last hole, each of us with his and her personal round, each smiling at the shared round – for an hour in this life something comes completely right, as when on a long approach putt the ball curves with the run of the green, takes one last revolution, and drops home.

And your bird can swing

'Your mother is happier than you think.'

'You think so?'

'*She* thinks so. Isn't that the point?'

The doctor sat at my bedside, short legs crossed, clipboard and stethoscope round his neck. He was familiar, something about the Irish accent, those little fervent eyes and plump, bad-tempered air . . .

Yes, Van Morrison!

'Do you still sing much?' I enquired.

He shrugged irritably. 'Nothing you'd understand. Too busy doing other things.'

'Like playing golf?'

A long, long pause. As his little round black eyes moved shiftily from side to side, I had time to note the long mauve beak, the thinning feathers of hair. My budgie was back, and for the first time, I seemed to have caught the bird off guard.

'Sometimes,' he admitted grudgingly.

'I bet you know nothing about golf.'

'I do so!'

I'd got it at last: the way to handle this bird was stay one step ahead, be unexpected, don't ask straight-on questions. I sat up in bed and peeled the bandages off my forehead. They'd been there too long.

I looked round my bedroom, the silvery bars. A big bright world was shining outside.

'Can't see the little neonate,' I said. 'I suppose he's left home.'

The bird began fiddling with the buttons of his faded tartan waistcoat. They looked very like ball-markers. I looked closely, read 'Royal Dornoch Golf Club'.

'The little un's gone down the fairway – took his clubs with him.'

'How could you let him? He doesn't know much about anything, and he looks like a monkfish!'

At this point the bird lost control. Buttons started flying off as he squawked. 'Andy-Pandy could always read and write! He was just pretending with those alphabet blocks! Just pretending to be stupid, stupid!'

I got out of bed. It was time to go. I'd been convalescing way too long. As I pushed open the window bars I said casually, 'I expect he wrote thirteen books. Any good?'

The budgie hopped down off its chair and pattered across the floor after me, the height of an average ostrich.

'No worse than you'd expect of a featherless biped.'

I dangled my legs over the sill. The ground looked a long way down. I could see fields, a burn, a loved woman and a familiar boy walking down the red dirt road.

'Eighteen stories, now,' he murmured in my ear. 'That's a lot.'

'You're telling me,' I said. 'Got to go.'

'Wait!' As I stared, he shuffled, seemed embarrassed, made a little grating sound in his craw, and then he half-sang, urgently: 'Swing the club that's yours to swing, and leave the others in the bag.'

I threw back my head and laughed. Real laughter but I didn't know where it would end.

'Wisdom! For the birds! Too late – I'm off!'

Then the bird's vast wing lay softly on my shoulder like a blessing.

'You cannot swing if you don't let go.'

Then he pushed. Time in falling down those eighteen stories to wave to Lesley and Leo by the river; time to turn on my back and pretend it was all right and it was meant to be like this, so as not to alarm them; time to remember Mal saying, 'Falling's not the problem – it's the ground that kills you, and I thought to myself, *Well that's all right then, while it lasts* . . .

'It's another great day!'

I opened my eyes, still flat on my back, in falling position, in bed. Nick was standing at the window, looking out at the dawn. I blinked, stirred. Still here.

'It certainly is,' I said.

16TH

'Extraction'

(CRUDEN BAY, NAIRN)

Reflections on the Day

Toothache again, Nick snoring – a poor night's sleep with peculiar dreams. Early start, quick veggie breakfast, wishing they at least had eggs. (After meat-withdrawal symptoms last night, Blair, Cynthia and I went into Findhorn and ordered carnivore specials.) Yet another improbably perfect day; it feels like a blessing.

Light breeze, sky clearing to pale September blue and big white clouds as our coach arrives at Cruden Bay. We spill out and gape: fairways, greens, marram grass, all bleached by salt and light to pale yellow and beige, fringed by the deep-red sand of the huge beach where the waves break. This course is *colossal*.

Bit intimidated to be with Tony and Rainer, both highly committed single-figure handicap players. Tony likes to play courses off the medal tees, which makes them harder but more authentic. His character note. I'm impressed but prefer the normal tees, further forward the better. My character note.

Decide not to keep scorecard – been getting too involved in scores, letting it determine what sort of day I've had. Poor score = poor day (like yesterday). Which is daft. We're not pros, this is not our living, it's not work. Made no notes either, tried to just play each shot as it came and *be here now*, like our meditation sessions.

Vivid moments, like on that towering high medal tee, looking across the whole course, the long red arcing beach rimmed by white surf, the tiny figures moving among the dunes, sun hot on my face. Cruden is so spectacular the golf is dwarfed; it becomes a sideshow to being there. Felt myself an enchanted child as we walked down narrow fairways between towering grass-covered dunes with smell of sea, marram grass, hot sand.

Swing is character. Tony was once a keen hurler, took up golf late. A natural athlete, loads of application, swing vigorous if not graceful – stiff legs, breaks his left elbow at top of backswing. Chats away volubly between shots, but once near his ball he goes into a bubble of total concentration. Very sensitive to movement or noise then – 'Andy, would you be still there?' Even Blair, clanking away 50 yards down the fairway, feels the stern forcefield and stops.

Rainer Tornow also a late learner. Again, great application and concentration. He has a very set routine, then a long pause over the ball, then a quick hit. He's consistent. They both are. Both play a lot, relish competing with themselves and others. Interesting to compare with brother David or Al McLeish, who both learned young and are far more natural players, all rhythm, less evident mental effort. They walk up to the ball, pause, hit it. With Tony and Rainer you can see the joins, the elements – stance, grip, alignment, rotation – as they were taught.

All the above considerably better than me. So I was gobsmacked when after a good driving day, on the 550-yard 17th (two consecutive beauties, a drive then probably the best 3 wood of my life to the fringe of the green) Tony looked at me and said, 'Andy, you are probably the best striker of the ball we've ever had on a "Fairway" course.' Rainer nods, 'Beautiful swing. Amazing club-head speed.' Tony takes up the gratifying theme: 'If I had your natural ability, I'd be playing off 3.'

I shrug, stunned with pleasure and surprise. Natural ability?

Blimey. Always think of David as the natural, my swing rather studied in comparison. I make a joke of it. 'Then I must be doing something very wrong – doubt if I've broken 90 today.'

Tony: 'I'm not joking you. You just need to play more, get some experience, and stop being so negative. If we meet up next year – and I hope you're coming to Ireland – and you're not playing off 7, you'd better start running.'

In fact, none of us played Cruden Bay well. Not one birdie between us. No putt holed longer than 10 feet. It turned into a driving day, where the pleasure was all in the tee shots. They whistled, they sang, they bounced and ran for ever. After that – poor stuff. Tony and Rainer both religiously kept scorecards, even after multiple bunker incidents. They were clearly bitterly disappointed at these. but struggled back to self-control, equilibrium. 'I allow myself to be angry for ten seconds, then put it away,' Tony remarked. They agree neither of them broke 90, yet how hard they kept trying, right to the end.

Tony went straight to the driving range afterwards, hit a bucket of balls, trying to sort out his swing. I drank beer in hot sun, trying to get used to this idea of myself as a natural player with a beautiful swing. Moi? Aw, Jeez, guys . . .

Well it's a nice idea but my game within 100 yards of the hole is full of bad decisions, misjudgements, crap really. And bad attitude, it seems! Tony again, somewhere near the 12th, a vicious dog-leg I parred to my surprise: 'Andy, you talk yourself down way too much.' Me: 'I'm just being realistic, Tony. It's a cultural thing.' 'I call it talking yourself out of good shots!' He seems heated, almost angry. 'You've got to *believe*. Be realistic about the shot you decide on, sure, but then commit to it. The way I look at it, it's not me that's failed when I slice into the rough. It doesn't make me a failure. It's simply something has gone wrong with my golf swing. But when I've failed to commit to the shot – then I really have let myself down.'

Interesting man, Tony Hegarty, much more complex than he presents. All that joking and blarney – then he goes quiet, almost melancholy. He's married to Maria, that fine golfer I went round Lundin Links with. As we talked on the coach to Cruden Bay, I found he squares being positive with being realistic in this way: *commitment without expectation*.

His outlook can seem rather simplistic and dogmatic – he's a great one for asserting, Tony, however charmingly. Then on the coach back I learned something of the traumas of his early life. Now I can understand and respect why he chose – why he had to choose, in order to survive – such an outlook. And respect too that he has chosen to try to help other damaged lives.

Commitment without expectation. I drink my pint sitting on the warm turf above the 18th green, and think on it. I've a feeling there's something for me here, something close to the heart of this golf-and-life quest, the recovery I'm looking for.

'If you're angry, you learn nothing,' Tony said on the 17th fairway. 'You see the pros when they hit a bad shot – they step back, try to work out what happened, then rehearse what they should have done. They try not to hate themselves for it.'

'But how do you do that? How can you change how you feel?'

It seemed the key question. What you feel is one of the great givens.

Tony looked intently at me. 'What you feel is one thing, Andy. What you *think* about what you feel is another. You are in charge of what you think.'

'Really?'

He grinned his big wolfish grin. 'Trust me,' he said. 'I'm an Irish psychotherapist. I *charge* for this advice and you're getting it free.'

Then he moved away into the concentration space he always went to for each shot. Looked at what he wanted to do. Long pause. Stepped briskly up to the ball. Steadied, committed with a tiny nod, hit it long and clean.

If he's right, there could be a way to fully embrace golf and life, the pains as well as the pleasures, to still want to do well, sometimes do badly and not be disgusted.

Blair whacked a long iron. A good shot but a bit right of the green.

'Darn it! The wind should have brought that in!'

But really there was no wind. The golf course is a theatre of self-delusion as much as self-discovery.

'Let me put it another way,' Tony said at my elbow. 'And I'm not joking you. How you feel about a shot is just your ego. It makes a lot of noise but it's not important. It's not you.'

Me not my ego – what's he saying here? You can find yourself in these dangling conversations on a course. I'm beginning to see it's a reason for playing with someone else who can provoke, or offer what you can't offer yourself.

That conversation concluded on the 18th green after the last putts had gurgled in. Tony handed me back my ball with a big grin.

'The difference is, Andy, your soul is immortal and your ego dies with you – just you remember that now.'

I've had curious conversations on golf courses, ranging from dinosaur hunting in the swamps of Zaire to Marxist theory, but this was the first for the immortal soul.

We shake hands, Cynthia hugs everyone. She's our silent witness every day, smiling quietly behind her shades, watching our little psychodramas. She doesn't seem in any hurry to play – maybe that's why, seeing us.

Blair marches off, a big hefty loud man in big shorts, big neck, former volleyball player in National League. His game got worse as the round went on – lashing the ball harder and harder into rough. Yet when he turns and says, 'Wow, that was a great day! Fantastic!', he means it. I admire his whole-heartedness. He and Cynthia recently moved in together, hold hands going down the fairway – sight not seen often enough on golf courses. Again, whole-hearted. And his unexpectedly soft putting touch . . .

You think you understand people when all you've done is put them in a box.

Rainer likewise. He's so neat, intense, disciplined – then suddenly Puckish. At our debriefing meeting this evening: 'I give today ten out of ten – and I should warn you, I'm feeling *very mischievous!*'

At our evening meeting, Blair, as always, rated his day eleven out of ten. When it came to my turn, I gave my current well-being rating as seven. People looked concerned. 'In my culture,' I explained, 'when someone asks how are you and you reply *Oh, not too bad*, that means you're very well. If it wasn't for this toothache, I'd even say I was an eight.'

My toothache has been niggling for some days now, getting steadily worse. I'm feeling slightly poisoned, alternating paraceta-mol and aspirin to keep it under control. Turns out both Torsten and Fritz Hey – lovely man, sweet self-deprecating smile – are holistic dentists. They examine me, confer. 'You must extract, I think,' Torsten says. 'Must be tomorrow. This is not good for you.'

When a holistic dentist says tooth must come out, you're in trouble. When a vehemently ex-Catholic starts talking about your immortal soul . . .

Today was like Cruden Bay itself – long, full of ups and downs, BIG.

Does your mantra lose its flavour on the golf course overnight?

Every golfer knows how it goes. You're playing quite well, you like this course, your swing tempo is leisurely, in fact, why hadn't you realised before this game is quite simple, uplifting, *easy?*

Then a drive slices out of bounds. Why makes no difference, for the world is about to turn dark. Tense now, your head comes up and a topped chip races across the green into a bad lie in an evil bunker. Then hands tighten on the putter and a three-foot putt slides past the hole. At the next tee, annoyed by it all and anxious about that slice, you hook your drive into the gorse and it's gone. You're gone.

You know how it goes and what it feels like. You know it in conversations, in work, in marriage: *losing it*. This is what we're dealing with here.

Whatever form your pain takes, that's where you go now. Some find themselves hacking about in a gorse of rage; others wander without hope through the rough of self-loathing. Others try in vain to keep the ball straight into cross-winds of self-delusion. (*That bunker shouldn't have been there; these greens are far too fast.*) But it's gone, that high equanimity. And from now on it just gets worse. Another ball is lost, another putt missed. The day's score is gone, and happiness has been thrown away and littered across these fairways like a torn-up scorecard.

Terrifying how quickly a good marriage or a good round goes bad. It takes just one moment's inattention, haste, anxiety, or simple miscalculation. If there is another game where one can fall so far so fast, tell me and I'll avoid it. (There is: rock- and ice-climbing. Maybe that's why I don't do it any more.)

No wonder the question *Can this last?* creeps across the thoughts of even the most positive golfer when things are going well. Which can tighten the hands, speed the swing . . . leading precisely to that feared disaster.

So it was on Old Nairn that Tuesday. After an early rise and drive to have my rotten molar pulled out in Elgin, I caught up with my 'Fairway to Heaven' group on the 9th. Big Blair in shorts, clubs clanking as he powered along, his partner Cynthia walking calm in shades behind him; Gisela with her long grey hair back in a band, warm and firm and methodical; Vin with a hint of chipmunk in his rounded red cheeks and merry, mischievous smile. Once again it's the most beautiful morning in history, the dew drying off, sun turning hot but air still fresh in the light breeze.

It's so good to see my friends, the course is clearly grand, already my jaw feels much better. Something poisoned has been removed, the pressure's coming off. I'm starting to feel strong and fit and up to it.

So in this positive and uplifted mood, I start to play with them. Missing half the round meant no point keeping a scorecard, so that pressure's off too. This one's purely for the enjoyment of it.

My first drive feels good but slides right into gorse bushes and is gone. Oh well. My approach shot feels good but sails over. The short putt on the green hits the side of the cup and spins away.

'Like frickin lightning,' Blair snorts. 'Frickin impossible!'

'What's the watchword for today?' I ask on the 11th tee.

'Grace and Ease,' Vin murmurs. 'Cynthia came up with it.'

'Grace and Ease. Nice. Thank you.'

Cynthia smiles, nods. She's been going round with us for four days now, watching, taking photos, not playing. She seems to be enjoying it. I wonder how we appear to her. Lunatics, I expect.

Vin drives. First time I've seen him play. Very easy, very within himself. Not long, but straight. No fuss. *Grace and Ease.*

'To hell with Grace and Ease,' Blair announces. 'Shock and Awe!'

He steps up with his big hollow-headed driver. Short fast swing from a big heavy man. Sometimes it works, sometimes it doesn't. When it doesn't, his response is to hit the next one harder. This time it works. He clouts it long and straight down the narrow fairway.

This time I pull my drive into the woods on the left. It's gone. Miss another short putt on the green. My sunny outlook is faltering, the old demons of disappointment, self-disgust, irritation, are stirring.

On the 12th I do it again – push the drive right, can't find it in the whin. I'm trying hard not to sulk as I drop another ball and play on. I don't really care, it's a lovely day, it's just great to be out here with these friends.

But I do care. It's like the toothache I'd been carrying the last few days, a bit worse all the time, grumbling away, poisoning my day. A decent 5 wood is followed by a fluffed chip. End up with a 6-foot putt which I know I'm going to miss, and do.

So here's the question: *How do you turn it around?* When you start going down that slope, hitting bad shots from an ever-worsening state of mind, how do you get it back?

'This is a signature hole of the course,' Vin says quietly. 'I always want to do well here.'

The 13th at Nairn is indeed a great-looking hole. Scots pines, cool and graceful, reddish trunks and deep-green shade, line the fairway on both sides. It's like hitting up a long narrow tunnel, rising to a distant plateau green: 'Crown', 412 yards.

I take my driver, tee up, look at what's ahead. Three lost balls in three holes. I don't care. Yes I do. What was it Tony said the other day? *I commit to hitting a good shot, open to the possibility that I won't.*

I address the ball.

'Grace and Ease,' Vin murmurs.

Sounds reasonable. Hands soften, shoulders drop.

Ball sings off straight, white globe vanishing down the green tunnel. That feels good. Next shot is challenging – about 165 yards onto the raised green, guarded by bunkers and a complex slope running right to left in front. A real golf shot on a real golf course, a James Braid special. *No one is as wise as James Braid looks.* Presumably not even James Braid.

Arms loose. Swing through. Grace and Ease.

Ball whizzes off as intended, lose it in the dazzling light above the green. Find it just over the back. I'm the only person thereabouts in two shots. I putt, slightly scared of the speed. End up 4 feet below the pin. I've missed three of these already today.

'Vin,' I say. 'Can you coach me on this?'

He stands beside me. 'You're jabbing at it,' he says quietly. 'Choose the line of the putt and make sure you follow through down the line. It's simple.'

I look at the putt. I really want par at this fine hole. If I miss it, I'll slip further into the pit. It's another test of character that golf keeps springing on you. I hate tests of character, but without them I get flat and bored. Maybe that's why I went to the Himalayas with Mal. The only thing I hate more than a challenge is not having a challenge.

I look sceptically at Vin. His eyes sparkle, he grins back merrily. 'Trust me,' he says. 'I'm a Buddhist.'

I inspect the putt, check the line, clear away a couple of bits of leaf. The world has narrowed though it feels enlarged, down to this dazzling green, the white hole, the white ball, and one simple clear intention. Time slows and bends. I'm thinking how much more *present* Vin is than the first time we met, when his mind was still blown by Tibet. Then I'm not thinking at all.

I stroke the putt, follow through the line as my ball curves and drops out of sight with a little rattling gurgle. 'Thanks, coach,' I said. 'You're hired.'

Vin laughs as he replaces the flag. 'It's a lot easier when someone else tells you. Wait till you see the next hole – it's a beauty!'

For the rest of that round, drives flew straight. The softer I swung, the longer and straighter they went. Approach shots bounced on those iron-hard corrugated links fairways, ran onto the huge greens. A series of 5 foot putts went in, all following the same simple mantra, *Follow through down the line*. Our Silent Hole had us all moving in harmony, at once alone with our effort, and conjoined. I had five par holes in the last six. More important, my concentration and equanimity had returned.

'Strength of mind' my dad would have called it. Back then I'd have made little sense of that. It would have sounded so old-fashioned, possibly a virtue when living through two world wars and the Depression, but surely not in the sixties. Now it sounds like an absolute necessity. I think golf is challenging me to develop, rather late in life, strength of mind. Whatever's up ahead, we're surely going to need it.

When we shook hands, then hugged, on the last green, I was a happy and thankful man.

How much we can give each other, I thought, looking round my companions as we drank beer and watched the others play out. Thanks to Gisela for her engagement, her methodicalness, her calm pleasure. To Cynthia, the compassionate observer, only wise sober sailor on a ship of intoxicated fools. To Blair, for his whole-heartedness, his total involvement, the way he wellies into a wedge shot. To Vin for a simple piece of coaching that runs as deep into life as you care to pursue it, *Follow through the line*.

Big thirst makes for good beer, great need for great companions. As I drink and relax, the day's messages start to come through. Each of us today had our own struggle, own game, own narrative, that's how it is – but we played with and for each other. Today wasn't diluted by company; instead it's been immeasurably enriched.

Today I *got it back*. How did it happen? Grace and Ease, and Vin's words. And the beauty of the day, the course, the relief of having that tooth pulled, the alert equanimity that seems to come with 'Fairway to Heaven'.

Getting it back when you meet with a friend, spouse, child, and get off on the wrong foot and nothing comes out right – that's the hard one. That's what we have to learn to do: get it back when the mind is full of pot bunkers and the heart is choked with gorse . . .

I drain my beer and watch the last group embrace on the 18th green, and it comes to me like a cascade of pennies dropping in a slot machine, the announcement of the bleeding obvious. Getting it back, in the end, is down to you, but it surely helps to be open to coaches, companions, friends, intimates who might offer you that hint, those words, that example that eases the way back up.

It is not necessary to play alone.

A Wilson cloud chamber of the mind

On the coach back to Findhorn we were talking about golf's honesty, the often unpleasant truths about yourself it reveals –

failure of nerve, over-ambition, lack of self-belief, mood swings, egotism, pettiness, impatience, fear of failure, distraction. Had we just meditated and done encounter sessions here for a week, it would have been possible to kid ourselves as to the nature of the experience. Instead we have played golf, as mindfully and open-heartedly as possible, and we are each left with a quiverful of remembered shots, the sublime and the ridiculous, that tell us everything we need to know about ourselves and how we work.

This notion of invisible inner processes having tangible external consequences made my brain briefly hyper-drive. 'Golf is a Wilson cloud chamber of the mind!' I cried.

Tony, a man who had some science, got it immediately. Joan and Vin looked baffled, so I tried to explain.

It is part of the lore of physics that in 1920 the physicist C. T. R. Wilson, visiting his laboratory after a party where drink had been taken (did I mention he was Scottish?), breathed beerily into an experimental chamber where he was researching alpha-particle radiation, and noticed silvery trails of water vapour appearing in the cloud of his breath. The alpha particles produced trails of ions, and those ions made the water vapour condense. What he was seeing was not the alpha particles themselves, but a marker of their passing.

'A bit like seeing the condensation trails of high aircraft, when you can't see the aircraft itself,' I suggested.

This happy-hour accident was developed into what Rutherford called 'the most original and wonderful instrument in scientific history', won Wilson a Nobel Prize, and made possible research into cosmic rays, those invisible particles that pierce us through continually as we stand over a short putt like St Sebastians, riddled with arrows so tiny, light and speedy they do us no harm.

A stray thought, a moment's doubt, a residual irritation, hope, anxiety – we don't see these inner events, but we know them by the shot they affect. We read our uncertainty in the wobbly putt, our fear in the topped shot into the bunker, our anger in the huge slice out of bounds – and our strength of mind in the 5-foot putt that runs straight and true into the cup.

The inner world traced in its visible results: a Wilson cloud chamber of the mind.

Off a tight lie

On a rare half-hour alone at NewBold House, I sat on my bed and took out the dog-eared, grass-stained notebook. I've learned to trust that most of what matters is in my head, learned by heart as they say. But over these 'Fairway' days, some kind of harvest of the last months was being gathered in, and I wanted to get it stored.

> Feel stronger now. In body of course, but more than that. When this whole ploy began, though I still walked and talked and breathed like before my brain got squashed, I felt *provisional*. After Susan Sontag unexpectedly survived cancer, she said she felt glad to be alive, but somehow 'posthumous'. I knew exactly what she meant. She's dead now, of course – the cancer returned.
>
> Somewhere along the fairways something has changed. I'm more solid, grounded, ready and willing to go on. Though I will die, I don't need to feel provisional while I live.
>
> Playing golf has had something to do with that.

How much of these on-course notes and drafts are in the present tense, automatically, instinctively! Because that's the way it's been. Perhaps golf – and any other sport – needs no further justification than this overwhelming presentness.

I seem to have ended up with two simple and rather old-fashioned principles for playing golf: Strength of Mind, and Equanimity. Virtues my father would have recognised. They weren't exactly the watchwords of the sixties, but I've come round to them, and him, at last. Something seems resolved there too. We've made our peace. I am not him but he is within me.

We need that strength of mind to face down our doubt, tension, impatience, irritation, overconfidence, distraction – all those little demons that rush into the vacuum created when the club head moves back from the ball.

The Equanimity we'll need when we're faced with the result! Most shots don't produce the outcome we committed to; some are just bloody awful, others 'unlucky', frustrating, unsatisfactory, posing new problems to adjust to. Golf (life) constantly challenges us to find this equanimity in face of results.

I do not admire competitiveness, in myself or others. But I do still admire the capacity to respond well to pressure, as if a psychological or even moral virtue. As though we sense, when we watch a hardened professional bracing himself to drive at the last hole to win the Open, or we line up a 4-foot putt in a 50p sweepstake with only one's dead father for a gallery, that one day we will need these qualities in earnest.

More than ever it seems quintessentially Scottish, this inner-directed individualistic pursuit. For whether played alone, in a team or against an opponent, golf remains essentially a solitary, private experience and struggle.

Yet in its core etiquette of regard, consideration, responsibility to whoever one plays with, partner or opponent, there's a social dimension. There are very few games where one can not only not put off or interfere with an opponent, but is positively obliged to aid them – follow where their ball went, help find it. Dad always stressed this is fundamental to golf.

I also like to think of the handicap system as making the

game particularly democratic. Players of wildly varying abilities can genuinely play together.

Mostly golf is about self-inflicted suffering, self-knowledge and hard-won (precious because hard-won) joy. Who but the Scots could evolve a game that offers such opportunities for humiliation and failure, and no one but oneself to blame for it? And such transcendent moments?

Why are low-handicap players often such a joyless, tight-lipped bunch? You'd think they'd revel in all those wonderful drives, fairway irons to the green, pitches and putts. Instead they fret over that one pushed drive, the misread putt. I never met a happier golfer than Dutch Paul, the day he broke 90 for the first time.

Bad golfers have much more room for improvement, and will once in a while pull off – usually when they're about to give up the game for ever – a truly wonderful shot.

Don't want to make golf into a moral/spiritual gymnasium, but times will come when we need all the strength of mind and equanimity we can muster. The day a spouse says she has something difficult to tell you, when the redundancy letter arrives or the policeman comes up the road with your kid, or the consultant takes you into a private room before giving you the test results.

Where will they come from then, the strength and equanimity? God knows. But occasionally I have glimpsed it on a golf course, felt it in me: the centre, the calm place, the core, the ground.

With these qualities we may better, in Vin's words, *invest in outcomes in a protected space*. Life isn't a protected space, but golf – like any game we choose to play – is.

Golf itself is a way of improving the lie of our life.

In art or on a golf course, in books, music or games, we seek a world more focused, ordered and meaningful than it normally (actually?) is.

It's not so much playing better as *better playing*. That's what 'Fairway' has been about. I'd ask no more than –

Then my mobile summonsed me with a very rare call from my mother. Heart lurched, of course, though she was calling only to ask anxiously again if she'd sent brother David a card. I replied, as the day before, I didn't know, and as we talked I could feel the gatherings of that 'Fairway to Heaven' week slipping through my fingers to be replaced by hopes, fears and sorrows that golf can't help.

And yet still there was a difference, something had been moved on, and my heart rate was constant, my balance was fine as I went down the staircase to gather one more time with my friends.

17TH
'The Zard'

(ROYAL DORNOCH, FORRES)

Those 'Fairway' days were intense, sustained, and left no time for TV, newspapers, radio, reading, phone calls. Instead, everything was lived at first hand. Remarkable how your life unclutters then, how much more clarity and energy become available.

When we weren't playing golf, we had group sessions for meditation, debriefing, sharing our experiences. John, Vin and Joan all led workshops. Each time we came together to sit on our chairs in the circle around the candles and the triangle of golf balls, the experience was more powerful. When we joined palms and looked at each other – grins, nods or simply looking – the energy that flowed through hands around the circle was palpable.

By the end of the Nairn day I felt we might all spontaneously combust or levitate, so powerful had the sensation become. Instead of feeling exhausted by cryptic yet suggestive budgie dreams and four consecutive days of golf on big courses, I felt fitter, stronger, more energised than I had for years. Easy to kid yourself, I thought, but it feels my last dream was true, and some kind of long convalescence is nearly over.

In our evening workshop session, Gisela and I interview each other from the 'Playing from your Centre' sheet. *Recall a peak experience when you experienced playing from the Centre – either in golf or in life. A time when you were uplifted, in love with life, completely alive, awake. Describe the story, what you were doing, where you were, who you were with.*

What flashed up first wasn't a golf course, or a time with Lesley. Perhaps because Mal's quip *Falling isn't the problem* was still resonating in me, what came up was a day I hadn't thought on in years. A day spent reconnoitring a route onto the main slopes of Lhotse Shar, above our base camp. Just Mal and me – Sandy Allan was sick that day – exploring with axes, crampons, minimal rope and gear, a day's provisions. The thin air was icy at 20,000 feet, so bright, diamond-sharp as we picked our way over glacier moraine, round crevasses, up chutes and funnels of snow, trying to find the best way onto the body of the mountain.

'What was special about that day?' Gisela asked.

That this was true exploration for us both. Far as we knew, no one had ever come this way and attempted Lhotse Shar by this route. That was the appeal for Mal and Sandy: a new route up an 8000-metre peak, first British ascent by any route. So no signposts, no route description, not even word of mouth as we went into the unknown.

We weren't yet fully acclimatised, and it was hard work, demanding constant alertness and judgement. But not fearsome. Nearest we came to danger was when a powder snow avalanche rushed by us like a ghost express train. We felt the suction of its passing, were briefly deafened, then left in its wake dusted with fine snow.

'I'd say that was good timing, wouldn't you?' Mal said. 'Of course, I knew one was due about then.' I glanced at him. He may have been serious or we may have just been lucky. In any case, we crossed the gully where it had passed and carried on up the gleaming ice buttress we christened 'The Zard' . . .

'What did you value most about the experience?'

Sense of going out into the unknown, being excited but comfortable with it. Closeness with Mal – we laughed, talked, shared, enjoyed each other and our work. I was doing something useful for the expedition, contributing more than words.

'What were the key qualities of the experience?'

I felt alive, alert, present. Concentrating hard, warmed by our friendship, the mutual trust when we roped up together for a dodgy snow-bridge or climbing 'The Zard'. Physically good, mentally sharp, emotionally open. I was Performing, Learning and Enjoying, all in balance with each other.

'I suppose I was living from the Centre that day,' I say to Gisela, and feel myself almost tearful.

'If you had three wishes that you could make to bring the qualities of that experience into your life, what would they be?'

1. Preparedness to go more often out of my comfort zone. This golf book, for instance. Friends assume I'm just coasting, but for me it's stranger and more challenging than another novel. I mean – golf? 2. To connect with someone else like that again. (I hope Lesley and I take that New Zealand trip into the mountains.) 3. To have again that excitement of being alive, fully physically and mentally connected. (Or maybe following trap lines in Alaska, or a canoe expedition in Northwest Territories.)

'If that's what the Centre felt like to you,' Gisela says, 'you don't have to look further than here.'

I stare at her, feeling something shift in my chest. She nods, twice, holding me with her dark eyes.

'And now,' she says, 'I am afraid you must listen to my sad story. It is about a long marriage . . .'

I went south in the middle of the 'Fairway' week – it was our rest day, so I wouldn't miss anything – to do a couple of readings at a festival near Perth. One novel reading, one poetry. I've been doing them for thirty years and still get severely nervous beforehand.

Maybe it was all that exercise. My body, heart, eyes were still full of golf courses, fairways, gorse, undulating greens. Whatever the reason, I've never been more relaxed, ready and steady. The energy and focus were there. At its best, performing is communion rather than communication, and this time it came from the Centre.

A good gig. Honest communion, without vanity, self-consciousness or phoniness. And good drinks and late talk afterwards with my old friend Brian from 'The Lost Poets' days, still writing, still in the game. Also still drinking and smoking, despite his heart attack. I now wince every time he lights up – I who enjoyed smoking for nearly thirty years. I'd had to stop in Intensive Care, and just never started again after I came out of hospital. It would have seemed ungrateful, somehow.

I got up early next morning, drove back up the A9 through the pre-dawn mist, still only half-awake, to join the 'Fairway' group at a lay-by north of Inverness as the coach went on to Dornoch. I felt burned out, wondered if I was up to another couple of days' golf. The fog was thick, headlights didn't help.

As I drove I was thinking about a conversation with Vin. My problem with Buddhism is that though I can see Desire is the problem and cause of Suffering, it's also human and great and gets things I value done (books written, hills climbed, babies born). It's the very core of our existence. Vin had laughed, pointed out that though Buddhism sounded a negative, dismal path, most of the practitioners he knew lived with great energy, warmth and humour. 'It's not about indifference, right?' Which I had to admit certainly seemed true of him. But still, he believed in the Void, the great Emptiness. Apparently it was all around us, like the fog.

At that moment – no kidding, I don't make this up – at that very moment the mist ended and I was abruptly driving through brilliant sunshine amid the mountains of the Drumochter Pass, the rising bulk of the Sow and the Boar on my left, radiant glittering streams leaping on my right, more heather-mottled purple haze hills and the shining road up ahead where my friends were waiting. And a great whoosh of happiness as though I'd struck a geyser of it underground shot up through me, and I thought, *No, Vin, the world is so FULL!*

On my car cassette player George Harrison's twelve-string electric played the gleaming intro to 'And Your Bird Can Sing'. I cranked it up loud, put my foot down for the rendezvous and sang my wee heart out, beating time on the wheel.

That's the way God planned it

From the opening drive and 7 iron onto the green 6 feet from the pin (missed the putt, but still), it was one of my best days, played on the most noble course I've ever known.

Began well, wobbled in the middle – that bent grass, the deep gorse, all those odd mounds and the inverted-saucer lightning-fast greens, all took their toll – got it back for a string of pars in the closing holes that felt like real golf, the way it's meant to be.

But that's just the score. The day was stunning – cool air, fair breeze off the sea, hot sun. The setting was ultimate: curving bay the length of the course all deep-blue water, red sand, surf breaking; the hills of Sutherland and Ross-shire rising clear and purple; the contoured dunes where the bent grass and marram grass swayed along the crests. Then the course itself . . .

On no other course is the nature of links golf so fully realised. Royal Dornoch is the Platonic form of links golf. Those narrow, undulating fairways throw up pits, curves, mounds; those greens at once vast and narrow, so fast, so true, often sitting on their own natural plateaux, all curving away at the edges. The course asks serious, legitimate golf questions, hole after hole, stroke after stroke. The challenges are so subtle, complex and fair, it's impossible to regret or resent them.

Old Tom Morris, Donald Ross and J. H. Taylor all made their contribution to this course, and I blessed them for it. Yet Dornoch isn't so much designed as discovered. If one wished to advance William Paley's Argument by Design for a Divine

Presence (though David Hume rather scuppered that one), I wouldn't argue from the analogy of the watch to the watchmaker. I'd go straight from Royal Dornoch to the fountainhead.

It's that good.

I'm not alone in thinking this. Donald Ross, probably the most famous golf-course architect in the world, came from Dornoch, learnt his golf here, took its principles to the United States to design some of the great classics there, including Pinehurst 2. J. H. Taylor took two weeks' holiday here every year just to play it. Harry Vardon called the 14th, 'Foxy', 'the finest natural hole in the world' (of which, more later). Tom Watson played three rounds in 24 hours here and called it 'the most fun I ever had playing golf'. The *New Yorker* called it 'the most natural golf course in the world' (though if you really want natural, try Iona and North Ronaldsay).

In short, it's one of the world's great championship courses.

I can't claim to be objective about Royal Dornoch. I had a very good day there, played well by my standards, in perfect conditions, with good friends, towards the end of a wonderful and revelatory week. I noted Rainer, who didn't play so well there, doesn't rate it as high as Nairn, where he did.

But playing well or poorly, there is something about this course. It's in the thin northern air, the light, the sea, the terrain itself. The words *noble* and *pure* rise in my mind whenever I think on it.

I remember too a number of horrible shots – a topped drive, a wild slice, the usual misjudged approach shots (the air's so clear it makes things look closer than they are; this is offset by the run on the cast-iron fairways, the speed of the greens: very tricky). But somehow my mind stayed steady, hands softened. Kept the head, kept my nerve, and holed a whole series of rescue putts from 20, 12, 15 feet.

Then on the back nine, as though they came through a hose nozzle, the drives abruptly switched from spray to straight-and-narrow mode. With the fairways flattering, a series of 280-yard sweeties off the tee, no effort required. Those long par 4s became a drive and short iron – though even then, such is the deep-level cunning and subtle complexity of the course, those second shots were a golfing challenge every time.

With the breeze behind, the second nine holes played shorter and shorter. At the 298-yard 15th, my drive finished in the valley at the bottom of the plateau green. The 16th at 395 yards was a drive and a 9 iron to the back of the green. The 446-yard 18th became a drive and a (poorly hit) 8 iron, which still ran over the back left of the green. It was like being briefly loaned new powers. (With the wind in the opposite direction, they'd be stripped away and I'd be a struggling infant.)

But the one I remember, the one that warms still, was 'Foxy'. Well named. A long par 4 at 439 yards, the fairway is littered with erupting mounds, like grass-covered acne. Then a series of grassy promontories jut across the fairway and guard the plateau green by running across the front of it *at an angle*. It's a bastard, it's beautiful, it's fair. Modern club technology has not ruined it.

'This is the signature hole,' Fritz announced. 'We must try to do well here.'

'Shock and Awe!' Blair announced, then beat a long drive into the bent grass on the right. 'Aww! Shock!'

I hit that drive sweet and straight, on automatic now. But the next shot posed another of those questions the course kept asking. Looking at it – wind behind, very fast greens, that skewed edge of the plateau – it wasn't so much a question as a riddle verging on a Zen koan.

I remember standing there, warm wind on my shoulders, sun into my face, suddenly aware of the ever-present susurration of the sea, waiting for Fritz to play his second while wondering whether to play a run-in 6 iron or a high 7, and for those long moments felt absolutely *here*, rejoicing in the challenge, hoping to do well but overwhelmingly happy just to be here at all. A Lhotse Shar moment, only this time a hundred feet above sea level.

I chose the 7 iron, pushed it a tad right, where it ran away off the green into a steep dip. Tried a new shot for me, the sand wedge off grass. Flipped it up to 8 feet. Took my time, cleaned the ball – another practice I'd never bothered with in the past – looked at the borrow of the green from both sides, committed to a line. Soft hands, hit through the line, holed it.

That was the Centre. Performance, learning and enjoyment all in balance. Yes there will be crap days, and merely disappointing days – I had several after the 'Fairway' week was over, maybe burn-out – but if it can be done once, it can be done again. You know you can find that place again, and that brings strength of mind amid the struggles of golf and life.

Strength of mind – though my father's mind was too stern for my temperament, and mine too emotional for his, we can now agree on this quality. I knew he'd played this course on our family holiday here around 1960, and I felt us converging as we played the last holes of Royal Dornoch into the yellow blaze of lowering sun.

I lay in my narrow single bed that night, replaying the day in that brief interval between memory and deep sleep. My last image was of my putt for par at 'Foxy'. Whether a putt is 8 or 30 feet, sometimes you just know as the ball leaves the putter blade something unexpected yet inevitable, longed for and gorgeously right is happening, like after five years' marriage falling asleep utterly in love with your spouse.

The Angel of Motivation

Wishful thinking leaves me sadder than negative thinking ever could. There's something bracing about the caustic pessimism of Emile Cioran or Schopenhauer's lyrical groans – but then I'm an East Coast Scot, and like to describe the razor-edged wind off the North Sea as 'fresh'. But wishful thinking – that soppy, lisping, backward cousin of positive thinking – is just pathetic, and doomed.

It is not a legitimate way to prefer your lie. Nor is calling someone 'differently empowered' when they're slowly losing their mind in old age. Or 'asleep' when you mean dead. My dead may be continually present, but they are really, really dead.

These thoughts prompted by a mural in the bathroom in NewBold House. Lying in the bath, I came to loathe it. The image was of a scene in an idealised tropical jungle (I've been in them; I know). It was like something from *The Jungle Book* – all the trees were magnificent and stately, the river transparent (there are no clear rivers in the tropics; they're tea-brown). No visible insects, lots of light (ravenous mosquitoes, Stygian gloom). This lovely scene is being looked upon by a wide-eyed naked child; it is the Jungle of Eden. But children do not go naked into jungles: they'd be bitten insane, and need footwear to protect them from the many poisonous and hurtful things there.

Tropical jungle is an overwhelming experience of life and death locked in one desperate embrace. It's eating itself, replicating, disintegrating. It may be awesome, but pretty, pleasant and wholesome it is not.

Lying in the cooling bath, I came to see this appalling painting as the very image of my reservations about the Findhorn project, about much New Age thinking. It's the wishful thinking, the idealised optimism, the assertion that, given half a chance, everything is wonderful or could be, in people and in the natural world and the universe, when clearly it isn't.

You might as well believe in fairies at the bottom of your garden – charming in a child, pathetic in an adult – a kind of psychological simpering I thought as I dressed to go down for another bland veggie dinner. Let's have a dose of pessimism, sarcasm, irony, and some honesty about how low and rotten and sad we can feel and be   now that might clear this over-scented air!

So I feared the worst when Joan announced that tomorrow for our last day we would be playing on Forres again, this time in competing groups, and we were competing (in a friendly manner, of course) in a Stapleford for the *Angel Cup*. I'd be with Gisela, Bruce and Tony, playing for the Angel of Motivation. The other Angels were Humour and Harmony.

I could see some of us – like Tony, Rainer, Bruce, Blair, even myself I confess – had a little spark in the eye at the prospect of a little of the red meat of competition. But these Angels? Surely not?

'Don't worry, Andy,' Joan assured me. 'You don't have to believe they exist. Think of them as symbols. Operating principles. Can you handle that?'

I thought about it. Motivation, Humour, Harmony, all competing over eighteen holes of golf to see which wins out. Well, it's more interesting than verbally debating the issue.

'Count me in,' I replied. 'But you'll have to explain what this Staplewhatsit is about.'

Tony explained, or tried to. I still don't think I entirely get it. Apparently golfers do this Stapleford a lot. It entailed each player playing for their foursome group, which sounded like competition with the hard edges rubbed off, each doing his or her best to contribute to the team.

The only thing I didn't look forward to was the 7 a.m. tee-off time.

Half-light on Forres' 1st tee. Air chill and moist on the hands. Silence. As far as we could see, the fairways and greens were spread with grey-gleaming dew, no footsteps breaking them. We were absolutely alone on a golf course at the break of day.

As we stretched, swished, loosened up quickly, there was a quick last-minute debate. Stapleford competition – most golfers will know how it works, and for non-golfers it's too technical to explain – depends on each player's handicap. I alone didn't have one, had never had one.

'Fourteen,' I suggested.

Someone made a remark linking my 14 handicap to eating golf hats. Tony, as our Angel of Motivation team captain, argued for

12. 'Andy's short game is not as bad as he thinks, but it's worse than it should be.'

Another team captain – could it have been Harmony? – said they'd accept 10 at a push.

As the argument went on, I remembered a retired man I'd played with at Beauchief. A golf handicap tends to be a golfer's virility symbol, except in this case men compete over how little theirs is. It could be compared to a currency's exchange rate, seen as that country's virility symbol. But a strong currency makes it hard to export and sucks in imports. In the same way a low handicap makes it harder to win.

That man I met up with on Beauchief, playing off 18 I think, had just won two monthly medals and the club's senior medal competition – and was indignant that the Handicap Committee were going to reduce his handicap to 15. 'How can I win anything with that?' he complained.

In the end I was assigned an 11 handicap, the first one I've ever had. Maybe I was finally becoming truly integrated into the human race.

Our Angel went off first. Tony called a group huddle. 'Support and Harmony,' Tony murmured. 'Commitment to the shot. We play this for each other.'

He led the way, hit an easy cracking drive off into the dawn. We followed as best possible. A quick clap on the back from Tony, and we were off.

Over the 'Fairway' days I'd been rethinking my attitude to competition, whether against others or oneself. It had ruined my enjoyment of golf in adolescence, and I didn't want to go back there again. At that age you're so unsure, and you have had no time to achieve much, that you tend to place all your self-worth on one thing. But surely to goodness by fifty you are a little more assured. A bad shot, a poor round, a lost match doesn't mean you're a worthless failure. That fluffed short putt was just a fluffed short putt, not the Final Judgement.

Even so, I wasn't convinced. Surely competing took the fun out of playing? Keeping score, playing only one ball, making yourself hole every putt – wasn't that making it all a bit like work, more grim Presbyterian struggle? Yet I could see Tony and Rainer or brother Sandy, even David, relished competition, however friendly. And not just because of a need to assert themselves, to beat others. It went deeper than that.

'When I'm out practising with no pressure I can put six balls out of six onto the green from eighty yards, and think I'm the great man,' Tony had said the other evening. 'But when it's just one ball, one shot, and there's a fiver on the game, that's when I find out.'

Rainer nodded emphatically. I was half-persuaded. Still, I was reluctant to let my competitive instincts off the leash – not because I didn't have them, but because they tend to devour me. I feared the perfectionism that could ruin this game for me again.

Then John Talbott spoke up. Quiet, balanced, self-contained, he was absolutely not someone who had to win in every situation.

'Sometimes there's a value in competition,' he said. 'It's a reality check.'

A reality check. That resonated. Without putting ourselves to the test, we can kid ourselves for years. The idea of the reality check spoke with my father's voice, though he'd never have used the phrase. Prefer lies by all means, but only legitimately. Don't kid yourself. Don't paint the jungle as all sweetness and light. Face things as they are.

Play for fun, but not to flatter. Compete to challenge your ego, not aggrandise it.

Play when something is at stake, but not your life's savings.

Gisela holed out from 20 feet on the 1st green for an eagle. Our exultation rang out over the silent, glittering course, fading up into the clear grey-blue air. Then Bruce contributed a birdie at the 2nd, myself one at the 3rd.

The light came full up gradually, as though in some invisible gantry a hand was pushing up the rheostats. Then the sun lit the tips of the Scots pines at the 4th. Walking up the fairway of the long 6th where I'd had that eagle at the beginning of the week – and how long ago that seemed! – the sunlight dipped into our eyes, warming hands chilly from the dew. No one up ahead, the course miraculously renewed, virginal again.

So we played for our Angel of Motivation. Tony was everywhere, like Ballesteros captaining the Ryder Cup team, encouraging, advising, doing the calculations, keeping the score. Team Stapleford sounds and is complicated, but it suited me. It was competition, but as a team we were playing for each other, trying to make our contribution.

For the first six holes, only the group's best score counted. This meant we could all go for our shots, take the risky option, try to hole the long putts. On the next six, the best two scores. On the last six, the best three.

Motivated? That Angel was all over me.

I was over-intense, or maybe just chilly, early on. Captain Tony coached my putts, reminded me to hit through the line and not stop on them. From then on, they started rolling in. Then he gently suggested I was swinging a bit fast, so I consciously slowed down and discovered yet again – for God's sake, how often do we have to learn the same simple truths? – the slower the swing, the sweeter and longer the shot.

It was great, playing for the team, with each shot counting. Though we were playing only for a battered silvery flower bowl found in a junk shop – and, of course, our Angel – competition still whetted an edge to the putter's blade. The pleasure of that 8-iron tee shot to 15 feet at the short 5th was all the greater because the team needed it. That 20-foot putt that curved towards the hole fell in more sweetly because it counted. Then again, heightened disappointment at the sliced drive, that approach shot misjudged, this putt sliding off-line.

Attachment, Desire, Pain and Pleasure! When will we solve you?

The day turned hot. And our golf, inspired early on, faltered towards the end. We were committed and supportive, but tiring. For some, this was the seventh consecutive day of golf.

In the closing holes, an elegiac feeling settled over us. This was farewell, a signing-off. Though we didn't know it, the late summer would come to an end next day in a series of gales and downpours. The company would scatter, the days become short, dark and golf-free. It was nearly over.

I stood on the last tee and hit my last drive, a good one. Hit my last approach shot, a poor one, short of the green. A slightly under-powered chip to 15 feet. Walking onto the green for the last time, yearning for a pint and some lunch, yet not wanting it to be over. Hoping we'd won.

Missed the putt. Oh well. Shook hands all round, then some spontaneous embraces.

We sat on a bench, watching Harmony then Humour play out while Tony did the maths.

'Our Humour golf was a bit of a joke,' Vin remarked. 'But we're still laughing.'

In the end, after all the calculations were done, the Angel of Motivation tied with that of Harmony. And why not?

End of the fairway

It's impossible to cover or do justice to all the events, people, conversations, jokes, delights, golf shots of improbable perfection or wince-worthy ineptness, learnings, forgettings of 'Fairway to Heaven'. I'll simply say it was a week of stunning weather, day after day of glittering dew-soaked greens drying into hot hard-baked fairways stretched under enormous blue skies, with the sound of the sea and scent of turf, seaweed, sand, gorse. At times the fairway wasn't so much *to* heaven as *in* heaven. It was Scottish links golf, friend.

Something happened there. By the end of that week, strangers were known, appreciated, entered into, loved. We permeated each others' golf games and psyches. I feel still the unexpected smoothness of Blair's putting stroke after the assault of his driving, the totality of Rainer's concentration, the pure sunburned joy on Torsten's face when he left the 18th green on Royal Dornoch. I hear Cynthia murmur, 'Grace and Ease, Andy,' see Joan on arrival running down the fairway towards Vin and Tony, arms spread in a child-playing-airplane . . .

Each and every one I owe thanks to. It was a special time that I hadn't seen coming. Something shifted in my head, something opened inside. I'd gone there hoping to be moved on while thinking it unlikely I would be. But I was, in ways I'm still working out.

I'll be playing alone less often. I no longer see playing solo as the paradigm of golf, though it has its special pleasures.

There is some merit in putting yourself to the test, in taking the reality check.

There is such a thing as firmness of mind, of steady resolve, of being committed without expectation. We can work at keeping the head still. It is possible to be engaged without being the slave of results.

You may prefer your lie in life through commitment, motivation, positive visualisation, self-belief. You can simply consider it differently. When someone dies, you may not say they have 'fallen asleep' but you may say their life is completed. It's not untrue, it's just a different image, and one that makes the loss more bearable.

The world is a given, but we live in it through metaphors, images and games – 'lies' if you will. These we can do something about, and they make a difference. I can do nothing about ageing, the dying and the dead, but I can deal with them better according to the picture I offer myself. I've a much better chance of hitting an approach shot right if I picture it so and commit, than if I allow the image of it trickling into the bunker to dominate.

But it must be honest, otherwise it's simply cheating and we're left with that sanitised jungle-and-child that so got on my nerves at NewBold House.

Here it is: through our games and our metaphors, our meditation, music or books, even our self-belief, we give ourselves a better chance at a decent shot. We can take a sad song and make it better. We can enlarge the area of forgiveness.

We can prefer our lie.

At the 15th hole at Royal Dornoch, I was told about a tradition, a superstition, a practice of teeing up a ball and driving it out to the sea. You make a wish, then hit. If you reach the water it may be granted. John Talbott wrote the name of his short-lived infant on his ball, which by some near-impossible freak hit and broke the chain surrounding the tee, then flew on into the water. 'A little letting go,' he said quietly. 'It helped.'

That kind of thing seems to happen a lot on 'Fairway to Heaven'.

I came back home unburdened, minus a decayed tooth and a few dodgy attitudes, energised, tanned and a few pounds lighter, recommitted to playing life and golf. I felt stronger in more than my legs.

The best was how we ended our last gathering in that hands-clasped circle. It ended not in solemn silence or deep thought, but in a contagious, helpless giggle that spread from John and rippled through all of us (following a true and uncharacteristically blue story Tony had pressed Vin to tell again five minutes earlier), till we were all heaving, gasping, near-crying with laughter. Then we dropped hands, embraced, went through for our big dinner followed by the night's partying, singing, drinking.

That was the way to end. Nothing po-faced and solemn, but hilarity, joy at the sweet ridiculousness of it all.

Thanks to all, you know who you are.

'Return'

(DOLLAR)

It was one of those October mornings when the sun is warm but the air is chilly. In the tree-lined streets an edgy wind whipped leaves that were yellow round the edges. In a hospital in Lichfield, my cousin Rosemary was dying in her late middle age. She was red-haired, loud, bossy, energising. She played the piano wonderfully, professionally, with great speed, verve, and unexpected sensitivity. The last time I'd heard her was at my mother's eightieth when she banged out the Grand March from *Aida*. Mum was still on great form then . . .

The leaves blow off, the river thunders under Friendship Bridge; another summer had become memory.

Driving through Dollar, I could see again how quietly prosperous, pretty, douce, verging on twee it was, this village of stone-built villas at the foot of the Ochils. Turning up the road running by Dollar Burn, the two decorative stone bridges, the clock tower, then the sandstone clubhouse at the top of the road, all were present and correct.

So why was I standing in the clubhouse lobby with my heart feeling soggy and heavy as a water-filled balloon? Why this displaced, sick, sinking feeling?

A friendly woman took my money for the round. The place was deserted, but cleaner and brighter than I'd remembered.

Everything used to be gloomy and brown, or maybe that was just me. There'd been a cigarette machine in the hall where on impulse I once pulled the handle, got ten Cadets *and* the change, and briefly felt life was on my side.

'Have you played here before?' she asked.

'I last played here forty years ago.' I never thought I'd get to an age where I could say things like that.

'You were at school here?'

'I hated it, loved the course.'

She nodded as she handed me a scorecard. 'Ah,' she said. 'Boarding.'

I'd been eleven when my parents left me at Dewar House, Dollar Academy. I see crowds of bigger boys charging round shouting. My father gives me a manly handshake, my mother a brief hug. I'll see them in a couple of months. Then they're gone and I'm sitting amid the din in my brand-new uniform on my trunk with my name stencilled on it, containing my new clothes for the year, each item with my name tag sewn onto it, down to the last sock and handkerchief. It might as well be a number.

I've left behind my parents, the dog, my wee brother, my games, the books, toys, clothes, freedoms of my former life. My big brother and sister are here, but in other boarding houses and our paths won't cross often. I'm on my own in this bewildering world and I have to survive it. My only luxury and friend is across my knee: a pencil bag containing half a dozen clubs, a few tees and some found balls. This golf bag has no name tag on it, but it at least is mine.

It comes back in flashes as I sort out my clubs, water, food, lace up the golf shoes in the sunny car park. Presumably everyone has a period in their lives they can identify as simply wretched, and those two years at Dollar were mine. Perhaps if I'd stayed on through the school, like my elder brother and sister, I'd have been more positive about it.

But I came in near the bottom and left near the bottom, and it was rotten. Something to be endured at best. Brother David reminded me at Glenbervie that I'd run away twice. I had absolutely no memory of this, but it seemed like a very good idea. When my dad retired and moved to Anstruther, he accepted it when I said I wanted to go to the local school. It couldn't possibly be any worse.

Anyway, it's done now and here I am, grown up and ready to have a go at this course again. Most of the time I don't even think of Dollar. The FP newsletter goes straight in the bin. And yet the memory surfaces once in a while, the pain and the anger still as freshly cut as the day they were stamped.

As I lug the trolley up the steep slope onto the dew-glittering, empty first tee, another single golfer comes up behind me. Damn. I came here to play this alone now as I did then, to take time to confront, comfort or overcome that miserable ghost.

'On you go,' I say. 'I'll be playing two balls sometimes, and making notes.'

'After you, please,' he replies. 'I am not a good golfer. In fact, I am quite bad.'

He sounds German. A neat, fit-looking man with gold-rimmed glasses, about sixty, wearing dark checked tartan trousers but a plain sweater and faded blue peaked cap. I appreciate his modesty. He looks the kind of person who tells things as he sees them. Perhaps he is quite bad.

'No, really,' I say. 'On you go. I'm in no hurry.'

He nods doubtfully, takes out a metal wood and begins to loosen up. I take a proper look at this first hole. It looks the same but different, like most childhood scenes revisited.

Interesting par 3, 186 yards. Built like the rest of the course on the side of the Ochils, the fairway slopes down steeply left to right. Trees and the river on the right, rough up on the left. The green is on a curious raised promontory, ending in a steep 20-foot bank. It's below this bank that most shots end up, unless they go directly onto the green. I remember that tricky blind pitch up the bank, trying to stop it in time with my cut-down niblick. I can feel the familiar coarse tape of the grip under my whitening fingers . . .

'If I should hold you up,' the man says, 'please play through.'

'Thank you.'

This used to be a hole for my trusty spoon, the 3 wood. Couldn't reach the green, of course, until the last few months at Dollar, when I'd got big enough to find that if I whacked it along the left side, it might stay up long enough to run onto the green, a triumph.

I take out the 5 iron, loosen up. With the sun warming our faces, I suddenly feel good. This shot is going to be OK, I know it. The day will be fine. I'm no longer a miserable, abandoned prisoner. I am a grown-up, and mostly this is good.

'Look, why don't we play round together?'

'Good,' he says. 'Perhaps you hit first.'

So there it is. Change of plan. It seemed somehow churlish to insist on playing alone. Perhaps it's something that happened in the 'Fairway' week.

I hold out my hand. 'Andrew Greig.'

'Guenter Schnorr.'

So here goes. Tee up at the 1st at Dollar. Swing a few times, arms feel loose, good steady feeling.

Nice contact, ball sails away as intended, slightly left of the flag. Lands on the raised green, disappears.

Guenter addresses the ball. Very methodical approach, reminds me of Rainer, though not nearly as accomplished. A stiff and slightly crabbed swing, but good contact. His ball pulls left, stays up in the light rough. As we walk down the fairway he tells me his handicap is 22, he took up golf in his fifties. As usual I reply it's a tough game to learn late. It's much easier when you're young and malleable and imitate easily.

Pleased to see my ball on the green some 20 feet from the pin, but as I wait for Guenter to play I think maybe some things weren't well learned back then. Maybe I was too affected by what happened.

OK, this putt. Unfortunately the greens have recently been gritted, which will make everything a bit random. Give it a good clip, then. Remember Vin: follow through down the line.

For some reason the words *strength of mind* go through my head as I stand up to the ball. Also Tony's maxim, commit to the shot. Calmly commit, while accepting the outcome.

The ball runs fast and smooth, arcs slightly left, pops into the middle of the hole. Blimey. A birdie for starters.

'This doesn't usually happen,' I assure Guenter.

Maybe it's time to finally accept, and outgrow, the things learned back then. We are so malleable, so porous in childhood. We're surprisingly tough, yet we mark easily.

When people talk, as they do in all sincerity, about the team spirit, self-reliance and self-confidence that can come from boarding school, I see the games room in Dewar House after the evening meal on that first day.

All us new boys were herded in by the head of the house and his cohorts (who I now see were only fifteen-year-old knobbly-kneed pimply youths but then were powerful, irresistible figures). The house master and matron had disappeared. The door was shut, the table-tennis table moved aside. There was an uneasy silence. Some heavy leather footballs were brought out. We were commanded to line up against the far wall, facing out.

'Right! The rules are you mustn't turn away or put your hands up to protect your face. Got that? Anyone who does will be beaten!'

Who were you, red-faced, shouting boy terrorising children in the name of tradition? What had they done to you? What did you go on to do? Did you become a bully in the army, or law, or a god-like consultant in medicine? Perhaps you became a director in the family firm, your wife detests you (I hope she's unfaithful), your children went to Dollar and became strangers to you, and now you sit sozzled most nights in the golf club bar, denouncing the world gone wrong as you down another gin. Or maybe, just maybe, you grew up and became a decent, useful human being, kind to friends, decent to strangers, loyal and close to your loving wife and children. Perhaps we passed in the street last week.

Whoever and wherever, the boy in me still loathes you.

So we were lined up against the wall at one end of the games room, the head of house and his prefects with the footballs at the other end 25 feet away. Whatever was coming, it wasn't going to be good.

'Wait!'

One of the prefects walked up, looked at me impassively, almost sympathetically, then carefully removed my glasses, put them in his pocket.

'You'll get these back later.'

Then they began kicking the heavy footballs at us as hard as possible. No turning away, no putting up hands. Mayhem of thudding, shouting, battering, crying. A ball hit me full on the face and I felt unreal after that, passive, went deep inside myself to outlast it. I sometimes wonder how long I stayed like that.

This initiation lasted maybe twenty minutes. Physical results: a few bloody noses, bruises, shocks and tears. No lasting physical damage, of course, but enough to break us in. To make it clear we no longer had any individual dignity, freedom, value. Here we would do what we were told because we were told, and take what was coming to us and not ask why.

Then it was over. The footballs bounced and were silent. A few boys were whimpering, one cried loudly. I was still far away, lying by the river at the bottom of our garden.

'SHUT UP!'

I was handed back my glasses. Whenever I read about torture chambers, beaten confessions, punishment beatings, it is that gloomy green-painted games room that I see. And it is one of the few of the many terrible things in our world that make me angry rather than sad: the power of the strong over the weak. Or put it simply: bullying.

'There's one reason I can never be a Buddhist,' I told Vin once: 'I still want to beat the shit out of some bastards.'

So: the 2nd hole at Dollar. This was a near-insoluble problem to a twelve-year-old with the cut-down clubs of the time. It's a short hole up and over a very steep rough bank maybe 120 feet high, onto a hidden green. From the forward tee, it wasn't possible to get the loft needed. From the men's tee further back, I could get the height but not the distance.

In time I found ways round the problem – teeing the balls very high, or laying the face of my niblick wide open. In my second year at Dollar, I could regularly get the ball up over that hill, but it seldom stopped on the green.

Now on this fine warm autumn morning I'm a grown-up man with a pitching wedge in my hand, and no one humiliates me except, occasionally, myself. This is surely an easy hole, a flip up over the direction marker with a half-hit wedge.

So it goes, straight and high but maybe a bit strong. Intimidated by the slope, Guenter lifts his head, tops his ball straight into the bank, mutters disappointment.

'Do you mind if I . . . ?'

'Not at all,' I say. 'I believe in second goes.'

His second attempt is good, flies high and clean over the direction marker. A quick smile passes over his serious face.

We find both balls at the back of the green. While he lines up his approach putt, I'm looking at the three huge beech trees that overshadow the green. I remember sheltering under them from the rain. Also on some occasions I played God in a small way. I'd wait till a ball came up over the hill, run onto the green and throw it away or put it in the hole, then I'd go back behind the trees and wait for the reaction when the golfers arrived.

It was the exercise of power in a place where I had none. I can only report that I gifted more holes in one than lost balls, that as a sneaky God on the whole I preferred to create glad, astonished cries than baffled rage.

The trees are still there, massive and autumnal. The wee boy in school uniform has hidden somewhere, but I know he's still around. Despite or because of him, maybe even in his name, I get two putts for my par.

Dollar is a short course at 5242 yards, designed by Ben Sayers whose cut-down clubs I used back then, and has no bunkers. What it does have is this persistent side-slope that comes into play again and again. It makes placement off the tee crucial and tricky, complicates approach shots to greens cut at an angle into the hillside, and the greens themselves have some awkward levels. Then again, most of the rough is non-lethal, the trees are decorative rather than hazardous. As I hit a series of sliced drives that fortunately end up on adjacent fairways, I have to admit Dollar is what you'd call a *forgiving* course. I have no problem with that.

As we work our way up and across the slope on the next few holes, Guenter endears himself to me by speaking warmly of the general affordability of golf in Scotland, and how it has been seen as a natural, non-exclusive pursuit.

'In Germany golf is so, so expensive, it is prohibitive. You can only play on a course through membership.' I nod, have heard this the other week from Fritz and Rainer. 'It is more about social climbing than golf. I do not care for these people.'

'I don't care for them either.'

The 3rd, 4th, 5th go by. We climb on fairways still soft and green from rain, so removed from the iron-hard baked links courses of the 'Fairway' week. Now the first brown leaves scurry across the fairway like eager mice, rustling over my shoes. Last summer on North Ronaldsay is a world away; chilly damp spring on Bathgate with Al McLeish is on another continent.

They run through my mind like a Powerpoint presentation: lovely, gloaming Shiskine; green humid Gigha; struggling with myself round lush Glenbervie with brother David; watching the trees that line Beauchief in Sheffield form deep-green shade as summer came on; the Firth of Forth deeply blue, lapping around Aberdour, Anstruther, Lundin Links and North Berwick; Iona on an other-worldly Hebridean afternoon. Then playing happily alone on Stromness that damp and chilly summer; south for the extended high of 'Fairway to Heaven', the flaming yellow gorse of Nairn, the glories of Dornoch, then Beauchief and Orkney again as autumn came on . . .

So many fairways, so much rough, gorse, whin; greens lumpy or glass-slick. How many balls have I hit? And lost? And found? I thought only to play golf and write about it, for a year, but it has become much more than that. And I'm now in the autumnal phase, the late harvesting . . .

The 5th is rightly called 'Prospect'. From up here at the far top end of the course, near the trees where generations of Dollar pupils went for a quick smoke, we can look up at Dollar Hill and the rest of the Ochils behind us, then down the sweep of the course at the small town, the school and playing fields, then south across the Devon valley to the hills of Fife, even the Pentland hills behind Edinburgh. Stirling is below the Hillfoots on my right, Glasgow out beyond that.

Mine is a very small country. Perhaps that's why we take it so personally.

Guenter and I hole out on the high 5th green for our pars and feel quietly pleased with ourselves. 'Honest par,' he says. 'This is better.'

It must be lunchtime, because dozens of black ant figures spill from the school buildings, scatter across the playing fields. Up here the voices, shouts, laughter, shrieks, echo faintly. They sound full of life and energy. Maybe the place isn't so bad. Maybe it never was.

But I didn't invent that games-room initiation.

Guenter glances at me, sun glinting on his gold rims. 'That could be you down there.'

'I used to come up here to get away from that.'

He laughs, but as we play down and across the hill on the next hole – I remember this one, that odd green in under the trees – I'm thinking how true that was. For in boarding school, like prison and the forces, all one's time is accounted for, and almost none of it is spent alone.

We slept in dorms of ten or so iron-framed beds. Maybe sixty boys in a building the size of a large house. Up with the bell, eat breakfast together. Bell to go to school together. Classes together. More bells. Back to the house for lunch together at long tables. Back to school. Back to house for prep – homework done sitting together, begun and ended with bells. Even set times for writing our compulsory bland letters home. We were like ruddy Pavlovian dogs, our living, eating, studying, playing games, sleeping, all regulated by bells. Lights out, sleep now, return thankfully to solitude amid the mutterings, heavy breathings, shiftings.

Good Christ, even the compulsory games were enforced company! As it happened, I loved cricket and didn't mind rugby – liked its dash and drama, didn't see the point of the pain – but I preferred tennis, table tennis and golf. My housemaster wrote, 'Greig should concentrate more on team sports and less on solo ones.'

So the golf course and the hills behind it were the one place I could be on my own. The only time I played with other people was during competition. Why on earth would I want to play golf with someone else?

As Guenter and I chat a little, play our way back across the course towards the woods of Dollar Glen, and the schoolchildren's cries rise and fall on the breeze, I see where my tendency towards solo golf began. This place, this course that now comes back to me in emotional flashes, this is where it became entrenched. Even when we moved to Anstruther and I went to a normal school and became relatively socialised, I kept on playing golf largely by myself or with brother Sandy and occasionally my dad. Solo golf has remained my default position.

Only now, forty years later, am I beginning to understand why, and to question it.

Light rain comes on while we play up the two satisfying short holes that run straight up the slope, Dollar Hill ahead, all khaki-coloured, the deep wooded glen on the right. I've turned fifty, I can hit the ball distances inconceivable to me back then (if not always terribly straight), I'm voluntarily playing with another golfer and enjoying his company, sharing his struggles as he shares mine, following and looking for each other's ball in the rough (no doubt about it, you lose far more balls on your own). Something has happened during this year of golf.

With a sense of release I loosen my arms, soften my grip, put a 6-iron tee shot directly onto the elevated 10th green.

Playing golf with someone else is a different experience. It dilutes a certain intensity but it lifts a burden. Following Guenter's shots – nice one, he may get a 3 from there – adds to my round, becomes part of it. Concentration can be harder, but then it's hard in another way with only the company of your own thoughts. Another person can be a balance, a reality check, a way of not over-burdening. It's called sharing, Andrew.

A quick flash of Lesley back in Sheffield. She'll be finishing her morning writing stint, maybe then going to meet a pal for lunch, or take that walk up through the woods at the end of our street. Most of this year, playing all this golf in so many places, I've been away too much from the centre of my life, which is wherever we are together. I share my life with her and Leo. The secret, unshareable inner-life apart, I live a social life. So maybe it's time my golf caught up with me.

We get our 3s and, feeling pleased with life despite the light rain, mount the tee for the only long holes on the course. As a boy these seemed to go on for ever, one spoon shot after another.

For the first time today I swing slowly enough to get everything behind the club head – wrists, arms, shoulders, hips, legs, *mind* – and the ball cracks off the blue driver without any effort, vanishes over the direction post.

*

'They say nice and easy, but I am not an easy guy.' Guenter has just lunged at his tee shot, topped the ball vigorously down the fairway. 'Always in business I am like a bulldozer, bam bam bam! This is why I like golf. It reminds me this should not be so.'

He explains he and his wife have rented a flat outside Dollar for a week. She has become a member of Dollar Golf Club. She found it on the Net, liked the look of it – short, hilly, lovely situation, no bunkers, very un-German – and took a year's membership.

'You mean she hadn't even seen it?'

'This is so,' Guenter affirms. He stands over his ball, swings stiffly but slower, sends the ball off firmly and straight.

'Less bulldozer, more Volkswagen,' I say.

He explains membership of their nearest course in Germany is so expensive, and the drive to it is so long, it isn't worth the hassle for the amount she plays. So she decided to join Dollar, come over for holidays. This is their first time; if they like it enough, they will keep coming back. They like it. Today she has gone for a long walk. He does not find walking interesting. Golf, however, is always interesting, always a problem.

My ball is sitting on a side slope, uphill lie. The red flag waves in the distance. Lunchtime must be over, for the children's voices have fallen silent. I check my card for distance, something I would have scorned a year ago but have got used to now. Playing on so many new courses – and in some ways I have changed so much and my memory is so fitful, this might as well be a new course – working out yardage and choosing the club accordingly makes sense, I have to admit it.

That flag should be about 200 yards. Uphill lie makes the ball fly higher. The fairway's soggy, the ball isn't running at all. So a soft 3 wood it is then. Something else has changed. A year ago I had no real idea how far I'd expect to hit the ball with each club. Now I find myself looking for distance markers – is that surrender, or just learning?

That 3 wood cracks, a thrill coursing from wrists to heart. I allowed for the side slope, committed to the shot (thanks, Tony), and the ball finishes level with the green, just below it.

'Great shot!' Guenter says.

'Thank you.'

And thank you, Joan, for reminding me how to accept praise. Thanks to so many people, I think as we walk towards the green. To brother David for getting me to slow the tempo. To Sandy Aird for correcting my shoulder alignment. To my father who first showed me how to play a fairway wood ('Like a broom, you see? Just brush the ball away'). To Vin Harris ('Golf is a safe place to invest in outcomes').

For the awkward pitch shot out of light rough, I play as brother Sandy showed me on the practice ground at St Andrews the other week. Drop hands, open stance, flip it up as if lobbing it there with the back of your right hand.

I do; ball drops like a poached egg and lies by the pin. (I don't do backspin, but I can manage the high flop.) As I tap it in I think, even when playing golf alone, there are many others present.

The rain moves on and sun returns, bright and yellow-green like olive oil streaked across the damp fairways. The whole course glitters, and a big divot from a full 9 iron heaves up the smell of earth. As we play out the closing holes, I think Dollar wasn't so bad. Well it was for me, but there was always this course, and the hills behind where in summer term you could take a packed lunch and disappear for half a day, which I did. Alone, of course.

And it taught me some useful lasting things. Cricket, for one. Also a life-long dislike of authority, enforced submission, tradition, hierarchy (for God's sake, the house posted up Seniority Lists at the start of each year). It taught me to keep my resistance stubborn, secret, underground. To withhold inner consent even when outer was enforced. It taught me how much I hate cruelty, bullying, mindless authority.

There were also day pupils at Dollar, 'real people' as I thought of them. People who had homes to go to, who could make toasted-cheese sandwiches when they wanted, who had bedrooms of their own, parents and brothers and sisters to argue with. Boarders were not allowed to go into the homes of day people. Was this to preserve class differences, or to enforce the true boarding-school experience? Who knows, but it was another hateful rule, and one I broke regularly. What few friends I had were invariably day people (though the lure of the toasted cheese and even a quick look at some television must have added to their appeal).

Looking down at the neat town from the 16th green, I can see some of the houses I used to visit. There's the MacFarlanes'; the Rankins'; that lad whose name I can't remember but he built hot-rod cars with his mechanic brother, tuning the engine as it roared. I'd visit them like a secret agent or a lover; stroll casually down the road, glance up and down, wait till no one in sight then – quick! – nip sideways through the gate, behind the hedge, up the path.

Day people weren't stiff and secretive; they didn't need to hide themselves. Because that was the most pernicious lesson boarding school taught, quite consciously: the suppression of personal emotion. For all the ethos of team spirit, it taught children to become self contained, isolated, withheld. You learned to keep your true thoughts and feelings, the hopes, fears, hatreds, angers, yearnings, to yourself, because showing them made you vulnerable.

My mother remarked casually the other night – we talk a lot about the distant past now, as it's more solid ground for her than the quagmire of an hour ago – 'I lost your elder brother and sister when they went to Dollar. I never really knew them after that.' That mask of self-control you learn to wear becomes near-impossible to remove. It's taken me a long time, God knows.

Maybe because my mind's elsewhere, I three-putt the 16th. Guenter makes a nice par, is pleased, and I'm pleased for him. Then on to the 17th. I remember this one – a great yawning down-and-side-hill hole, across a burn and its gully, rising to a difficult green. 287 yards. It's called 'McNabb', the name of my second boarding house. It had a decent house master, Adam Robson, who had been a Scottish rugby international but despite this was a calm, gentle man with a passion for painting. That second year was marginally less miserable than my first.

In those days, this hole was simpler because there was no chance of reaching the burn with my spoon. The challenging shot was the next one, a mid-iron, aiming to run onto the green from the left. Being grown-up with these new clubs, the amazing shafts, club heads, balls, we have lost some of the true challenge and interest of these holes.

But we're here and this is now, and I fancy a go with the big blue driver. Not a percentage shot, but this one's for the fun of it. Soft hands, swing slow, sweet carrion crow. Grace and Ease, Cynthia . . .

'Blimey!'

'It is bad?' Guenter asks, lowering the camera.

'No – good always takes me by surprise.'

Over the closing holes Guenter has been talking about his working life. He worked for IBM, computer systems, big contracts – the world of business that is foreign to me but still as real as my own. He must have been part of the economic resurgence of West Germany. I glance at him as we search for his ball down in the gully – serious, concentrating, diligent.

Then came the changes – the unification of Germany, the rise of the personal computer. Difficult times, everything uncertain.

Here's his ball, in a horrible lie amid some rushes. I'd be tempted to prefer it, but Guenter gives the greenery a big thump, dislodges the ball a few feet, puts his next shot nicely onto the green. Not a man to give himself easy breaks. He never gave himself a short putt the entire round, despite the grit on the greens that made it all uncertain. I'm rather impressed by that.

We eventually find my ball in turn, just as I was about to give up on it. It's in light rough, some 20 yards short of the green. Awkward shot across the side-slope, but a chance for a second birdie. So put aside thoughts of the German economic miracle, Adam Robson, toasted cheese at the Rankins'; also of what will happen if I hit this shot thin. Soften hands, decide where the ball should land, commit to the shot, play it.

As we inspect the putts that both of us will hole, Guenter finishes his story. Now he is a systems consultant, has some projects of his own. He wipes clean his putter blade, smiles up at me. 'I am moving towards less work, more golf.'

'Sounds sound to me,' I say as we move towards the 18th tee, pleased with that birdie putt. 'Reckon I'll do the same. There's more to life than writing.'

'Even writing about golf?'

'Even that.'

The last hole, yes I remember this one. Not just the topography – a vicious side-slope dipping steeply down below the elevated green – but a welter of emotions and memories. The hole always intrigued me. The second shot was very tricky for a boy. Too soft and the ball ran back down into that gully. Just a tad hard and it scuttered over the crown green and over the back, which was so steep and coarse a drop as to be almost unplayable. Also at that point a sense of sorrow and loss – the round almost finished, I'd be going back to boarding house, back into the system, the bells, the idiocy, hysteria, indifference and casual cruelty.

My drive ends up in that gully below the green, just in from the trees; Guenter's is in the light rough up on the left – a tricky approach.

As I wait for him to play, a name floats across my mind for the first time in nearly forty years. *Neil Bryson.* In my last term at Dollar, we'd played against each other in the Under-14s. A day boy, dark hair, witty and quick. I think he beat me in the semi-final – or did I beat him? Certainly it was close.

We became friendly. In those last weeks of that last summer

term in 1963 we played golf together several times, went to his house once. Talked about Telstar, the satellite and the tune, about going to the moon, about flying model planes, bike expeditions, climbing hills on family holidays . . .

Neil Bryson, yes. Weighing up the pitch shot out of the depths of the gully below the last green, I remember our last awkward goodbye, right up ahead on the 18th green. Leaving behind that possibility of real friendship was the only reason I regretted leaving Dollar. Wonder where you are now, Neil.

Guenter's approach is good, solidly on the green. Mine is slightly heavy but crests the hill and stays on, maybe 20 feet short.

Lining it up, waiting while Guenter takes his putt, it comes back: my last day at Dollar. My trunk was packed, my parents were at the prize-giving watching my sister getting piles of books and my brother various sporting cups. I'd said I felt ill and skipped the prize-giving. McNabb was near-empty. I'd never be coming back. I was going to a new school, a new life at a normal school called Waid Academy.

On impulse I took a couple of clubs and some balls and slipped away to the course. I wiled away my last Dollar hours practising chip shots onto the 18th green, waiting for the hubbub in the town below when the prize-giving was over.

My approach putt is feeble, 3 feet short. I look at Guenter, he looks at me.

'I can give you that,' he says. 'These greens are difficult, so much grit.'

'I'd better finish it properly.'

I can almost see the shade of that boy in short trousers, his round-rimmed National Health specs, short Brylcreemed hair, earnestly absorbed in hitting one chip after another across the green; feel his excitement, his relief, impatience, even some odd sorrow at leaving. I don't know if he'll ever entirely leave.

I hit the ball firmly. It bounces over the grit, catches the rim of the cup, swerves in. Guenter and I shake hands.

'Thank you for this playing together.'

'I'm really glad we did,' I reply, and mean it.

As we bump our trolleys together down the steep path to the clubhouse, Guenter adjusts his gold-rimmed-glasses and turns to me.

'How many more rounds you must play for your book?'

'I've no idea, Guenter.'

He looks perplexed.

There'd never been a plan. Whether ending a book or a phase in life, I can only hope to recognise the right moment when I get there. Crisp brown leaves rattle over our shoes as we come down the steps. The last time I came down here was to be picked up by my parents and taken on to a new life. There'd be no more of that. Any more new lives I have to make for myself.

Before leaving Dollar, I take a look at Dewar House. It's been sold and converted into flats. They should have razed it to the ground. I wonder what happened to that games room? McNabb looks improbably small, not much bigger than a large family house. Through the windows, the rooms look more . . . domestic. Curtains, posters, lamps. It seems now it's twin or single rooms. I hope most of the rest of the hogwash has gone with the big dorms, the freezing showers and terrible food. Maybe boarders can now mix with day pupils, enter their houses, taste normal family life.

Anyway, I'm out of here, even if it's never entirely out of me. As I drive through afternoon sunlight back to Liz Duff's in Culross, I think through the day. Seven pars, two birdies, 75. Good by my standards. I got to play Dollar again, and play it better than I could have then. And I met another human being, one I respected and enjoyed.

I got to return to the old battlefield and have a second go. To reconnect to that miserable, stubborn, angry wee boy, and assert I'm beyond him.

As I drive down the back roads, leaves are flying everywhere. The great beech trees I remember by the bridge will soon be bare. Something is coming to an end.

Endgame

After Liz had left for work next morning, I'd intended to drive to Anstruther, spend another day and night with Mum, then get on down to Sheffield. Then there was Machrihanish to organise with Vin, the course at Brora I'd been recommended, the chance of a round at Balcomie with Sandy. Perhaps that would wind up the book. Guenter was right. It had to end somewhere.

But when I went out to the car and put my overnight bag alongside the clubs, still earthy from yesterday, a new option occurred to me. Perhaps it was the morning sun warm on the back of my neck, the dew-damp gardens, the remaining leaves still now the wind had blown out. It was a perfect autumn morning; there wouldn't be many more.

I made a quick phone call. Mum had mislaid the note she'd made to herself to say I was due back by lunch.

'I wish you wouldn't all worry about me.'

'You're eighty-five, Mum, and some days you don't feel yourself. Of course I worry about you.'

Her impatient laugh on my mobile. Clearly a good morning, then.

'The only thing I worry about is people worrying about me. You go and do what you want. Oh, and cousin Rosemary is dead. You remember her?'

'Yes, Mum, I remember her.'

I turned north out of Culross, and headed back to Dollar.

No birdie at the 1st today, but a chip and putt rescued par. At the second, my tee shot was straight and too strong, but another chip and putt for par.

It was that kind of day, that kind of round, a lot of rescuing going on.

Though the course had some people out on it, there was no one with me, or ahead, or behind. Though I'd come to appreciate playing in company these last months, it was good to be back on my own on a golf course.

Unencumbered too by the past. A lot of that had got worked through the day before, and today all I did was play the course.

Windless, the sun hot for a while, the dew had vanished after the first few holes and the ball ran on a bit on the autumn fairways. The greens were still gritty as an urban Scottish novel, but the ball kept finding the hole. Six times in the first seven holes, wayward tee shots or slightly misjudged second shots were made up for by 'rescue' chips and putts.

I was in that ideal space, at once absent-minded and concentrating, involved yet removed, simply playing. All the time, in the back of my head, something was resolving.

At 'Castle', the bonnie par 3 that runs up alongside Dollar Glen, I pushed my tee shot, chipped dead, knocked in from a foot with the back of Dad's putter, the way he used to. I didn't need the scorecard to tell me I was 'one under 4s', meaning 35 shots, two over par for the opening half of the round. Well above my standard. I'd try not to let that frighten me.

The next hole is much the same but shorter. I hit a three-quarter 6 iron onto the back of the green. On impulse, teed up another ball, and tried a full 7 iron. Pulled it a bit, but it finished on the left edge of the green. Interesting.

It came to me then: this book, this exploration, was never going to be one clear-cut quest. It has turned out to be more like one those summer evenings on Stromness, when I'd take a few clubs and a handful of balls out onto the 15th fairway, and just try things out, then walk over the rise and see the result.

Yes, that's what this book would be. Not one shot, but a number of differently flighted shots to a hidden green.

But how many shots? When to call an end? Brooding on this, I let things slip and had two bogey holes. At the second one, I hit a truly awful fairway wood, and had to scramble for my 5.

I took a break on the 13th tee. Sat and drank water and ate chocolate in the autumn sun, looking down over the douce town while I had myself a think. Where to stop? At Balcomie with Sandy?

A week earlier I'd finally got round to reading Michael Murphy's *Golf in the Kingdom* after so many people at 'Fairway' raved about it. It had been great fun, a kind of Carlos Castenada, with crusty, elusive Scottish golf pro Chivas Irons (what a triumph of naming) in place of Castenada's trickster mage Don Juan. It was generally agreed that Balcomie outside Crail was the model for 'Burningbush'. Apparently the bonnie, slightly couthy course of my youth had become a place of pilgrimage. Graeme Lennie the pro there had talked of looking up from his counter one morning to see Clint Eastwood.

'You're looking for Burningbush?' Graeme asked.

Eastwood had no poncho, no cigar, but was still commendably taciturn. 'Yup.'

Yes, it might be interesting to revisit Balcomie, playing with Sandy. See again the Gay Trophy, find my name on it, 1966. See if I felt any of the other-wordly occult, magical vibes ascribed to the place, play some supernatural shots or merely an assortment of good and poor ones. I'd taken the drugs in my time, I could be open to magical realms. Remembering 'The Shot' at Lundin Links, or that 50-foot putt I knew was going in the hole the moment it left the blade . . . Yes, strange things happen on a golf course, though the strangest things on it are ourselves.

But last night I'd stayed up late at Liz's, reading *In Search of*

Burningbush by Michael Konik. A fine, moving book, a human story told through golf, easy on the supernatural. It had been at once reassuring and worrying to find his protagonists playing some of the ones I'd played. The book climaxed, inevitably, at Balcomie. Which on balance ruled out my doing the same.

Ever since I'd started on this, people kept suggesting courses I must play. Machrihanish, Brora, Murcar, Troon, Golspie, Prestwick. And the truly remote and unsung – that one in Shetland mainland, another up in Unst, the most northerly course in Britain. Islay, Barra, Benbecula . . .

But I'd known from the outset this was not going to be a guide, nor a survey. It would be absolutely non-definitive. The R & A in their wisdom have decreed a limit to the number of clubs you can carry. Things have to stop somewhere; this venture is no exception.

But the daylight is burning and there are six holes of golf left to play. I finish the last of the water, have a stretch and let the questions go for now. I trust the part of my mind that works these things out in the background, then steps forward and tells me how it's going to be.

Distractions over, I start playing good golf. As always when it's good, there's no effort, mental or physical. You look at the shot, decide, then turn it over to your wonderful, doomed, clever body, and on good days it does the deed. A good honest par at the 13th is followed – two straight shots and one streaky putt – by the only birdie of the day. The 15th involves a blind drive over a direction post. I crest the hill to see my ball down there, just off the green. *A number of differently flighted shots to a hidden green . . .*

Drop a shot on 'Quarry' with a silly three-putt. I think again on Irish Tony: *It's only your ego that's hurting, not your immortal soul.* I'm still smiling inwardly as 'McNabb' gives up to a clean drive, a steady pitch, a birdie putt that hits the rim and kicks away.

Then it's down to the last hole. On the tee I think about Mum, decide we'll have fish suppers to save cooking (she hates me keeping an eye on her, but I can't take any more raw potatoes), wonder if she'll be in calm or anxious mood. After all those years when 'home' meant reassurance, sanctuary, restoration, now it's a place where I go with trepidation, to give rather than receive.

I love and owe her so much. At least enjoy and make the most of what's left, and be there for the rest. The point of strength of mind – equanimity, the *balance* my father saw in Harry Vardon – is not to resist failure, sorrow and loss, but to allow them and not be overwhelmed.

So my last drive rolls down into the swale below the 18th green. My pitch up the bank is not too hard and not too soft. A brief nod to that absorbed, unhappy shade of a boy playing out his last hours here, then I putt to inches, knock it in, hear that last gurgle.

My card records 35 OUT, 37 IN. Total 72, six over par. Not that I was counting.

Of course I'm counting. There is still something at stake. There aye will be.

I'd assumed there'd be one clear pursuit to this book. Instead what came up – along with umpteen golfing moments I'd record and sift in the months to come – were my mother and father, childhood and family, adolescence and friendship, love and sex, my country and a lot of dead people. And not being dead when I could so easily have been, knowing now that I will soon be gone. As will my mother, Lesley and all my friends. And still we make love and play golf.

Any better ideas, pal?

I trundle down the steps to the clubhouse through yellow autumn light, tired yet curiously light-hearted, thinking back on all today's up-and-downs from wayward shots. Rescue, emotional rescue; it can be done.

Then I pack up trolley and clubs, and drive on to the rest of life.

A Long Shot

As your lover on waking recounts her dreams,
unruly, striking, unfathomable as herself,
your attention wanders
to her moving lips, throat, those slim shoulders
draped in a shawl of light, and what's being christened here
is not what is said but who is saying it,
the overwhelming fact
she lives and breathes beside you another day.

Other folks' golf shots are even less interesting
than their dreams. I'll be brief.
While she spoke I thought of a putt yesterday at the 4th,
as many feet from the pin as I am years from my birth
definitely more than I am from my death:
one stiff clip, it birled across the green,
curved up the rise, swung down the dip
like a miniature planet heading home,

and the strangest thing is not what's going to happen
but your dazed, incredulous knowing it will,
long before the ball reaches the cup then drops,
that it's turned out right after all,
like waking one morning to find yourself
unerringly in love with your wife.

Andrew Greig grew up on the east coast of Scotland, the birthplace of golf. He is the author of six acclaimed books of poetry, two Himalayan mountaineering expedition books, and five novels. He lives in Orkney and Sheffield with his wife, the novelist Lesley Glaister.